MIDRASHIC WOMEN

BRANDEIS SERIES ON JEWISH WOMEN

Shulamit Reinharz, General Editor

Joyce Antler, Associate Editor

Sylvia Barack Fishman, Associate Editor

Susan Kahn, Associate Editor

The Hadassah International Research Institute on Jewish Women, established at Brandeis University in 1997 by Hadassah, the Women's Zionist Organization of America, Inc., supports interdisciplinary basic and applied research as well as cultural projects on Jewish women around the world. Under the auspices of the Institute, the Brandeis Series on Jewish Women publishes a wide range of books by and about Jewish women in diverse contexts and time periods.

MARJORIE AGOSÍN
Uncertain Travelers: Conversations with Jewish Women Immigrants to America, 1999

RAHEL R. WASSERFALL
Women and Water: Menstruation in Jewish Life and Law, 1999

SUSAN STARR SERED
What Makes Women Sick: Militarism, Maternity, and Modesty in Israeli Society, 2000

LUDMILA SHTERN
Leaving Leningrad: The True Adventures of a Soviet Émigré, 2001

PAMELA S. NADELL AND JONATHAN D. SARNA, EDITORS
Women and American Judaism: Historical Perspectives, 2001

CHAERAN Y. FREEZE
Jewish Marriage and Divorce in Imperial Russia, 2001

MARK A. RAIDER AND MIRIAM B. RAIDER-ROTH
The Plough Woman: Records of the Pioneer Women of Palestine, 2002

JUDITH R. BASKIN
Midrashic Women: Formations of the Feminine in Rabbinic Literature, 2002

MIDRASHIC WOMEN

FORMATIONS OF THE FEMININE
IN RABBINIC LITERATURE

JUDITH R. BASKIN

BRANDEIS UNIVERSITY PRESS

PUBLISHED BY UNIVERSITY PRESS OF NEW ENGLAND

HANOVER AND LONDON

BRANDEIS UNIVERSITY PRESS
PUBLISHED BY THE UNIVERSITY PRESS OF NEW ENGLAND,
HANOVER, NH 03755
© 2002 BY BRANDEIS UNIVERSITY PRESS

Library of Congress Cataloging-in-Publication Data

Baskin, Judith Reesa, 1950–
Midrashic women : formations of the feminine in Rabbinic literature / Judith R. Baskin
    p. cm.—(Brandeis series on Jewish women)
Includes bibliographical references.
 ISBN 1–58465–177–6 (cloth : alk. paper)—ISBN 1–58465–178–4
(pbk. : alk. paper)
 1. Women in rabbinical literature. 2. Aggada—Commentaries. 3.
Midrash—History and criticism. 4. Feminism—Religious
aspects—Judaism. 5. Women in the Bible. I. Title. II. Series.
 BM509.W7 B37 2002
 296.1'406'082–dc21

                                                    2002002979

For Warren

A husband of valor who shall find?

CONTENTS

Acknowledgments ix

Note on Translations and Abbreviations xi

Introduction 1

1 Distinguishing Differences: The Otherness of Women in
   Rabbinic Judaism 13

2 Constructing Eve: Midrashic Revisions of Human Creation 44

3 Eve's Curses: Female Disadvantages and Their Justifications 65

4 Fruitful Vines and Silent Partners: Women as Wives in
   Rabbinic Literature 88

5 "Why Were the Matriarchs Barren?": Resolving the Anomaly
   of Female Infertility 119

6 "A Separate People": Rabbinic Delineations of the Worlds
   of Women 141

Afterword 161

Notes 165

Bibliography 203

Subject Index 213

Index of Primary Sources 223

ACKNOWLEDGMENTS

This book has been in progress for many years. I am grateful to my teacher, Judah Goldin, *z"l*, in whose graduate seminars at Yale University I first undertook the study of midrash and who encouraged me to write about Rahab. I am glad to thank friends and colleagues who read parts of this volume, or listened to papers based on its contents, and offered helpful suggestions; these include Alan Avery-Peck, Jennifer Fleischner, Mayer Gruber, Paula Hyman, Tal Ilan, Ross Shepard Kraemer, Susan Niditch, Vanessa Ochs, Miriam Peskowitz, Laura Levitt, Maurie Sachs, Jonathan Seidel, Susan Shapiro, Cheryl Tallan, Judith Romney Wegner, and Walter Zenner. I would also like to thank Jacob Neusner, who has offered generous encouragement of my research and writing over the years. I owe a special debt to Berel Lang, who encouraged me to undertake this project, and I am grateful to Sylvia Barack Fishman and Shulamit Reinharz for welcoming my work into the Brandeis Series on Jewish Women, with the support of the Hadassah International Research Institute on Jewish Women. I offer special thanks to my editor Phyllis Deutsch for her patience.

My work in the Women's Caucus of the Association for Jewish Studies throughout the 1990s and my collaborations with other scholars investigating Jewish women's history and literature have been significant sources of inspiration to me. I would particularly like to acknowledge the support and friendship of Howard Adelman, Sarah Blacher Cohen, Judith Hauptman, Deborah Hertz, Sara Horowitz, Carole Kessner, Miri Kubovy, Rochelle Millen, Pamela Nadell, Frances Malino, Renée Levine Melammed, Riv-Ellen Prell, Ellen Schiff, Emily Taitz, Shelly Tenenbaum, Ellen Umansky, Dvora Weisberg, Chava Weissler, and Laura Wexler. I am grateful, as well, to the University at Albany, State University of New York, for a sabbatical leave in the Fall of 1999, which allowed me to complete important work on this book.

My uncle, the American sculptor and graphic artist Leonard Baskin, *z"l*, was a man of immense learning and outsized talent and personality. He took great pleasure in rabbinic *aggadah* and was always interested in my work. I am delighted that his illustration, "Four is the Number of the Matriarchs" (*A Passover Haggadah. The New Union Haggadah*, ed. Herbert Bronstein [New York: Central Conference of American Rabbis, 1974]) is reproduced on the cover of this book. I would like to thank the Central Conference of American Rabbis for permission to reprint this stunning image here.

It is a great honor to be the first Director of the Harold Schnitzer Family Program at the University of Oregon. I am grateful to the Schnitzer family for their vision and for their generous support of the publication of this volume.

My son Sam and my daughter Shira are great sources of pride and happiness to me. I thank them for tolerating my preoccupation with this project over a long period of time. I am most blessed in my parents, Marjorie and Rabbi Bernard Baskin; they have always been models to me of committed engagement to life and learning. My husband Warren Ginsberg and I first met thirty years ago as fellow graduate students in the Medieval Studies doctoral program at Yale. It has been a great joy and privilege to share my life with Warren, a genuine scholar and a true mensch, and I dedicate this volume to him with all my love.

NOTE ON TRANSLATIONS AND
ABBREVIATIONS

All biblical quotations are from *Tanakh: A New Translation of the Holy Scriptures According to the Traditional Hebrew Text* (Philadelphia: The Jewish Publication Society of America, 1985), except in those instances where changes were necessitated by the midrashic context. Biblical quotations appear throughout the book in an alternative font so that they will stand out from the rest of the text. Non-English words appear in transliteration within biblical or rabbinic quotations when the Hebrew or Aramaic is central to the passage's exegetical argument.

Translations from the Mishnah are based on those in *The Mishnah: Translated from the Hebrew with Introduction and Brief Explanatory Notes* by Herbert Danby (Oxford: Oxford University Press, 1933). Translations from the Babylonian Talmud are grounded in *The Babylonian Talmud*, ed. I. Epstein, 18 vols. (London: The Soncino Press, 1936). Translations from *Midrash Rabbah* are grounded in *Midrash Rabbah*, trans. H. Freedman, 9 vols. (London: The Soncino Press, 1938). Translations from *Avot de-Rabbi Nathan* A are informed by *The Fathers According to Rabbi Nathan*, translated from the Hebrew by Judah Goldin (New Haven: Yale University Press); those from *Avot de-Rabbi Nathan* B are informed by *The Fathers According to Rabbi Nathan. A Translation and Commentary* by Anthony J. Saldarini (Leiden: E. J. Brill, 1975). Translations from *Pesiqta de-Rav Kahana* are grounded in *Pesikta de-Rab Kahana: R. Kahana's Compilation of Discourses for Sabbaths and Festal Days*, translated from Hebrew and Aramaic by William G. Braude and Israel Kapstein (Philadelphia: Jewish Publication Society, 1975). Translation from *Tanna Deve Eliyyahu* are informed by *Tanna Debe Eliyyahu*, translated by William G. Braude and Israel Kapstein (Philadelphia: Jewish Publication Society, 1981). Translations from other rabbinic texts are my own unless otherwise indicated.

The following abbreviations are used for biblical books: Gen. (Genesis), Ex. (Exodus,), Lev. (Leviticus), Num. (Numbers), Deut. (Deuteronomy), Josh. (Joshua), Judg. (Judges), Sam. (Samuel), Kgs. (Kings), Isa. (Isaiah), Jer. (Jeremiah), Ezek. (Ezekiel), Zeph. (Zephaniah), Zech. (Zechariah), Mal. (Malachi), Ps. (Psalms), Prov. (Proverbs), Song (Song of Songs), Lam. (Lamentations), Ecc. (Ecclesiastes), and Chron. (Chronicles). The apocryphal book, The Wisdom of Ben Sira, is abbreviated as Ben Sira.

These abbreviations are used in citing rabbinic works: M. (the Mishnah), B. (the Babylonian Talmud), J. (the Talmud of the Land of Israel), and T. (Tosefta). Square brackets within quotations from rabbinic texts generally indicate words added in order to clarify the meaning of the passage.

MIDRASHIC WOMEN

INTRODUCTION

The Lord God said, "It is not good for man to be alone; I will make a fitting helper for him." . . . So the Lord God cast a deep sleep upon the man; and, while he slept, He took one of his ribs and closed up the flesh at that spot. And the Lord God built the rib that He had taken from the man into a woman; and He brought her to the man.

(Genesis 2:18, 21–22)

R. Hisda said: He built more chambers in her than in man, fashioning her broad below and narrow at the top, so that she could receive child.

(*Genesis Rabbah* 18:3 on Genesis 2:22)

Biology is not enough to give an answer to the question that is before us: why is woman the *Other*? (Simone de Beauvoir, *The Second Sex*)[1]

Genesis 2:22 describes the divine fashioning of the first woman from the rib of God's initial creation, the male Adam. The Hebrew verb form for God's action is *vayyiven*, literally "and He built." Although the midrash collection *Genesis Rabbah* offers several metaphorical interpretations of this process of "building," it may be that R. Hisda's literal exegesis in *Genesis Rabbah* 18:3 provides the most apt expression of rabbinic Judaism's understanding of appropriate female functions and of women's essential alterity from men. In this short statement R. Hisda imagines God constructing the first female from the body of an already created male entity. She is to be the man's companion, but she is quite different from him since she has been deliberately formed as a vessel for the reception and nurturing of male-generated new life. Described as "broad below" and "narrow at the top," a woman is understood to be destined for purposes neither possible nor desirable for a man. In the pages that follow, I suggest that just as aggadic midrash, non-legal rabbinic biblical interpretation, was layered on the rib of the biblical text as a requisite accompaniment to the written word, so the rabbinic sages deliberately constructed women as ancillary beings, shaped on the rib of the primordial man to fulfil essential social and sexual functions in an androcentric society.

While the conviction of male superiority was built into rabbinic ways of reading divinely revealed texts and of ordering human affairs, this book demonstrates that the framers of rabbinic literature were not oblivious to the implications of forming the feminine as essentially other and implicitly lesser than the masculine. Midrashic authors, acutely aware of the extent and nature of the limitations imposed on females, rationalized woman's less desirable place in their society as divinely intended. The rabbis' justifications of the patriarchy they themselves maintained and fostered relied on establishing the secondary nature of females from the moment of their creation. The results, both positive and negative for Jewish societies past and present, have been profound. As Shaye J. D. Cohen has succinctly observed of the privileged centrality of men in this social system:

Classical rabbinic Judaism has always been, and in many circles still is, a male-dominated culture, whose virtuosi and authorities are males, whose paragon of normality in all legal discussions is the adult Jewish male, whose legal rulings in many areas of life (notably marriage and ritual observance) accord men greater privilege than women, and whose values define public communal space as male space. Within this culture women are unable to initiate a marriage or a divorce, are obligated to dress modestly in public and to segregate themselves behind a partition in synagogue, and are excluded from the regimen of prayer and Torah study that characterizes, and in the rabbinic perspective sanctifies, the life of Jewish men. In this culture women are socially and legally inferior to men.[2]

In this volume, I demonstrate the ways in which this insistence on female alterity and marginalization underlies and informs midrashic traditions concerning the "second" sex.

Reading Rabbinic Literature

Like the biblical literature it interprets and builds up, the documents of rabbinic Judaism are complex and multi-stranded texts which interweave traditions, motifs, and influences from a variety of sources, time periods, and diverse environments, reflective of the extended duration of their composition and redaction. Far from monolithic in the views and attitudes expressed within its canon, rabbinic discourse preserves a variety of competing interpretations and opinions. While majority views are generally honored, minority opinions are preserved as well. Some of these legal and literary traditions were composed in the Land of Israel and incorporate both Greco-Roman and early Christian cultural influences. Others were shaped in the very different world of Sassanian Iran and Iraq. This oral Torah, diverse and variegated as it is, received sanctity in Jewish tradition and practice through the rabbinic insistence that it was part of the revelation at Sinai and constituted the crucial accompaniment to the written Torah, the Hebrew Scriptures.

The shapers and expositors of rabbinic Judaism were men and the ideal human society they imagined was decidedly oriented towards their own sex. With few exceptions, female voices are not heard in rabbinic literature. When they are, they are usually mediated through male assumptions about women's lesser intellectual, spiritual, and moral capacities, as well as their appropriate roles in life, which were presumed to differ from those of men. Indeed, the rabbinic written tradition believes that Judaism is the Judaism prescribed and practiced by men. Women played no active part in its development, nor were they granted a significant role in any aspect of rabbinic Judaism's communal life of leadership, study, and worship. Neither women's religious rituals, which undoubtedly existed, nor female understandings of their lives, experiences, and spirituality are retrievable in any significant way from rabbinic Judaism's male-directed writings which became so pivotal for ensuing patterns of Jewish life.

The basic literary method of the rabbinic enterprise was midrash. This expansion and elaboration of the canonized Hebrew Scriptures sought to interpret not only the events and revelations of the past but to reveal all of their ramifications for the present and future of the people of Israel. The midrashic writers took for granted that biblical texts contained neither contradiction nor repetition and creatively exercised their interpretive powers to demonstrate that this was so. The earliest written document of rabbinic Judaism is the Mishnah, a compilation of legal rulings, each of which is individually designated as a *mishnah*. Based on biblical law, actual practice, and spiritual vision, the Mishnah is organized by subject matter and was edited in the Land of Israel in the early third century C.E. The Tosefta, a somewhat later collection of legal rulings, follows the order of the Mishnah and supplements it. In the centuries following the completion of these two works, rabbinic communities in the land of Israel and in Babylon (the ancient Jewish communities in the Tigris and Euphrates river valleys) produced extensive commentaries on the Mishnah known as Gemara; the Gemara produced in the rabbinic academies of Babylon was far more voluminous than that produced in the Land of Israel. When the Mishnah and this more extensive Gemara were combined and redacted to form the Babylonian Talmud sometime in the sixth century C.E., the definitive compilation of Jewish law and traditions for centuries to come had been concluded. The Talmud of the Land of Israel, completed at the end of the fourth century C.E., although less comprehensive than the Babylonian Talmud, also became a part of the larger body of rabbinic literature.

Parallel to the Mishnah, Tosefta, and Talmuds are midrash collections, exegetical compilations of interpretive traditions, which are organized either according to the order of biblical books, or follow cycles of scriptural readings. These midrash compilations, which share numerous textual traditions in common with the Mishnah and Talmuds, were mainly redacted in the Land of Israel and are difficult to date; the range of their composition extends from the period of the Mishnah into the early Middle Ages.[3]

The content of rabbinic literature, encyclopedic in its compass and incorporating a variety of literary genres, is generally apportioned between *halakhah* and *aggadah*. *Halakhah* is concerned with the statement and elaboration of authoritative legal directives. This body of legislation, which goes far beyond any biblical imperative in its intent to ordain practice in every realm of human existence, is in many ways extra-historical, often depicting an ideal vision of how people *should* live rather than reflecting any contemporary reality. Indeed, the idealized vision of social policy these documents portray was frequently at odds with the everyday practices of the functioning Jewish cultures in the different times and places in which the literature of rabbinic Judaism was produced and edited. As Jacob Neusner has written concerning the Mishnah, "the social parameters of the system are defined by the people who made it up, not by the world in which they lived."[4]

Although rabbinic writings reveal very little about the actualities of Jewish activities in any particular era or locale, in the course of the Middle Ages mandates of the Babylonian Talmud became normative for virtually all Jewish communities. Thus, the models of the relation between male and female, as between the divine and the human, which were imagined but not necessarily lived in every detail by a few groups of particularly pious male sages, ultimately became the central authority and practical pattern for almost a millennium and a half of Jewish existence, with enduring consequences for Jewish women as well as Jewish men.

Aggadah includes all non-legal material in rabbinic literature, including legendary expansions of biblical stories, allusions to popular folklore, personal and historical anecdotes, and homiletical and ethical teachings. While *halakhah* is characterized by carefully framed and exhaustively debated legal mandates, both proscriptive and prescriptive, the more variegated *aggadah* offers occasional glimpses into contemporary circumstances and daily practice, illuminating the outlines of lived experience in all of its good and bad intentions and improvisational disarray. As I argue in this book, aggadic literature frequently preserves a more nuanced and complex view of women and their activities than the impersonal dictates of halakhic discourse. Given the complex formation of rabbinic texts, however, situating any of these sporadic glimpses of female lives in a particular time or place is usually impossible.

Studies based on non-legal midrashic traditions run the risk of replicating the episodic nature of the *aggadah* itself by jumping from statement to statement and text to text. I have tried to avoid that tendency in these pages by focusing, in each chapter, on one or two lengthy and contextualized aggadic passages from either the Babylonian Talmud or a midrash collection, in which the particular themes I wish to address are elucidated. The talmudic texts explicated here generally constitute all or part of a discrete *sugya*, that is, a discussion devoted to a particular *mishnah*. As I work through each passage, parallel and contrasting statements from other rabbinic texts are introduced to support my ideas and arguments. Nevertheless, one cannot work with the *aggadah* and aspire to a high degree of systematic exposition. Rabbinic literature in the best of circumstances is characterized by a multivocal dialectical structure that preserves not only the definitive opinions of the majority, but also retains minority points of view.

Sometimes, as Daniel Boyarin has pointed out, these "finally redacted and authoritative texts encode an inability or unwillingness to decide between competing views."[5] Yet, while the inclusion of contending opinions may indicate that there is not always a final privileging of one possibility over another, it is also evident that some views predominate while other strands of opinion are secondary. Among the multiplicity of rabbinic remarks concerning women, the convictions of female alterity and women's innate inferiority to men emerge as primary. These central themes are the focus of this book.

The attribution of individual passages of rabbinic literature to particular authors, times, or places is an extremely demanding and controversial enterprise. Such endeavors are beyond the scope of the present work. Similarly, this volume does not intend to recover specific information about actual women who lived during the different historical and geographic phases of the rabbinic period[6], nor to offer extended comparisons with attitudes towards women and women's roles in the larger cultural contexts in which late antique Jewry lived.[7] While I am sensitive to differences in rabbinic attitudes about women and sexuality expressed in the Jewish communities of the Land of Israel as opposed to those of Babylonia, where these can be discerned, such distinctions are also not my focus.[8] Rather my goal in this book is to recover from selected passages found in rabbinic literature those attitudes towards women which became authoritative in informing subsequent Jewish values and practices. Certainly other views existed as well, and some may argue that those rabbinic strands I have chosen to emphasize are less central than I maintain or that they allow for other interpretations. Such is the protean nature of rabbinic literature which often constrains final determinations.

This book primarily analyzes texts found within the canon of the Mishnah, Babylonian Talmud, and late antique midrash compilations. Just as Jews have traditionally read the Hebrew Bible through the lens of rabbinic midrash, so too, traditional understandings of many rabbinic teachings have been significantly shaped by the contributions of later interpreters. Important subsequent exegetes include the magisterial medieval commentator Shlomo ben Isaac (Rashi), who died in France in 1104, and the school of Talmud scholars who immediately succeeded him, the Tosafists. A study of how rabbinic views of women were shaped and altered for later students by these medieval interpreters is a scholarly project in itself which would be of great value. I have not attempted it here.

Reading through a Feminist Lens

This is a feminist book. I approach rabbinic literature, an inarguably androcentric gathering of writings, with the knowledge that women's lives and experiences will find little resonance in these documents. I am also aware that until quite recently women have not been part of the intellectual, communal, and religious endeavors that have been deemed central and worthy of record by authoritative Jewish tradition. Inspired, nonetheless, by the impact of modern feminism on academic fields of inquiry and the widespread recognition of the importance of gender as a category of historical and literary analysis, I am part of a growing cadre of contemporary scholars who are taking a variety of approaches to the study of women and rabbinic dicta.[9] What sets my work apart is its particular interest in aggadic texts. Much of the work in this field has dealt with women in Jewish legal writings. This volume differs in its emphasis on non-halakhic rabbinic exegesis, a literary genre which not only maintains the constant potential to enter the realms of the imagination and even the fantastic, but can also add ethical dimensions to halakhic rulings. While the women who figure in halakhic legislation tend to be generic female ciphers without distinctive personalities or characteristics, the aggadic mode occasionally allows for more subtle portrayals of distinct human characters. Often the *aggadah* seems more reflective of the complexities of actual human relationships as they are lived, while the *halakhah* appears to point toward an ideal, but not yet achieved, condition of order. Biblical exemplars of the attributes the rabbinic interpreters believed were most appropriate for women, as well as glimpses of the real women who shared their everyday lives, are revealed in the relaxed and unpredictable arena of aggadic texts.

Throughout the pages of this volume, I interrogate rabbinic writings from the point of view of gender. I ask who the authors of these texts might have been and I wonder about their intended audience as well. Were some portions of this literature accessible to broad audiences including women, perhaps through oral sermons? Can we discern the roles women played in the lives of those who formulated and studied these documents? When are women portrayed as helpful enablers and when are they seen as impediments to the male life of the mind? To what extent do the representations of women in rabbinic texts reflect social realities in particular times and places and to what extent are they projections of men's sexual and political anxieties and fantasies? While I cannot answer each of these questions for every text I discuss, they are the issues I try to examine.

Every scholar is a product of her or his own time. Our reasons for choosing our subjects and for writing what we write are both acknowledged and submerged. During the first half of the 1970s when I was completing my graduate training, women were still a decided minority among those entering the scholarly ranks. The subsequent growth of Women's Studies as a field of academic inquiry and the increasing number of women who have embarked on academic careers in Judaic Studies established a new atmosphere in which asking questions as and about women became possible. Like many female colleagues of my generation, much of my professional life has been devoted to the study of women in Judaism and Jewish history. Like them, I have discovered that scholarly investigations of the lives and experiences of Jewish women of previous eras can often shed light on modern dilemmas and concerns.

This volume does not overtly address the present day situations of women in the wide variety of modes of Jewish practice that flourish at the beginning of the twenty-first century, although it may be that its conclusions will be of use in clarifying contemporary issues as well as in explicating the past. I would note that I approach rabbinic texts with no commitment to the special status with which they have been invested in traditional Judaism. My respect for the extensive richness, the highly attuned spirituality, and the multi-faceted genius of rabbinic literature is boundless. I have no stake, however, in affirming its divine origins or in justifying its prescriptive imperatives. Rather, I hope I am a careful observer who accurately reports the content of the texts I analyze in these pages.

In recent years, a number of very creative minds have worked to formulate Jewish feminist theologies that have the potential to redefine contemporary and future forms of Judaism and Jewish religious practice. Such Jewish feminist theologies challenge theories of Judaism that view male experience as universal. Based on a hermeneutics of suspicion, feminist theologians assume that Judaism's traditional texts and their interpretations reinforce male hegemony and justify the traditional roles to which women have been assigned. Some of these theologians have written about texts I discuss in the pages that follow and have analyzed them in compelling and perceptive ways. However, the feminist theologian utilizes her studies of received texts from the past for purposes of religious reconstruction in the present and future. While I admire the scholarly acumen, contemporary relevance, and transformative potential of thinkers like Rachel Adler, Judith Plaskow, and Ellen Umansky,[10] my own endeavor in this volume is neither theological nor redemptive in nature. Rather, I wish to understand how women are portrayed in the aggadic midrash of late antiquity and, where possible, to suggest why.

Women in Rabbinic Literature

In the pages that follow, I approach rabbinic formations of the feminine from a number of directions. Chapter 1, "Distinguishing Differences: The Otherness of Women in Rabbinic Judaism," provides an overview of the place of females in the rabbinic ordering of human affairs, demonstrating that as nurturing mothers and supportive spouses, they were acknowledged as indispensable to the smooth functioning of everyday life in the present and for the continuity of the Jewish people in the future. These essential enablers were often portrayed as cherished beings who were loved and protected by the men of their families. Nevertheless, rabbinic perceptions of females as inherently different from men in undesirable ways excluded women from full partnership in the divine covenant and rendered them ineligible for significant participation in most of the communal ritual, spiritual, and intellectual aspects of Jewish life. Moreover, by virtue of their bodies, which were seen to incorporate both sexual attractiveness and potential pollution, women represented constant sources of enticement and societal disorder that had to be carefully controlled. Whatever the diverse origins of the rabbinic constructions of women delineated in this chapter—and a number of theories are examined—there can be no doubt of their enduring unfortunate consequences for Jewish life and gender relations.

"Constructing Eve: Midrashic Revisions of Human Creation," chapter 2 of this volume, examines aggadic traditions that attempt to unravel the apparent contradictions between two biblical creation stories: the vision of an equal creation by divine fiat of both male and female human beings in Genesis 1, and the version preserved in Genesis 2, where female creation is a secondary and subsequent event. As this chapter shows, rabbinic literature privileged the second account, while generally disregarding the challenging implications of the first. Still, midrashic tradition was not oblivious to the problems raised by the initial creation story. Alternative aggadic responses suggested that the first human entity was an androgyne, combining female and male characteristics, or conversely that the juxtaposed narratives referred to two different female creations. This figure of the "first Eve," who refused to be subordinate to her husband, ultimately merged with ancient traditions about the female night demon Lilith and in this guise became a central character in post-rabbinic Jewish folklore. Rabbinic references to the "first Eve," however, are few and obscure; the preponderance of rabbinic opinion agreed that the first woman was created from her husband's rib and that this belated and secondary origin accounted for the many manifestations of female inferiority aggadic writers took for granted.

The third chapter of this book, "Eve's Curses: Female Disadvantages and their Justifications," reveals rabbinic recognition that women were hobbled in comparison to men and delineates midrashic enumerations of the drawbacks they believed were the inevitable accompaniment to being a female. I find it striking that significant voices within the rabbinic enterprise were moved to rationalize why women were barred from the prestige-conferring activities available to men in areas of communal worship, study, and leadership. Yet rabbinic empathy had its limits and convincing explanations for female exclusion reinforced a separationist social policy. Aggadic traditions affirm that few rabbinic sages were prepared to grant any woman entrance into their circles, regardless of unusual intellectual gifts, significant economic resources, or access to political power.

In my discussion in chapter 2, I suggest that the narrative of the primeval androgyne appealed to rabbinic exegetes as an endorsement of marriage. According to this discourse, the divine intention for human completeness and continuity is only achieved when the female and male components of the original human creation are reunited so that procre-

ation becomes possible. At the same time as marriage is strongly encouraged, however, the *aggadah* makes clear that the husband is the
dominant partner. Chapter 4, "Fruitful Vines and Silent Partners:
Women as Wives in Rabbinic Literature," in many ways the central section of this work, deals directly with rabbinic assertions of the essential
role of matrimony in both halakhic and aggadic writings. One significant
strand of midrash on marriage delineates the qualities of good and bad
wives as assessed from a male perspective. A good wife is portrayed as
a woman who enables her spouse to devote himself to Torah study, the
highest source of cultural esteem in rabbinic society. Yet a husband's
commitment to learning often meant long absences from home. Rabbinic
literature reflects the severe tensions generated by conflicts between male
obligations to family and the imperative to study. While a good wife
waited patiently at home for her husband's return, bad wives ventured
immodestly into the public domain where they threatened their husband's honor. It is telling that, while discontented wives had few effective
strategies, unhappy husbands had halakhic options, including divorcing
an unsatisfactory spouse or taking a second wife as a means to humble
a difficult partner. Nevertheless, the *aggadah* deprecates divorce on ethical grounds and counsels preservation of marital ties by invoking the
metaphor of marriage as a human model of the unbreakable covenant
between God and the people of Israel.

A major purpose of marriage was procreation. Although reproduction
was regarded as a legal obligation for men and not for women, many
midrashic traditions make clear that the infertile wife was in a miserable
situation. Chapter 5, " 'Why Were the Matriarchs Barren?': Resolving
the Anomaly of Female Infertility," details the ways in which aggadic
texts taught that compassion and faith could sometimes prevail over the
halakhic prescription to divorce an infertile wife after ten years of marriage. Such midrashic exempla illuminate the rift which frequently separated rabbinic theory and actual practice. Moreover, a review of homiletical reflections on childless women also yields suggestive insights into
the dilemma of suffering and the efficacy of prayer, as well as the ways
in which biblical models could become paradigms and symbols of empowerment in women's lives.

Chapter 6, " 'A Separate People': Rabbinic Delineations of the Worlds
of Women," explores aggadic representations of women among women
and a woman on her own. Rabbinic literature exhibits a marked anxiety
in connection with female associations in the public domain, connecting
women among women with witchcraft and pagan rituals. This pertur-
bation regarding women colluding extends to the domestic realm, as
well, since all groups of women, including co-wives, sisters, mother and

daughter, and mistress and maidservant, are constructed as fundamentally untrustworthy. Aggadic traditions about Leah and Rachel, and Leah and Dinah, evoke concerns about female propensities for deception and immodesty. The aggadic counter-traditions concerning the daughters of Zelophehad (Num. 27), on the other hand, offer high praise for a group of women who successfully acted together to clarify the laws of inheritance. No common cause is found in midrashic adumbrations of the troubled biblical saga of Sarah and Hagar. Here the midrash privileges Sarah's central role in the history of the Jewish people and invokes the right of a mistress over her servant, impugning Hagar for her insufferable behavior and gentile origins. Similar opprobrium is reserved for Cozbi (Num. 25), another foreign woman who is blamed for leading Israelite men into sin.

Not all gentile women fared so poorly. The rabbis invested the biblical prostitute Rahab with the sanctioned female qualities they most valued in order to transform this Canaanite woman who accepted the God of Israel into an estimable model of female piety and virtue. Their exegetical efforts to domesticate a fallen woman into a submissive wife and mother in Israel not only reveal a favorable rabbinic attitude towards converts, whose welcome into the nurturing care of God was seen as a presage of Israel's ultimate reconciliation with the divine, but also demonstrate an aggadic willingness to attenuate the alterity of both gender and foreign origin when it served a homiletical purpose.

To study women in rabbinic literature is actually to study men. Since women's voices and actions are reflected only through the mediation of male constructions of their views and behavior, this book reveals far more about men's assumptions and anxieties than actual female concerns. Moreover, rabbinic *aggadah* preserves many voices. Comprised of discrete segments written, rewritten, and constantly edited over many centuries, across vast distances and in response to a variety of cultural environments and pressures, it is not surprising that this literature expresses diverse attitudes towards women and their activities. The multivocality of rabbinic literature on the nature of women, as on other topics, can be daunting. Judith Hauptman has suggested that almost every negative aggadic statement about women can be offset by another that says just the opposite.[11]

Yet, while the tendency of rabbinic editors to include contending opinions may indicate that there is not always a final privileging of one possibility over another, on some topics specific views predominate, while other strands of tradition and belief are subdued. As I argue in the chapters that follow, I find that certain dominant themes emerge out of the multiplicity of opinions preserved in aggadic literature concerning women. Primary among them—whether expressed as legal ordinance, anecdote, folklore, or midrashic expansion of a bibical text, and whether reflecting biblical, Greco-Roman, or Sassanian influences—is the conviction that "women are a separate people" (B. Shabbat 62a), a created entity essentially unlike men in physical form, in innate capacities, and in social and religious significance. These biological, intellectual, and spiritual differences are understood to be inherent in a woman's very essence: they are a consequence of how God created her. The conviction of the inherent alterity of women, and the inferior nature of their abilities and qualities, is invoked throughout rabbinic writings to justify female subordination to male control as essential for social order in the present and Jewish continuity in the future.

DISTINGUISHING DIFFERENCES:
THE OTHERNESS OF WOMEN
IN RABBINIC LITERATURE

Rabbinic literature evolved over a long sweep of time and reflects influences from a variety of cultural settings. Ostensibly an expansion and adumbration of divine revelations received at Sinai, this extensive body of writings encompasses a range of competing interpretations and opinions; while majority views are privileged, minority opinions are preserved as well. Rabbinic writings are not historical documents.[1] Highly edited over many centuries, this multivocal literature was created by men whose personal piety, individual experiences of the world, and vivid imaginations shaped an idealized social order which often had scant connection to the actual realities of Jewish life in the environments in which they lived.

Rabbinic views about women are as varied as rabbinic opinions on other subjects, but they rest on the conviction of women's essential otherness from men. The talmudic statement that "women are a separate people" (B. Shabbat 62a) conveys the basic rabbinic conviction that females are human entities created by God with physical characteristics, human qualities, and social functions inherently dissimilar from those of males. Moreover, the ways in which women are perceived to be essentially different are not only ineradicable but problematic for men. It is not surprising that women occupied a subordinate place in rabbinic Judaism's visionary world view in which free unblemished Jewish males alone participated fully in Israel's covenant with God.[2]

Woman as Other

The differences between the status and roles of men and women in rabbinic social policy were so marked that some rabbis believed that female alterity began at conception. In M. Niddah 3:7, a *mishnah* discussing how long a woman remains in a state of ritual impurity following a miscarriage, R. Ishmael explained that postpartum female ritual impurity is significantly longer following the birth of a daughter[3] because "a male is fully fashioned on the forty-first day [after conception] while the female is not fully formed until the eighty-first day." Although this opinion is ultimately rejected by the majority of the sages, who maintain "that both the fashioning of the male and the fashioning of the female take the same course, each lasting forty-one days," the preservation of R. Ishmael's minority position indicates that it accorded with rabbinic views about the essential differences between male and female.

The patently appealing notion that the process of fashioning a female took twice as long as fashioning a male is also considered at length in B. Niddah 30b, part of the extensive talmudic discussion about human conception and embryology based on M. Niddah 3:7 in B. Niddah 30a–31b. Here, too, R. Ishmael's view is finally rejected, this time on the grounds that "The duration of the fashioning period cannot be derived from that of [the period of] uncleaness." Nevertheless, even if a majority of rabbis could not find convincing evidence that the essential distinctions between male and female were reflected in each gender's development from the moment of conception, dominant views confirm that the dissimilar social roles and destinies of each gender were evident from birth.

The following segment of B. Niddah 31b, in particular, raises many of the areas of woman's profound otherness from man that will be discussed in detail in this chapter:

R. Isaac citing R. Ammi further stated: As soon as a male comes into the world peace comes into the world, for it is said, "**Send a gift (_khar_) to the ruler of the land**" (Isa. 16:1), [and the Hebrew word for] "male" (_zakhar_) [is composed of the consonants of the words for] "this is a gift" (_zeh khar_). R. Isaac citing R. Ammi further stated: When a male comes into the world his provisions come with him, [the Hebrew for] "male" (_zakhar_) [being composed of the consonants for the words for], "this is provision (_zeh khar_)," for it is written, "**And he prepared a great provision (_kherah_) for them**" (2 Kings 6:23). [Conversely] a female has nothing with her, [the Hebrew for] "female" (_n'qevah_) implying "she comes with nothing" (_n'qiyyah ba'ah_). Unless she demands her food nothing is given to her, for it is written, "**Name (_naq'vah_) the wages due from me and I will pay you**" (Gen. 30:28).

R. Simeon b. Yohai was asked by his disciples: Why did the Torah ordain that a woman after childbirth should bring a sacrifice? He replied: When she is giving birth she swears impetuously that she will never again have intercourse with her husband. The Torah, therefore, ordained that she should bring a sacrifice[4]. . . . And why did the Torah ordain that in the case of giving birth to a male [a woman may resume sexual relations with her husband] after seven days but in the case of a female [relations may not resume until] after fourteen days?

[On the birth of] a male, with whom all rejoice, she regrets her oath after seven days, [but on the birth of] a female, about whom everybody is upset, she does not regret her oath [of abstaining from sexual relations] until after fourteen days. And why did the Torah ordain circumcision on the eighth day? In order that the guests should not enjoy themselves while his father and mother are not in the mood for it.

It was taught: R. Meir used to say, Why did the Torah ordain that the uncleanness of menstruation should continue for seven [additional] days? Because being in constant contact with his wife [a husband might] develop a loathing towards her. The Torah, therefore, ordained: Let her be unclean for seven days in order that she shall be beloved by her husband as at the time of her first entry into the bridal chamber.[5]

R. Dostai son of R. Jannai was asked by his disciples: Why does a man go in search of a woman and no woman goes in search of a man? This is analogous to the case of a man who lost something. Who goes in search of what? He who lost a thing [his rib] goes in search of what he lost. And why does the man lie face downwards [during sexual intercourse] and woman face upwards towards the man? He [faces the elements] from which he was created and she [faces the man] from whom she was created. And why is a man easily pacified and a woman is not easily pacified? He [derives his nature] from the place from which he was created and [she derives hers] from the place from which she was created. Why is a woman's voice sweet and a man's voice is not sweet? He [derives his] from the place from which he was created and she [derives hers] from the place from which she was created. Thus it is said, "**Let me hear your voice; / For your voice is sweet / And your face is comely**" (Song of Songs 2:14).

A number of themes having to do with distinctions between males and females are raised in this passage. They include the views that the birth of a male excites celebration while the birth of a female is a cause for disappointment. Males are said to come into the world well equipped to function fully in society and to leave progeny after them. Women, conversely, come into the world with nothing; they are dependent upon male largesse for their very survival and, as empty wombs, they must wait for male agency in order to become bearers of children. A male child is circumcised on the eighth day of life to the great delight of all; indeed, on that day his parents may resume sexual relations. No rituals await new born daughters and, as a sign of grief at her gender, marital relations may only resume fourteen days after her birth. Women must be separated from their husbands during their menstrual periods, and, as the *halakhah* evolved, for a week afterward. R. Meir is credited with the view that this enforced hiatus maintains marital romance since it prevents the husband from finding his wife distasteful.

The final segment of B. Niddah 31b attributes distinctions between man and woman to differences in their modes of creation, a topic discussed in depth in chapter 2 of this book. The passage suggests that the preferred position for sexual intercourse is that in which the man, on top, looks towards his origins in the earth (i.e., to the cosmic substance from which God created him) while the woman, facing upward, looks toward the man from whose body she was created. Men communicate directly with God and the cosmos while women experience that relationship only vicariously, if at all, through their subordinate relationship to their husbands.[6] Moreover, because woman was created from a bone, which can be used as a musical instrument, her voice is described here as sweet. A woman's sweet voice can be as much of a sexual incitement as her physical beauty and B. Niddah 31b concludes with a proof text from Song of Songs evoking the pleasant and the problematic aspects of woman's sexual attractiveness to men, both of which play significant roles in rabbinic formations of the feminine.

The Centrality of Men

The interpreters and expositors of rabbinic Judaism were men, and the divinely mandated society they imagined was decidedly oriented towards their own sex. As B. Niddah 31b elucidates, rabbinic Judaism literally saw men as God's gift to the world. When female voices are heard in rabbinic literature, they are usually mediated through male assumptions of female difference and inferiority. Women did not play any active part in shaping rabbinic Judaism's idealized design for an androcentric communal life centered on worship, study, and governance according to divinely revealed mandates. In this religious system, men expound the divine rulings that affect women's lives; women, the objects of some these directives, have no standing to legislate for themselves or others.[7] One of the most succinct statements of the difference in the status of men and women in rabbinic Judaism is found in B. Menahot 43b, in a discussion of the various ritual obligations incumbent on the adult male Jew:

It was taught: R. Judah [in some sources R. Meir] used to say, A man is bound to say the following three blessing daily: "[Blessed are you . . .] who has not made me a gentile," "who has not made me a woman," and "who has not made me a brutish man," R. Aha ben Jacob once overheard his son saying "[Blessed are you . . .] who has not made me a brutish man," whereupon [struck by the arrogance of the statement since brutish men are also bound by the commandments] he said to him, "And this too?" Said the other, "Then what blessing should I say instead?" [He replied] ". . . who has not made me a slave." [Objectors asked] and isn't that the same as a woman [since a woman and a slave are of the same status regarding performance of commandments]? [It was answered] A slave is more contemptible.

These three blessing ultimately became part of the daily liturgy for morning prayers in traditional Jewish practice, enshrining the difference in the status of men and women in rabbinic Judaism for centuries to come.[8]

Certainly there were rabbinic voices sympathetic to women and their situations. Scholars including Judith Hauptman and Jacob Neusner have demonstrated how rabbinic legislation enhanced women's rights in various areas of social and economic life, eliminated glaring injustices, and often eased problematic legal situations.[9] Such mitigations, however, should not be understood as indicating any fundamental alterations in the overwhelming rabbinic consensus of women's essential otherness and lesser capabilities. Moreover, neither women's important economic activities, nor their religious rituals, which undoubtedly existed, nor female understandings of their lives, experiences, or spirituality are retrievable in any significant way from this male-centered literary corpus, which represents an idealized vision of how life should be lived more than it reflects the actual realities of everyday existence.[10]

B. Niddah 31b suggests that a man, despite all his advantages, is somehow incomplete without a woman; she was formed from his rib and he must recover what he has lost in order to fulfil his legal obligation to procreate. To devalue women in comparison with men is not to devalue them altogether. Rabbinic literature affirms that individual women, who are indispensable to reproduction and are required to provide essential family support services, were not only necessary for the smooth functioning of everyday life in the present and for Jewish continuity in the future, but could also be cherished beings who were loved and protected by specific men. Indeed, as long as women satisfied their essential domestic expectations, they were revered and honored for enhancing the lives of their families, and particularly for enabling male relatives to fulfil their religious obligations of prayer and study. B. Berakhot 17a relates that women earn merit "by making their sons go to the synagogue to learn Scripture, and their husbands to the studyhouse to learn Mishnah, and by waiting for their husbands until they return from the studyhouse."[11] B. Yoma 47a preserves several anecdotes attributing the achievements of high priests to the valor and modesty of their mothers.

While numerous texts condemn immodest and light minded women who do not conform to patriarchal expectations, rabbinic literature praises the supportive, resourceful, and self-sacrificing wife and mother, and expresses concern for her physical and emotional needs and welfare.[12] Rabbinic jurisprudence frequently moved beyond biblical precedents in its efforts to ameliorate some of the disadvantages and hardships women faced as a consequence of biblical legislation, particularly in extending protection to women in personal status areas.[13] Moreover, many halakhic authorities sought to be flexible in easing difficulties which individual women encountered because of their disadvantaged position in rabbinic legislation, including complications resulting from levirate marriage, desertion, and the inability to divorce a husband or to contest an undesired divorce.[14] Still, despite some willingness to consider an individual woman's personal situation sympathetically, the purport of rabbinic opinion is that a woman best contributes to a smoothly functioning society when she is submissive to and supportive of male authority. As B. Niddah 31b advises, woman, who is inherently inflexible due to her creation from the bone of a rib, must look to the more adaptable man from whose body she was created for guidance and security.

Circumcision and Male Potency

Male anxiety about female corporeality and its functions played a significant part in the relegation of women to a secondary place in rabbinic Judaism's public and ritual life. Many rabbinic authorities believed women's bodies were irredeemably deficient since they lacked the ability to generate life. As B. Niddah 31b put it, a woman comes into the world with nothing while man is well equipped for his stay on earth. Essentially passive, a female depends on male potency for everything, including the production of progeny. The metaphorical configuration of a wife as a "house," a vessel for the bearing and nurturing of children, already found in numerous biblical passages, is a rabbinic commonplace.[15]

Establishing the active agency of men and the passivity of women in reproduction was an important component of rabbinic constructions of female otherness. One aspect of this discourse argued that men were most like God in their ability to generate new life, while women, as submissive nurturers, were subordinate not only in relation to men but in their lack of resemblance to the divine. This dialectic of differentiation was based on the conviction that being like God required fully functioning male sexual organs.[16] In the ancient world, virility and the physical parts that made it possible were accorded enormous reverence. The English words "testify" and "testimony" derive from the Latin *testes* because men invoked their most defining parts in swearing oaths and entering into contracts. Possession of male genitals was central not only to rabbinic Judaism's understanding of what it meant to be created in the divine image but also to Judaism's defining initiation event, physical circumcision, the joyous ritual following the birth of a son referred to in B. Niddah 31b.

Beginning with Genesis 17, *b'rit milah*, the covenant of circumcision, became the prerequisite for full entry into the *b'rit*, the covenant between God and Israel, whose primary obligation came to be understood as obedience to the legal code revealed at Sinai. This covenantal alliance, marked on the flesh of the eight-day-old male infant, debarred women, for lack of the organ of reproduction with which they were not created, from complete participation in Jewish worship and religious service. Howard Eilberg-Schwartz has written that "since circumcision binds together men within and across generations, it also establishes an opposition between men and women."[17]

As Shaye J. D. Cohen has shown, the rabbis were quite aware that the privileging of circumcision as the central marker of Jewish identity rendered half of the Jewish people ineligible. He suggests they evinced little concern about it because in rabbinic thinking to be a Jew was to be born into an ethnic community. Even if a woman could not be circumcised, she did not need circumcision or any other ritual to be accepted as a Jew.[18] Secondly, Cohen suggests that for rabbinic Judaism Jewish women were not Jews in the way Jewish men were Jews:

The normal Jew for the rabbis, as the "normal" Israelite of the Torah, was the free adult male. The exclusion of women from circumcision typifies their exclusion from the observance of numerous commandments. . . . A woman's place is to facilitate acts of piety by her menfolk, acts of piety from which she herself is excluded. Therefore it should occasion no surprise if only men are marked by circumcision—only men are really Jews in all respects.[19]

As Cohen observes, the rabbis were so convinced of "the fundamental inferiority, marginality and Otherness of women" that "the presence of a covenantal mark on the bodies of men, and its absence from the bodies of women, seemed natural and inevitable."[20]

Moreover, circumcision was synonymous in rabbinic thinking with the linked themes of male fertility, procreation, and intergenerational continuity. As Eilberg-Schwartz has written of the biblical origins of this ritual:

As a ceremony of birth, Israelite circumcision did not incorporate themes of virility and social maturity. But it did symbolize the initiate's fertility. As the priests saw it, a boy's procreative powers were granted by God as a privilege for having been born into Abraham's line. They were granted in fulfillment of the divine promise that Abraham and his descendants would be fruitful, multiply, and inherit the land. A male's ability to reproduce was not simply the outcome of his maturation but also a privilege of having a certain genealogy. Circumcision was thus a rite which simultaneously conferred and confirmed one's pedigree.[21]

Indeed, so close are the connections among fertility, maleness, and creation in the divine image, that some rabbinic texts, like the following excerpt from a discussion in B. Shevuot 18b on the ways in which a man can guarantee the generation of male progeny, link the production of male children with obedience to divine mandates of sanctity:

Rabbi Benjamin bar Yapat said in the name of R. Eleazar, all who make themselves holy at intercourse will have male children, as it is written, "For I the Lord am your God: you shall sanctify yourselves and be holy, for I am holy . . ." (Lev. 11:44), and near it is written "The Lord spoke to Moses, saying: Speak to the Israelite people thus: When a woman at childbirth bears a male, she shall be unclean seven days; she shall be unclean as at the time of her menstrual infirmity. On the eighth day the flesh of his foreskin shall be circumcised" (Lev. 12:1–3).[22]

B. Shevuot 18b assumes that the male role in reproduction is the crucial component in the birth of children and that particular attention to following divinely ordained mandates of sanctity will guarantee male offspring who will continue the dialogue of holiness between God and Jewish men.

Most rabbinic texts maintained the model reflected in B. Shevuot 18b of the active male and the passive female in human procreation. However, it is worth noting that a few rabbinic passages reflect a more nuanced awareness of the respective reproductive roles of each sex, probably indicative of some knowledge of Greco-Roman medical debates over the male and female contributions to reproduction. Ancient Greek medicine preserved two conflicting views of the female role in conception, that of Hippocrates and his school and that of Aristotle. The school of Hippocrates, which maintained that woman was a creature completely different from man, held that both men and women released seed during sexual relations. While the man's role was more important, each sex contributed to the constitution of the embryo. Aristotle, on the other hand, insisted that woman was a substandard or defective man. He believed that only men could produce seed and generate the new life which grew in the female's body until the moment of birth.[23] As Jan Blayney has written:

To briefly elaborate: in Aristotle's view, the male contribution to generation was semen, whilst that of the female was menstrual fluid; and given that the male was the one who generated, and the female the one out of whom the male generated, and that the male was naturally the active partner, whilst the female was the passive partner, then, in Aristotle's mind, it was only reasonable that the male provided the movement and form, the female the body or matter.[24]

The most influential Roman medical writer, Galen, who lived during the second century C.E., tried to reconcile these two conflicting outlooks. He preserved the Hippocratic view that both men and women produced seed, while also insisting that the maternal semen was less important than the paternal and served primarily to provide nourishment for the male semen. In the later stages of embryonic growth, Galen held that this sustaining function was assumed by the menstrual blood, a theory originating with Aristotle.[25]

It is striking to see how aspects of both schools of thought appear in rabbinic texts. In B. Berakhot 51b, a passage discussed in more detail in chapter 3, the Palestinian sage 'Ulla explained his refusal to allow a woman to participate in sharing the cup of benediction that concludes the recitation of grace after a meal on the grounds that the blessing did not apply to her because of her passive role in reproduction:

Thus said R. Johanan: The fruit of a woman's body is blessed only from the fruit of a man's body, since it says, **"He will bless the fruit of your** [masculine singular] **body"** (Deut. 7:13). It does not say the fruit of "her body," but the fruit of **"your body."**

In this apparent appropriation of the Aristotelian approach to conception, woman's secondary responsibility in the performance of commandments is proved by reference to her secondary role in reproduction. In each case, her husband is the active partner while she is the passive recipient of the benefits of his performance. The children she bears are the fruit of the man who impregnated her and she may take no credit in their origination. Indeed, since he is commanded to procreate and she is not, she is objectified as a vessel through which he can fulfil his obligation.

Genesis Rabbah 18:3 preserves a similar comment on the creation of woman from man's rib in Genesis 2:22, in which R. Hisda is quoted as saying: "He built more chambers in her than in man, fashioning her broad below and narrow at the top, so that she could receive child." Here, too, the female is constructed both literally and metaphorically as the passive participant in the generation of new life, housing and nourishing the man's child until it is ready to be born.

While B. Niddah 31b appears to support the view of female passivity in its statement that women come into the world with nothing while men are well-provided for their earthly responsibilities, some alternate views of conception and the formation of the embryo, maintaining Hippocrates' theory that both men and women emit semen, appear earlier in the same extended *sugya*. Thus, B. Niddah 31a quotes R. Isaac citing R. Ammi as follows:

If the woman emits her semen first she bears a male child; if the man emits his semen first she bears a female child, for it is said, **"When a woman brings forth seed and bears a male"** (Lev. 12:2)[26]

Several related teachings cited immediately after this saying reinforce the contention that if a woman achieved orgasm, which was understood to be the meaning of her "emitting seed," prior to her partner, she would conceive a male child. Two goals of rabbinic social policy are linked here: the achievement of male offspring and the mutuality of sexual pleasure within marriage.

B. Niddah 31a also preserves a rabbinic variation on Galen's theory of how the embryo is constituted. In this version, "there are three partners in a child":

God, the father and the mother. The father supplies the white substance [semen] of which the child's bones, sinews, nails, brain and the white of the eyes are formed. The mother supplies the red substance [menstrual blood] of which are formed the skin, flesh, hair, blood, and the dark of the eyes. God supplies the spirit, the breath, beauty of features, eyesight, hearing, and the ability to speak and to walk, understanding, and discernment. When his time to depart from the world approaches, the Holy One, blessed be He, takes away his share and leaves the shares of his father and his mother with him. R. Papa observed: It is this that people have in mind when they say, "Shake off the salt and cast the flesh to the dog."

In this model, which incorporates marked similarities to Galen's compromise theory of human generation, the male seed is planted in the woman's womb where it is nurtured by the female's menstrual blood. What differentiates this rabbinic representation of the origins of human life from its Roman counterpart, however, is the addition of the indispensable third party, God, who supplies the essential attributes of animation, cognition, and communication.

Certainly, no rabbinic teacher would argue with assigning the primary part in the genesis of each new human life to God. The second most important role, however, was unquestionably that of the male whose role in human continuity imitated God's creative powers. The prerequisite of circumcision for inclusion in the covenant established between God and Israel reinforced this link between male fertility and fully Jewish status. Such a preeminent emphasis on male generativity devalued and minimized a woman's roles in reproduction and in Jewish communal life in general, even as it diminished her connection to God.

Woman as Source of Pollution

It was taught: R. Meir used to say, Why did the Torah ordain that the uncleanness of menstruation should continue for seven [additional] days? Because being in constant contact with his wife [a husband might] develop a loathing towards her. The Torah, therefore, ordained: Let her be unclean for seven days in order that she shall be beloved by her husband as at the time of her first entry into the bridal chamber. (B. Niddah 31b)

A major question in B. Niddah 31b is how long a woman must remain in a state of ritual impurity following the births of a son and a daughter, respectively. In connection to this topic, R. Meir asserts that marital separation during menstruation is a positive aspect of conjugality, because it will prevent a wife from becoming abhorrent to her husband. His statement offers an apologetic explanation for the barriers to marital intimacy imposed by biblical and rabbinic ritual purity strictures[27] by suggesting that the stored up sexual longings and ardent anticipation generated by a forced separation maintain the romance in a marriage. However, the compliment is backhanded, as well, since it implies that a man in unremitting contact with his wife and her natural processes will soon find his spouse repugnant. R. Meir's teaching further suggests that women are problematic for men not only in what their bodies lack. The physical features and functions that distinguish the female body also evoke contradictory male responses of repulsion and attraction.

Certainly, rabbinic Judaism is not unique in relegating women to the margins of its intellectual and spiritual world as a result of their biological differences from men. Anthropologists have noted that numerous societies have designated women as distant from culture and closer to nature because of the "natural procreative functions specific to women alone," including fertility, maternity, and menstrual blood. Although this perception of women's otherness based on physical and biological differences is a human construct rather than a scientific reality, it is often reflected in institutional structures and barriers that reinforce this vision of the female as an essentially physical being.[28] In many cultures, women have been defined almost exclusively in terms of their sexual and reproductive functions, many of which may be frightening or unpleasant to men.[29] Again 'Ulla's statement that "women are a separate people" must be taken literally. In the system of dialectics through which rabbinic thinkers defined reality, women embody their otherness from men just as God is other than human beings; similarly, human beings are contrasted with other creatures, and Jews with gentiles. In each case, the dissimilarities of the outer forms indicate the differences within and point, as well, to the cultural consequences of those differences.

An analogous approach to understanding rabbinic distinctions between men and women has to do with rabbinic categories of normality and the anomalous. In his discussion of what constitutes clean and unclean in Jewish tradition, Jean Soler has argued that Judaism strictly defines human beings, God, the animals, and the plants through their relationship with one another in a series of opposites. Entities which are seen as capable of causing uncleanness and disorder can upset this cosmic taxonomy. He writes that in the biblical dietary laws, which became the basis of the system of permitted and forbidden foods in rabbinic Judaism, animals which do not fit into any designated category, or fit into two classes at once, are considered unclean because they are anomalous in their relation to the perceived order which underlies the created world.[30] Soler goes on to say that the dietary and the sexual prohibitions of the Hebrew Bible are coordinated and that both are based on separating classes of being. To abolish differentiations would be to subvert the order of the world.[31] One may extrapolate from Soler's model that, in the rabbinic vision of men as whole and women as incomplete, men represent order and control while women, who are connected with disorder in themselves and others, are demonstrably a secondary and, in some ways, an anomalous category of creation.

Women evoke repulsion and fear of disorder because their biological processes can be seen as threatening to men. In a religious system which likens ritual impurity to a state of spiritual death, periodic female flows of blood are central to male anxieties about women as sources of potential pollution and as portents of physical extinction. Such fears, deeply rooted in the cultures of the ancient Near East, are voiced in various rulings found in Leviticus 11–15, in which the *niddah*, the menstruating or postpartum woman,[32] is listed among a number of biblical sources of potential danger to male ritual purity.[33] Although males are also subject to discharges and states of ritual impurity, their physical manifestations are understood to be unusual and sporadic. For women, as Howard Eilberg-Schwartz has pointed out, such discharges are characteristic; they are normal and expected rather than an accident which may temporarily affect and disable a man. The fact that women regularly menstruate constitutes an indispensable component of biblical and rabbinic constructions of the female. Nor, as he notes, is menstruation seen as a positive part of women's natural cycle of fruitfulness; menstruation indicates a failure of fertility. Unlike the blood of circumcision, which is associated with fecundity, the blood of menstruation may be linked with defilement, estrangement from God, and death.[34] The seriousness with which separation from a *niddah* was taken in biblical times is evident in the fact that sexual contact with a *niddah* is also forbidden in Leviticus 18:19 as among those sinful acts punished severely by *karet*, or extirpation from the community (Lev. 18:29). As Shaye J. D. Cohen writes, "The prohibition of 'drawing near' to a menstruant for sexual purposes (Lev. 18:19 and 20:18) is part of a list of prohibited sexual unions and has nothing to do with ritual purity. Even when the purity system would lapse after the destruction of the second temple in 70 C.E., the prohibition of union with a menstruant would not."[35]

During the rabbinic era, the prohibition of sexual relations with a menstruating wife was expanded. At some point after the codification of the Mishnah, seven further "white" days of separation between husband and wife were added, following the end of the menstrual period itself. It is impossible to know to what degree these prohibitions were observed at any point during the various eras or in the various locales of rabbinic Judaism. These strictures became normative only in post-talmudic Jewish societies. Still, they probably encountered considerable resistance when they were first promulgated, as indicated by the threatening tone of much of the discussion exhorting their observance. *Avot de-Rabbi Nathan* A, ch. 2 advises the following precautions to preserve separation between spouses:

What is the fence which the Torah made about its words? Lo, it says, "Do not come near a woman during her period of uncleanness to uncover her nakedness" (Lev. 18:19). May her husband perhaps embrace her or kiss her or engage in idle chattter? The verse says, "Do not come near." May she perhaps sleep with him in her clothes on the couch? The verse says, "Do not come near." May she perhaps wash her face and paint her eyes? The verse says "And concerning her who is in menstrual infirmity" (Lev. 15:33): all the days of her impurity let her be in isolation. Hence it was said: She that neglects herself in the days of her impurity, with her the Sages are pleased; but she that adorns herself in the days of her impurity, with her the Sages are displeased.

In response to the question of whether a *niddah*, during her "white" days may sleep in the same bed as her husband, each wrapped in her or his own garment, even when no physical contact takes place, parallel passages in *Avot de-Rabbi Nathan* A, ch. 2 and B. Shabbat 13a recount the cautionary tale of a worthy scholar who died young. The prophet Elijah asked the mourning wife about the husband's conduct with her during her "white days." She answered, "He ate with me, drank with me, and slept with me in bodily contact, and it did not occur to him to do other." Elijah responds:

"Blessed be the Omnipresent for slaying him, that He did not condone [his wrong behavior] on account of the Torah [this man had learned]! For lo! the Torah says, 'Do not come near a woman during her period of uncleanness' (Lev. 18:19)."

B. Shabbat 13a continues, "When R. Dimi came, he said, It was a broad bed. In the West [Palestine] they said, R. Isaac. b. Joseph said: An apron interposed between them. [And even so, he was punished]." According to this *aggadah*, the possibility of coming into contact with a *niddah* is dangerous in itself. Neither a broad bed nor an actual textile separation can provide adequate protection. The separation from the *niddah* had to be complete, regardless of the human cost.

It is instructive that *Avot de-Rabbi Nathan* A concludes its version of the story with an emphasis on the dangers of female/male proximity and an admonition about close association with any women, even family members:

Lo, Scripture says, "None of you shall come near anyone of his own flesh to uncover nakedness: I am the Lord" (Lev. 18:6). Hence it was said: Let no man be alone with any woman in an inn, even with his sister or his daughter or his mother-in-law, because of public opinion. Let no man chat with a woman in the marketplace, even is she is his wife, and needless to say, with another woman, because of public opinion. Let no man walk behind a woman in the market place, even behind his wife, and, needless to say, another woman, because of public opinion.

Marital sexual separation entails at least as much hardship for men as for women. The rabbinic prolongation by a week, without biblical justification, of the length of time a wife and husband are to abstain from all physical contact, not only sexual activity, indicates how seriously later formulators of rabbinic literature and Jewish social practice took the prospect of even accidental contact with a *niddah*. Evidence that this separation was regarded as onerous and was resented is evident in the following aggadic comment from *Midrash on Psalms* 146:4 about the benefits of the world to come, commenting on "He sets free the bound" (Psalm 146:4):

Although nothing is more strongly forbidden than intercourse with a menstruant . . . in the time-to-come, God will permit such intercourse. As Scripture says, "In that day, too—declares the Lord of Hosts— . . . I will also make the 'prophets' and the unclean spirit vanish from the land" (Zech. 13:2); the "unclean" clearly refers to a menstruant, and of such it is said, "Do not come near a woman during her period of uncleanness to uncover her nakedness" (Lev. 18:19).

Although this minority view is immediately countered by the ascetic statement that it is sexual intercourse itself which will be forbidden in the messianic era, David Biale suggests that this midrash may be read as one "voice of protest raised against the legal strictures on sexuality and perhaps also against the rabbinic obsession with procreation."[36]

Why were these rules of separation so crucial to rabbinic Judasim? Judith Hauptman suggests that rabbinic social policy preserved the rules of separation during actual menstruation when other ritual purity separations lapsed both because levitical legislation specifically banned sexual intercourse with a menstruating woman, separate from any ritual considerations (Lev. 18:19, 20:18), and because of a general revulsion to menstrual blood common throughout the ancient Near East.[37] The addition of the seven days of further separation, the so-called "white days," is more problematic.

Tirzah Meacham has proposed that this innovation reflected a trend of thinking in which the category of normal menstruation was eliminated and all uterine bleeding came to fall in the category of abnormal bleeding. All *niddot* therefore become *zavot*, who are required to wait seven clean days after a flow of blood. The motivation may have been to provide further safeguards against any possible contact with a woman with a flow of blood, and perhaps to eliminate the need for rabbinic discrimination among categories of different kinds of blood. She notes that there were probably objections to this increased stringency, since it goes far beyond biblical requirements for the menstruating woman and significantly reduced the possibilities of normative halakhic sexual contact. Perhaps an atmosphere of asceticism, possibly related to mourning for the continued state of exile and the destruction of the Temple eased its acceptance, at least among the sages themselves.[38] As both Hauptman and Meacham point out, the tendency towards expanding prohibitions in this area of Jewish law continued and increased in the post-talmudic period.[39]

Separation from the *niddah* is often presented as a matter which is of concern only to husband and wife. However, both biblical and rabbinic sources link contact with any menstruating woman to defilement and even to danger. M. Shabbat 9:1 quotes Isaiah 30:22 in equating the desecration conveyed by carrying either an idol or a *niddah*:

R. Aqiva said: Whence do we know that an idol defiles by carriage like a *niddah*? Because it is said, "And you will treat as unclean the silver overlay of your images and the golden plating of your idols. You will cast them away like a menstruous woman. 'Out' you will call to them." So does an idol defile by carriage.

In this instance, simply conveying the body of a menstruating woman from one place to another, even without actually touching her, is considered equivalent pollution to contact with an idol. In a discussion of various numerically based superstitions, including the statement that a woman is among those who may not pass between two men, B. Pesahim 111a preserves the following tradition: "If a menstruating woman passes between two [men], if it is at the beginning of her menses she will slay one of them, and if it is at the end of her menses she will cause strife between them. What is the remedy? Let them commence a [biblical] verse [beginning] with *el* [a Hebrew word element for God] and ending with *el.*" Similarly, B. Shabbat 110a advises how a woman threatened by a snake can frighten it away: she should throw some of her hair and nails at the snake while saying, "I am menstruous."

Shaye Cohen has pointed out that such attitudes, more expressive of folk piety than legal formulation, confirm "the marginality of all women, menstruating or not, in the organized, public expressions of Jewish piety." As he writes of their consequences, "In Judaism (at least until recently) public sacred space is male space, and the exclusion of menstruants from that space confirms that women, because they are women, are not its natural occupants."[40] Cohen states that in his view the menstruant is constructed in rabbinic literature as impure and as capable of transmitting impurity but not as a source of danger. It seems to me, however, that he does not go far enough: significant voices within rabbinic literature believe that the *niddah* herself can be dangerous. The linkage of the menstruating woman, and hence all women, with peril and death for men is an ancient belief, which is deeply embedded in biblical and rabbinic thinking.[41]

Charlotte Fonrobert does not believe that rabbinic literature constructs menstruating woman as either a source of general impurity or of danger to the community at large. She argues that following the destruction of the Temple all ritual purity legislation lapsed. It was only the second levitical prohibition concerning the *niddah*, forbidden marital contact, that continued in force. *Niddah* observance, accordingly, is best understood as part of a rabbinic effort to preserve the biblical community of Israel as an ethnically distinct, embodied community distinguished by corporeal practices. Thus, Fonrobert suggests that discussions in B. Niddah about ways in which a menstruating woman transfers states of impurity to objects and other persons had no practical relevance. While Fonrobert acknowledges that references to the harmful propensities of menstruating women remain in rabbinic literature, I am not convinced by her dismissal of such statements as "folklore," rather than as actual expressions of anxiety about the *niddah* as a source of danger to men in general.[42]

It is important to remember that menstruating women constituted no danger to other women, nor were they halakhically prohibited from taking part in rituals or in study. T. Berakhot 2:12 is quite clear on this matter:

Men who have experienced an abnormal genital discharge and women who have experienced an abnormal genital discharge as well as menstruating women and women who have recently given birth are permitted to chant Torah, Prophets, and Writings out of a scroll and to chant from memory Mishnah, midrash, *ha-*

lakhot, and *aggadot*. Men who have experienced an emission of semen are barred from all of these activities.

Yet, this statement permitting female engagement with all of the revealed writings of Jewish tradition does not appear in the Babylonian Talmud. Scholars, including Daniel Boyarin and Mayer Gruber, have pointed out that although the Tosefta accepts that women may be involved in chanting scriptures and rabbinic teachings, even when in a state of *niddah*, the Talmud at B. Berakhot 22a omits any mention of the licit participation of women in such activities, whether *niddah* or not, and takes for granted that these acts of worship and study are exclusively male prerogatives. Since B. Berakhot 22a affirms that words of Torah are not susceptible to uncleanness, it seems clear that the exclusion of women from these activities does not reflect any apprehension that they might defile the divine word. Based on this point, Mayer Gruber argues that the systematic disempowerment of women from rabbinic Judaism's central communal spiritual actitivities cannot be explained by their periodic states of *niddah*, and must have its origins elsewhere.[43]

I would disagree. The issue is not whether or not women might pollute the Torah scrolls. They cannot. Rather the rabbis' fear is that women might defile the men with whom they would come into contact, if their presence were encouraged in sites of worship and learning. In effect, the rabbis have written male piety on female bodies. In order to construct fences to protect male ritual sanctity from the *niddah*, all potential contacts with women had to be eliminated from places of holiness. There can be little doubt that the perceived dangers associated with the *niddah* represent one important thread in rabbinic Judaism's formation of the feminine as something quite separate from the world of unblemished adult Jewish males.

Woman as Temptress

Why is a woman's voice sweet and a man's voice is not sweet? He [derives his] from the place from which he was created [the earth] and she [derives hers] from the place from which she was created [a bone]. Thus it is said, "Let me hear your voice; / For your voice is sweet / And your face is comely" (Song of Songs 2:14).

B. Niddah 31b concludes an extensive talmudic discussion with an evocation of female sexuality, an indication that women are also problematic in rabbinic thinking because they are sexually attractive to men. Consciousness of the strength of human sexuality and its capacity to cause social disorder permeates rabbinic literature. It is not surprising that significant strands of rabbinic legislation are motivated by a desire to circumscribe, defuse, and control the female not only as potential polluter but also as sexual temptress.[44]

Jacob Neusner has discussed the part played by rabbinic Judaism's heightened awareness of sexuality and its potential consequences in his analysis of mishnaic texts concerned with the contracting and dissolving of marriages. He argues that in the patriarchal world of rabbinic Judaism man is normal and woman is abnormal, since she is always capable of upsetting the rabbis' ordered program for reality. Thus, rabbinic Judaism is especially anxious to keep women subject to men and to establish rules that regulate the transfer of a woman from one man to another at liminal moments when her situation is likely to be most disturbing and disruptive, particularly the contracting of marriages.[45]

As Michael Satlow has demonstrated, rabbinic literature portrays women not only as sexually attractive to men, but also as more sexually avid and as less able to control their overwhelming desires.[46] This "light mindedness" inherent in women is why M. Qiddushin 4:12 rules that a man cannot be alone with two women (unless one is his wife) while a woman may be alone with two men, since one man's presence will restrain the other. In fact, certain remarks in rabbinic discourse offer high praise to men who are able to resist sexual temptation. One such passage in B. Sanhedrin 19b–20a occurs in the context of a discussion of David's tangled relations with Saul's daughters Merab and Michal. Of particular interest to the rabbis is Palti (1 Sam. 25:44) or Paltiel (2 Sam. 3:15), the man to whom Saul gave Michal after her marriage to David, who is said to have resisted the temptation of consummating his relationship with Michal over a long period of time, since she was not officially divorced from David. This second husband is favorably compared to other biblical figures who braved similar but less taxing enticements:

R. Johanan said: Joseph's strong temptation [by Potiphar's wife recounted in Gen. 39:7–13] was but a petty trial to that of Boaz [Ruth 3:8–15], and that of Boaz was small in comparison with that of Palti son of Layish. . . . R. Johanan said: What is meant by the verse, "Many women have done well, / But you surpass them all" (Prov. 31:29)? "Many women" refers to Joseph and Boaz; "But you surpass them all" refers to Palti son of Layish. R. Samuel b. Nahmani said in R. Jonathan's name: What is meant by the verse, "Grace is deceptive, / Beauty is illusory; / It is for her fear of the Lord / That a woman is to be praised" (Prov. 31:30)? "Grace is deceptive," refers to the temptation of Joseph; and "Beauty is illusory," to Boaz; while "It is for her fear of the Lord / That a woman is to be praised" refers to the case of Palti son of Layish.

The most striking aspect of this testimony to male triumph over sexual desire is its transgendered reading of Proverbs 31:29–30. The irony of invoking one of the most positive statements of female qualities found in biblical literature as a proof text for praise of men who resisted the seductive allurements of women seems to be lost on the rabbinic compilers. The end of this *sugya*, which concludes the discussion of M. Sanhedrin 2:2, uses these same verses from Proverbs to praise various generations of men who eschewed the pleasures of women in order to devote their lives to Torah study, a topic discussed in more detail in chapter 4 of this volume.

Not all men are as strong as the biblical exemplars described in B. Sanhedrin 19b–20a. A preponderance of voices within rabbinic Judaism advise the construction of legal boundaries limiting contact between men and women in all circumstances to prevent the possibility of sexual arousal or contact between inappropriate partners, to avert adulterous or incestuous relationships and the conception and birth of illegitimate children (*mamzerim*). B. Nedarim 20a advises that a man must not converse much with women as this will ultimately lead him to unchastity. It goes on to say:

> R. Aha of the school of R. Josiah said: He who gazes at a woman eventually comes to sin, and he who looks even at a woman's heel will beget degenerate children. R. Joseph said: This applies even to one's own wife when she is a *niddah*. R. Simeon b. Lakish said: "Heel" that is stated means the unclean part, which is directly opposite the heel.[47]

As Judith Hauptman has written in another context, these texts written by men and for men make a very simple point: "Seeing and being with women arouses men sexually. Often, the woman who arouses a man is forbidden to him. Since his arousal demands resolution, it is better for him not to put himself in circumstances in which arousal is likely."[48]

Aggadic passages that define a number of biblical women simply by how they were imagined to have affected men sexually are part of the same discourse. Thus, B. Megillah 15a, in a discussion of some specific biblical women, preserves the remark that "Rahab inspired lust by her name; Yael by her voice; Abigail by her memory; and Michal, daughter of Saul, by her appearance." Here, as elsewhere in midrashic exegesis, biblical women of courage and action are objectifed and reduced to their imagined sexual impact on men, whether by reputation, voice, nostalgia, or outer beauty. Similarly, other admirable biblical women are represented in negative terms because their actions question rabbinic Judaism's constructions of appropriate female roles. Thus, B. Megillah 14b criticizes the judge Deborah and the prophet Huldah for arrogance in their dealings with men: "R. Nahman said: Haughtiness does not befit women. There were two haughty women, and their names are hateful, one being called a hornet [Deborah, usually translated as "bee"] and the other a weasel [the literal meaning of Huldah]."

A similar negative construction of the female, this time as complicit in attracting sexual attention, is evident in an anecdote in B. Ta'anit 24a about the beautiful daughter of R. Jose b. Abin. This aggadic traditon also alludes to the potential weakness of all barriers, both literal and legal:

One day [R. Jose] saw a man boring a hole in the fence so that he might catch a glimpse [of R. Jose's daughter]. He said to the man, What is this? And the man answered: Master, if I am not worthy enough to marry her, may I not at least be worthy to catch a glimpse of her? Thereupon [R. Jose] exclaimed: My daughter, you are a source of trouble to mankind; return to the dust so that men may not sin because of you.

Although R. Jose is criticized in context for his callousness in expressing a desire for his daughter's death, one cannot escape the conclusion that, in at least one of its aspects, rabbinic Judaism perceives of women as essentially no more than sexual snares with the potential to lead a man into sinful behavior simply by virtue of their physical being.

Blaming women for male lust does not originate in rabbinic literature. This theme is well established in biblical and post-biblical writings, as well as in the cultures among whom Jews lived. An extended passage in B. Sanhedrin 100b offers an example of how rabbinic authorities justified such attitudes by building on the proof texts of earlier authorities. In this case, the context is whether or not the non-canonical book, The Wisdom of Ben Sira, written a few centuries before the rabbinic period, could be licitly read. The rabbis concluded that, at least on the subject of women, Ben Sira said nothing that diverged in any significant way from their own traditions. In fact, they adumbrated his comments when appropriate:

But if you take exception to the passage: "A daughter is a secret anxiety to her father, and worry over her robs him of sleep; when she is young, for fear she may not marry, or if married, for fear she may be disliked; while a virgin, for fear she may be seduced and become pregnant in her father's house; or having a husband, for fear she may go astray, or though married for fear she may be barren" (Wisdom of Ben Sira 42:9–10); if she grows old, lest she engage in witchcraft.[49] But the Rabbis have said the same: The world cannot exist without males and females; yet happy is he whose children are males, and woe to him whose children are females. . . . R. Joseph said: We may expound to them the good things it [Wisdom of Ben Sira] contains, for example, "A good wife is a great blessing" (26:3); "A bad wife is a chafing yoke" (26:7). How shall he mend matters? Let him banish her from his house: so shall he be healed of his plague. "Happy the man whose wife is good: the number of his days is doubled" (26:1). "Turn away your eyes from a shapely woman, and do not gaze at beauty belonging to another; many have been seduced by a woman's beauty, and by it passion is kindled like a fire. Never dine with another man's wife, or revel with her at wine; or your heart may turn aside to her, and in blood you may be plunged into destruction" (9:8–9), and many are the blows sustained by itinerant peddlars. "Those who seduce to adultery are as the spark that kindles the ember" (11:32).

The rabbis agree with Ben Sira on the anxieties connected with daughters and on their undesirability compared to sons (a sentiment also expressed in B. Bava Batra 16b), and add the fear that an elderly daughter may engage in witchcraft. Moreover, they offer further advice to the man enduring an incompatible spouse: She should be divorced as quickly as possible. While not arguing with the premise that a good wife doubles a man's life, they do comment on the temptations to adulterous behavior confronting the traveling salesman.

Ben Sira's frequent negative declarations about women also include the statement that "From woman sin had its beginning, and because of her, we all die" (25:24). Similar attitudes are evident in his warnings about headstrong daughters:

Do not let her parade her beauty before any man, or spend her time among married women; for from garments comes the moth, and from a woman comes woman's wickedness. Better is the wickedness of a man than a woman who does good; it is a woman who brings shame and disgrace (Ben Sira 42:12–14).

These remarks continue a biblical thread, warning against female sexual wiles (e.g., Prov. 31), which found a sympathetic resonance in many rabbinic speculations about the sexual untrustworthiness of women. Thus, B. Gittin 45a combines male fears of female infidelity and female involvement in witchcraft in the tale of the daughters of R. Nahman who were taken captive. They were known even before their captivity for their mysterious ability to stir a boiling cauldron with their bare hands. During their captivity, a fellow prisoner resolved that he would rescue the women, if he could determine that they had retained their virtue:

Said he to himself: Women talk about their business in the privy. He [followed them and] overheard them saying, These men [their captors] are [our] husbands. Let us tell our captors to remove us to a distance from here, so that our [legal] husbands may not come and hear [where we are] and ransom us . . . When the daughters of R. Nahman came back, [this man] said, They stirred the cauldron by witchcraft.

It is no accident that the man in this story chose to eavesdrop on the women when they were in the privy. The outhouse is seen in rabbinic literature as a place of danger where demons and unclean spirits lurk. Associating the privy with women's intimate conversations is to associate their conversations with licentious and supernatural topics, an expression of the perils the sages link with women who have strayed outside of their preferred location in the domestic realm.[50]

A related aspect of this rabbinic conviction of the potentially dangerous power of women's sexuality is the ways in which men denigrate and imbue with peril the disturbing female body, which both attracts and repels, subsequently reducing all women to sources of possible temptation, anxiety, and even disgust. The rabbinic remark that woman is "a pitcher full of filth with its mouth full of blood, yet all run after her" (B. Shabbat 152a) is in its own terms less a misogynistic opinion than a bewildered statement of fact. A similar expression of corporeal repugnance is the tradition that female pubic hair is a divine punishment for women's transgressions. According to B. Sanhedrin 21a and B. Shabbat 62b, Israelite women had virtually no pubic hair until the time of Isaiah when they became sinful; this is based on reading Isaiah 3:17 as **"My Lord afforested with hair the pubic regions / Of the daughters of Zion"** (B. Shabbat 62b). In B. Shabbat 62b, this statement is part of an extended exegesis of the passage beginning at Isaiah 3:16: **"Because the daughters of Zion are so vain / And walk with heads thrown back, / With roving eyes, / And with mincing gait / Making a tinkling** (te'akhasnah) **of their feet . . ."** This description of women as sexual temptresses intent on seduction is further demonstrated by the following excerpt from this text:

R. Isaac of the School of R. Ammi said: This teaches that they placed myrrh and balsam in their shoes and walked through the market-places of Jerusalem, and on coming near to the young men of Israel, they kicked their feet and spurted it on them, thus instilling them with passionate desire like with a serpent's ('akhus) poison. And what is their punishment? As Rabbah b. 'Ulla lectured: **"And then / Instead of perfume, there shall be rot"** (Isa. 3:23), the place where they perfumed themselves shall be decaying sores. **"And instead of an apron, a rope,"** the place where they girdled themselves shall become full of bruises. . . . Said Raba, Thus, men say, Ulcers instead of beauty.

This enthusiastic accumulation of physical humiliations of the female body is indicative of significant repulsion and even misogyny.[51] The passage ends with a discussion of the sexual license and vulgarity of the men of Jerusalem prior to the destruction of the city. The message of this *sugya* is clear. Adorned and perfumed women seduced men into ever greater degrees of sexual immorality and the result was ruination. This is why men must strictly limit their converse and contacts with women.

B. Sanhedrin 21a continues its discourse on the dangers of the female body in a discussion of the story of Tamar who was raped by her half-brother Amnon, commenting on Amnon's subsequent contempt for Tamar: **"Then Amnon hated her with exceeding great hatred"** (2 Sam. 13:

15). As is often the case in rabbinic literature, a wronged biblical woman is held responsible for the misfortunes which befell her. The dominant interpretation preserved here is that Amnon's hate was justified because Tamar caused mutilation of his genitals with her pubic hair. When a counter claim is raised that the daughters of Israel in that era did not have pubic hair, the answer is given that "it was otherwise with Tamar, for she was the daughter of a captive woman." B. Gittin 6b also expresses the view that a man who has intercourse with a woman with pubic hair risks castration, while B. Nazir 59a confirms that women in talmudic times practiced the custom of removing their armpit and pubic hair by shaving or depilation.[52]

Rabbinic Judaism's system of controlled oppositions, then, is predicated on an overwhelming consciousness of the disruptive potentialities of human sexuality. Moreover the interlinked projections of male desire and male resentment onto women, in conjunction with the conviction of women's lesser intellectual capacities and general flightiness, is sufficient to establish the particularities of female sexual unreliability and women's potential danger to men. Certainly for rabbinic social policy, women's very existence suggests their capacity for disrupting an ordered male world. Left unchecked as a focus for male sexual interest, an unattached woman is a constant reminder of untamed nature in a society which aspires to the divine, while the impure woman is at any moment a potential source of pollution.

B. Niddah 31b referred particularly to the appeal of a woman's sweet voice which evoked her attractive and disturbing presence. B. Megillah 15a, cited above, confirmed that even the mention of the sweet qualities of Yael's voice prompted sexual desire in men. The statement in B. Berakhot 24a that "The voice of woman is indecent," deriving from a ruling that a man may not recite the *Shema* if he hears a woman singing, since her voice might divert his concentration from the prayer, is a further indication that even hearing a female could be hazardous and had to be controlled.

Such specific references to the dangers of the female voice underlie one of the halakhic justifications for exempting women from full participation in communal prayer. Extrapolating from the perils of hearing women to the risks of seeing them, rabbinic prohibitions on male/female contact in worship eventually led to a physical barrier (*mehitzah*) between men and women in the synagogue to preserve men from sexual distraction during worship. The similar concern, rooted in post-talmudic popular piety, that a menstruating woman should not enter the synagogue, may also have contributed to the insistence that the non-menstruant, too, must sit separately and out of sight and sound.[53] Since rabbinic Judaism was solely concerned with the quality of male worship in the communal sphere, the deleterious effects on female spirituality as a consequence of this isolation were not considered.

Explaining Rabbinic Attitudes

Some scholars have looked to the influence of Greek/Hellenistic culture, which became increasingly predominant in the Middle East following the conquests of Alexander the Great in the early fourth century B.C.E., as the source of negative views of women as lesser beings whose sexuality and physical functions occasion male apprehension. Tikva Frymer-Kensky suggests that post-biblical Judaism was significantly influenced by Greek thought, which "portrayed females as inherently and essentially different from men, and fundamentally less valued," and as representative of what is " 'natural,' and untamed, even animal-like," while men "represented civilized humanity."[54] She believes that in the ways in which it conceives of women and sex, rabbinic Judaism is dramatically different from the literature of the Hebrew Bible, since "in place of the Bible's portrayal of women and men as fundamentally similar, the rabbis express a gender-polarized view of humanity. In place of the Bible's silence about sexual attraction, the rabbis portray sexual attraction as a mighty, at times dangerous and irresistible, force." Frymer-Kensky states that in the absence of an integrated biblical vision of the experience of human sexuality, Greek concepts of sex and gender filled the vacuum in "decidedly antiwoman, anticarnal ways that have long influenced the Western religious tradition." She suggests that rabbinic conceptions of women as totally other from men, rabbinic expressions of misogyny, and rabbinic wariness of the disruptive possibilities of erotic desire, may be seen as direct influences from Greek civilization.[55] While this approach is persuasive it does not wholly account for the thoroughness with which women are delegated to the category of other in rabbinic Judaism, nor for the eager continuation of such traditions in Western Asia, where Greco-Roman influences were far less dominant than in the Land of Israel. Rather, it seems more likely that highly negative views towards women and their physicality, together with ambivalence and anxiety about female sexuality and fidelity, were endemic throughout the ancient world in Middle Eastern, Mesopotamian, and Greco-Roman cultural settings. While the theme of woman as dangerous temptress may be muted in biblical writings, it is certainly not absent.

Daniel Boyarin, who also acknowledges the impact of Greek thinking about women and sexuality in rabbinic literature, is less convinced that its effect was overwhelming. He has argued that while rabbinic thinking is androcentric and patriarchal, it is not gynophobic in the ways that typify much Greek writing about women. In rabbinic Judaism, he writes, the flesh is not abhorred and women and sexuality were not feared, as was the case in some strands of Greek and Hellenistic thought. Rather women, at least those who fall within rabbinic definitions of "good wives," are highly valued as social, sexual, and economic partners, and as mothers of children. Boyarin attempts to demonstrate that in the instances where gynophobic statements appear in rabbinic texts, they are highly influenced by Greek sources, often mediated through sympathetic Hellenistic Jewish writers such as Ben Sira, but he believes that where such themes do appear they have generally been moderated in ways that dilute their gynophobic intent.[56]

Boyarin does not dispute that there are highly unpleasant misogynistic remarks recorded in rabbinic literature, but he maintains that rabbinic tradition as a whole does not see women as essentially impure and contaminating. Thus, he denies the contention of some scholars that fear of women's sexuality played a significant part in the construction of rabbinic patriarchy.[57] Boyarin acknowledges, however, that talmudic statements which construct women as essentially evil snares for male virtue function far more significantly "in the genuine and open misogyny of much of medieval Jewish discourse."[58] He believes that while "legends, fears, and terrors of women's sexuality" existed, they were not officially contenanced by mainstream rabbinic culture. However, he makes clear that "from the early Middle Ages on, they became well entrenched in rabbinic culture and official religion, paralleled exactly by similar changes in the discourse of menstruation from cultic disability to near-demonic contamination."[59]

In minimizing the significance in rabbinic discourse of this particular approach to women, Boyarin is caught in a dilemma. He admits that misogyny was present within rabbinic culture, but he insists that it was not a "key symbol" the way it was in Hellenistic thought.[60] Therefore, he discounts gynophobic/misogynistic teachings as uncharacteristic of rabbinic thought as a whole. However, if one accepts the multivocal nature of rabbinic literature in which a variety of apparently equally authoritative voices are represented, one cannot deny that such statements represent one strand of rabbinic thinking about women which was deemed worthy of preservation.[61]

Moreover, while rabbinic Judaism may not have depicted all women as essentially injurious by virtue of their gender, it does admit the possibility that some women are dangerous on just those grounds. Mordechai A. Friedman, for example, has traced recurring superstitions associating particular women with "life-endangering demonic forces" through biblical, rabbinic, and medieval sources. While such views, he argues, were never mainstream and were generally rejected by authoritative voices, the fact that they keep reappearing in various rabbinic associations of women and death indicates the deep resonance they found within rabbinic culture. In fact, the connection of women with the angel of death and claims that women are responsible for bringing death into the world are central components of rabbinic discourse about the feminine.[62]

Mayer Gruber finds the rationale for excluding women from the central activities of Judaism in those brutal external circumstances of Jewish life at the time the Mishnah was composed. He suggests that following the devastating failures of the First and Second Revolts of 66–70 C.E. and 132–135 C.E., Jewish men in Roman Palestine were not only physically defeated and humiliated by the Romans, but were also psychologically emasculated by their helplessness to defend themselves and their families from Roman depradations.[63] This political impotence of the Jews continued throughout late antiquity, no matter where they made their homes. Building on earlier arguments put forth by Jacob Neusner about the deliberate self-feminization of Israel in this era,[64] Gruber argues:

Jewish men sought and found in the study of Torah, the Rabbinic courts of law, which had jurisdiction over marriage and divorce and petty economic transactions, a new arena to assert their manliness, which is to say their power to influence the world . . . it is no wonder that they sought to banish women from these few areas in which, under the Roman-Byzantine and Parthian and Sassanian yoke, they could feel like powerful men rather than powerless little boys."[65]

The following set of comments in *Song of Songs Rabbah* 1.5, §3 reinforces that rabbinic thinkers believed they had been compelled to accept the female role and that they were conscious of all the disadvantages that followed from it. This aggadic consolation text ultimately promises resolution for the discomfort Jewish men palpably felt about their "female" powerlessness. At the same time, however, this passage also gives a graphic representation of how dismal and unappealing women and their lives appeared to the androcentric formulators of these words, a topic discussed in detail in chapter 3 of this volume.

R. Berekhiah said in the name of R. Samuel b. Nahman: Israel are compared to a female. Just as a female child takes a tenth part of the property of her father [when she marries] and departs, so Israel inherited the land of the seven peoples which is a tenth of that of the seventy nations. And because Israel inherited like a female, the song they uttered is called by the feminine form *shirah*, as it says, **"Then Moses and the Israelites sang this song (*shirah*) to the Lord"** (Exod. 15:

1). But in the days to come they will inherit like a male who inherits all the property of his father . . . They will then utter a song in the masculine form, as it says, "**Sing to the Lord a new song (***shir***)**" (Ps. 96:1). It is not written there *shirah hadashah* ["new song" in the feminine] but *shir hadash* ["new song" in the masculine].

R. Berekhiah and R. Joshua b. Levi said: Why is Israel likened to a female? Because just as a female receives a burden and discharges it, receives and discharges, and then receives no more [that is, becomes pregnant and gives birth until she becomes too old for childbearing], so Israel are enslaved and delivered, enslaved and delivered, and are delivered again and enslaved no more forever. In this world, because their pains are like those of a female in childbirth, they utter before God a song (*shirah*) in the feminine form but in the world to come, because their pains will not be like those of a woman in childbirth, they will utter a song in the masculine form (*shir*), and so it says, "**In that day this song (shir) shall be sung**" (Isa. 26:1).

In this extended *aggadah*, it is accepted that in many ways the oppressed Israel of this world has been feminized with all the disabilities that implies. However, as this consolation text promises, ultimately the male community of Israel will be redeemed and return once more to their proper masculine state. No mention is made of what women have to look forward to.

Boyarin has proposed a similar thesis that the political realities of the subordinate and marginalized position of the Jews, no matter where they lived in the ancient world, led rabbinic culture to privilege gentle, passive, and emotional men, at the same time as it formed a social system based on subordinating women and keeping them separate from the privileged spheres of study and communal worship.[66] He argues that because non-Jewish cultures in later historical periods understood studying Torah, the quintessential activity of rabbinic Jewish maleness, as female, internalized ambivalence within Jewish culture itself required the elimination of women from male domains of worship and study. Since the passive and studious men were already occupying women's internal space, women had to be limited to crucial but culturally diminished roles as family caretakers and economic entrepreneurs.[67] Boyarin maintains that this exclusion of women from Torah was a sociological development which was not intended to keep women in ignorance, "nor was it the product of a sense that women were contaminated and contaminating." Rather, he argues, "it was purely and simply a means for the maintenance of a male power-structure via the symbolic exclusion of women from the single practice most valued in the culture, the study of Talmud."[68] Whatever, the initial cause, however, he affirms the consequences: Separating women from Torah study produced "an ideology of women as contaminated and contaminating, which men have disseminated and women internalized."

I disagree with Boyarin's insistence that limiting the study of revealed texts to men was only a result of the circumstances in which Jewish men found themselves, rather than also predicated by profound convictions of female difference. However, I cannot quarrel with his conclusion that "it is thus nonetheless certain that women have been made in historical Judaism to experience themselves as impure, dangerous, and devalued through these exclusions."[69]

While Gruber, Neusner, and Boyarin provide a suggestive historical context in which rabbinic Judaism's effort to exclude women from communal roles and cultural esteem was formed, I do not think their explanations can claim completeness. The deeply entrenched convictions and suspicions of female alterity in all the cultures of the ancient world, including biblical and rabbinic Judaism, begin and find their strongest resonance in woman's disturbing physical otherness from man. Rabbinic social policy finesses the dilemma of woman by assigning her to male control whenever possible and by justifying her limitations with references to the inferior nature of her innate qualities. Similarly, female socialization and female collusion in maintaining male imposed norms were also important factors.[70] That women were seen to accept the premises of the system is confirmed by the talmudic story in B. Sotah 22a which praises a "young girl who fervently prayed that no man would unwittingly be led astray by her and thus lose his place in Paradise."

Another talmudic illustration of this phenomenon of female collusion with a tradition of subordination is found in B. Ketubbot 65a. This aggadic anecdote, which also reflects on the anomalous state of the unprotected widow, recounts the story of Homa, the widow of R. Abaye, who came to the sage Rava in his role as a communal judge, asking for an allowance of board and an allowance of wine from her husband's estate. At one point, Homa was demonstrating the amount of wine her husband was accustomed to give her and her arm became uncovered. When Rava went home he made sexual overtures to his wife who inquired, "Who has been in court today?" "Homa, the widow of Abaye," he replied. Thereupon, his wife, unnamed beyond being designated as "the daughter of R. Hisda," pursued the widow, striking her with the straps of a chest until she chased her out of Mahuza. "You have already killed three husbands," she said to her, "and now you come to kill another man!" Here, as Friedman has demonstrated, remnants of traditional "killer wife" stories are discernible.[71] At the same time, the perilous position of the independent woman, subject to sexual projection and sexual predation by men and social ostracism from women who feared a similar fate, is also obvious.

Women in Other Judaisms

The strong rabbinic insistence on the desirability of confining women to domestic and enabling activities, preferably as wives subject to a husband's authority, a theme discussed in more detail in chapter 4 of this volume, may have been influenced, at least in part, by knowledge of the prominent public roles undertaken by some women in contemporaneous Jewish communities in the Greek-speaking Jewish Diaspora of the Roman Empire. Increasing information about such alternate social configurations demonstrates that the rabbinic separation of women from arenas of endeavor constituted as male was a deliberate choice, since this was not the only Jewish communal model available, at least for those who lived within the boundaries of the Roman Empire. Moreover, such knowledge provides a context for the pattern, discussed above and documented by such scholars as Gruber, of deliberately removing women from a public domain in which they had functioned during biblical and Second Temple times.[72]

Ross Shepard Kraemer and Bernadette Brooten are among scholars who have shown that in the first centuries of the Common Era many Jewish communities did not conform to rabbinic norms regarding women and their social roles. From the third century B.C.E. on, large numbers of Jews lived in highly hellenized environments in areas including present-day Egypt, Syria, Turkey, Greece, and Italy. Evidence suggests that a number of aspects of Jewish life in these settings, including possibilities available for women, diverged significantly from the norms and prescriptions found in rabbinic Judaism. While it seems likely that most Jewish women in these milieus lived their lives in the relative seclusion of the domestic realm, Ross Shepard Kraemer's examination of funerary and other inscriptions, as well as her analyses of the roles of women in Greco-Jewish literary texts, demonstrates that some Jewish women in the Greek-speaking diaspora world of late antiquity acted as autonomous entitities in social, economic, and religious capacities.[73] Moreover, documentary evidence connected with some specific women in the land of Israel, including Berenice of the first century C.E., and Babatha of the second century C.E., delineates female lives of independent agency apparently at odds with rabbinic ideals.[74]

On the basis of a number of inscriptions in Greek and Latin, dating from the first century B.C.E. to the sixth century C.E., and ranging from Italy to Asia Minor, Egypt, and Phoenicia—where women bear such titles as "head of the synagogue," "leader," "elder," "mother of the synagogue," and "priestess"—Bernadette Brooten has similarly suggested that contrary to the previous scholarly consensus, which was significantly informed by rabbinic texts, Jewish women assumed positions of leadership in the very public sphere of the ancient synagogue.[75] Although it is not clear if these synagogue titles were simply honorific in recognition of significant philanthropy or whether they imply that women had meaningful leadership and/or ritual obligations, Kraemer has proposed that Jewish communities in the Greco-Roman Diaspora may have been particularly accepting of women's leadership in areas of public affairs where "civic responsibility and religion intersected," as in synagogue activities. She also notes the possibility "that women's leadership was particularly likely in Jewish synagogues with relatively high numbers of proselytes (both male and female) for whom the participation of women in public life, including religious *collegia*, was familiar and acceptable."[76] It seems probable that many of the women who held such communal roles were widows or divorcées, since most of these individuals appear to have controlled significant economic resources and are not mentioned in connection with men.

As Brooten has remarked, all that is known about women from rabbinic Judaism is what its male authors thought about them. She predicts that "As we begin to evaluate all the sources for Jewish women's history in the period in question, including inscriptions and papyri, a much more differentiated picture will emerge."[77] Kraemer has also suggested that the strong objections to women in the public domain expressed in rabbinic literature may reflect some "rabbinic opposition to the power and prestige of women in Jewish communities" which were just beginning to come under the influence and authority of rabbinic traditions. Kraemer's observation, "that intensification of prescriptions against women is often a response to the increased autonomy and authority of women,"[78] is an important reminder that the social policies of the rabbinic sages were not formed in a vacuum but were considerably affected, positively and negatively, consciously and unconsciously, by the environments in which they lived. The evidence already available for these different alternatives for Jewish women in Greco-Roman Diaspora communities demonstrates that in their desire to eliminate women from the sphere of communal authority, the rabbis were not simply sanctifying accepted traditions and norms of life but constructing a congenial reality of their own. Their vision of an ideal society, believed to conform to the divine will, compelled them to deliberately reject a number of features of the wider Jewish and gentile worlds around them, including traditions of female legal autonomy, women's religious rituals, and female communal leadership, because of the dangers they perceived to be connected with such options.

The Consequences of Alterity

The rabbinic formation of the feminine is a highly complex and many-layered phenomenon constructed from numerous attitudes, convictions, and deliberate choices. It was significantly shaped, too, by a variety of political and social realities. In the rabbinic taxonomy of human beings, women were constructed as other than men in a number of ways. As a secondary creation, physically incapable of virility and generation, they were excluded from the responsibilities, privileges, and power conferred by full partnership in the divine covenant. Perceived as both sexually attractive to men and as fundamentally untrustworthy, they represented constant sources of enticement and societal disorder that had to be maintained under male control in the safety of the domestic realm. Moreover, women's periodic uncleanness presented recurrent threats not only to their husbands' persons but to others around them. Rabbinic *halakhah*, committed to strictly limiting women's presence in the communal domains of worship, study, and leadership roles, deliberately disempowered women in areas of ritual participation and personal status issues and consciously rejected other social models which sanctioned women's participation in community life.

There can be little dispute that the formulators of rabbinic literature believed that to be female was significantly less desirable than to be male. Yet, different as they were imagined to be, women were also acknowledged as essential to men, since they constituted the indispensable social mortar which sustained rabbinic society. As subsequent chapters of this book will demonstrate, women as wives, mothers, and economic partners were indeed indispensable "bolsters to their husbands," eminently worthy of recognition and appreciation.[79] Nevertheless, women's spiritual and intellectual qualities and needs were generally seen as inferior and subordinate to those of men. Women themselves were often shown as having the potential to lead men towards immorality and death. For many aggadic writers, the explanations for these mysterious differences between women and men could be found in the nature of female creation itself, a topic explored in depth in chapter 2.

CONSTRUCTING EVE:
MIDRASHIC REVISIONS
OF HUMAN CREATION

The conviction of women's otherness established in chapter 1 is more than a foundation of rabbinic social policy. It is also a central component in rabbinic understandings of the relationship between God and Jewish men. Rabbinic Judaism's belief in a special alliance between God and the people of Israel does not extend equally to males and females; rather Jewish men are understood to be connected with the divine in ways unavailable to Jewish women. In chapter 1, I suggested that the central ritual of circumcision through which Jewish males entered the covenant between God and the Jewish people excluded women by virtue of the organ they lacked. This chapter discusses midrashic validations of women's subordinate status based on the inferior nature of female creation. Moreover, the insistence that the formation of the first woman was flawed and secondary is also employed to explain and justify the marginalization of females in the ideal society imagined in rabbinic literature.

Building a Woman

The initial chapters of Genesis contain two separate versions of the creation of men and women. In the first account, contained within the cosmology of Genesis 1–2:4, unnamed human creatures, male and female, are simultaneously created by God's word, in the divine image and likeness (Gen. 1:26–27), as the ultimate act of six days of creation:

(26) And God said, "Let us make a humanity[1] in our image, after our likeness. They shall rule the fish of the sea, the birds of the sky, the cattle, the whole earth, and all the creeping things that creep on earth.
(27) And God created humanity in His image, in the image of God He created them; male and female He created them.

These creatures, and it is never stated explicitly that there are only two, are blessed by God and instructed to "**Be fertile and increase, fill the earth and master it; and rule the fish of the sea, the birds of the sky, and all the living things that creep on earth**" (Gen. 1:28). In this sophisticated theological narrative, attributed to the Priestly source of Pentateuchal traditions,[2] the creation of human beings, both female and male, as uniquely sentient among other living things and as dominant over all other creatures, signifies the climax of God's creation of "**heaven and earth and all their array**" (2:1).

The second and quite different narrative, attributed to the so-called Yahwist writer, describes how the Lord God formed a man from the dust of the earth and animated him with the breath of life (Gen. 2:7), even before vegetation had appeared on the earth. The Lord God planted a garden in Eden and placed the man in the garden to tend it. At this point, the Lord God noticed the man's solitary state and, proposing to make a "**fitting helper for him**" (Gen. 2:18), formed all the beasts and birds out of the earth. Although the man gave these new creatures names, no appropriate partner was found among them and man remained solitary.

(21) So the Lord God cast a deep sleep upon the man; and while he slept, He took one of his ribs and closed up the flesh at that spot.
(22) And the Lord God fashioned the rib that He had taken from the man into a woman; and He brought her to the man.

Adam proclaims this female being to be "**Bone of my bones and flesh of my flesh / This one shall be called woman, for from man was she taken**" (Gen. 2:23). Here the biblical redactor editorializes, "**Hence a man leaves his father and mother and clings to his wife, so that they become one flesh**" (Gen. 2:24). Although Adam names his companion "woman," he does not give his "fitting helper" a personal name until after the episode of human disobedience that leads to the expulsion from the garden and the assumption of the mortal burden of a life characterized by frustration and suffering. Only then does Adam name his wife Eve. In a folk etymology, the biblical author connects the name Eve (*Havvah*) with the word for life (*hai*), explaining, "**The man named his wife Eve, because she was the mother of all the living**" (Gen. 3:20).

Modern scholarship has debated the separate origins and purposes of the two Genesis cosmologies which were conflated at some point into one seamless narrative by biblical redactors. These stories were probably seen as complementary rather than contradictory, since each account provided information about God, God's creatures, and the nature of the human condition absent in the other.[3] The effort to merge these divergent documents is evident when the redactor summarizes the origins of the first human family in Genesis 5:1–2: "This is the record of Adam's line. / When God created humanity He made it in the likeness of God; male and female He created them. And when they were created, He blessed them and called them 'adam."

Among the rabbis, certainly, biblical accounts of human beginnings were read as part of one continuous text. Rabbinic exegetical principles did not accept the possibility of either repetition or contradiction in divine revelation. The male and female created in the divine image in Genesis 1 were obviously the Adam and Eve of Genesis 2:4–3, and their later actions are referred back to the circumstances of their origins. Similarly, rabbinic readers understood Adam and Eve to be married. Thus, rabbinic comments on the nature of the first woman also reflect broader rabbinic views on the roles and status of women as wives. Nevertheless, questions about the details of human creation remained and had to be dealt with. The sages wondered particularly whether both men and women were created simultaneously in the divine image or if woman was a later and essentially lesser creation. They pondered what the nature of the first human creature might have been and they considered whether two different women were being referred to in these competing narratives.

The issue of simultaneous creation is addressed by *Genesis Rabbah* 8:1 which begins its discussion of human creation with the divine decision in the first story, "And God said: Let us make humanity . . ." (Gen. 1:26):

R. Johanan commenced [by introducing the biblical verse]: "You have formed me before and behind" (Ps. 139:5). Said R. Johanan: If a man is worthy enough, he enjoys both worlds, for it says, "You have formed me for a later [world] and an earlier [world]. But if not he will have to render a full account [of his misdeeds] as it says, "You lay your hand upon me" (Ps. 139:5).[4]

[Another interpretation of this verse, "You have formed me before and behind," is now offered.] R. Jeremiah b. Leazar said: When the Holy One, blessed be He, created the first 'adam, He created it with both male and female sexual organs as it is written, "Male and female He created them, and He called their name 'adam" (Gen. 5:2). R. Samuel b. Nahmani said, "When the Holy One, blessed be He, created the first 'adam, He created him with two faces, then split him and made him two backs—a back for each side. To this it is objected: But it is written, "He took one of his ribs (mi-tzalotav)" (Gen. 2:21) [a reference to the second biblical story of the creation of woman from the man's body]. He replied, ["One of his ribs" means] one of his *sides*, as you read [in an analogy from the similar use of the same word elsewhere], "And for the other side wall (tzel'a) of the Tabernacle" (Ex. 26:20).

The second group of comments in this midrash, based on exegeses of Psalm 139:5, offers explanations for the apparent contradictions in the biblical accounts of the origins of man and woman. R. Jeremiah b. Leazar suggests that God created one entity with both male and female genitalia. However, in this vision of a primal androgyne, which imagines human male and female sexual characteristics as originating in one simultaneous creation, the primary being is still constructed as male. Only afterwards, as R. Samuel b. Nahmani elaborates, did God separate the female "side" from the male entity to create a new and independent being. In these interpretations, both biblical versions of human creation are accounted for, while any possibility of imagining an initial female creation separate from the original man is obviated. The idea of an essentially male being with male and female characteristics is the closest the rabbis will come to acknowledging the simultaneous and co-equal creation of man and woman described in Genesis 1:26, and even this view is a decidedly minority opinion.[5]

The assumption that the initial human creation was a solitary male is the view that most commonly appears in the rabbinic aggadah. *Genesis Rabbah* 17:4, for example, confirms and explains the subsequent creation of woman in the context of a discussion of Adam's naming of the animals (Gen. 2:19–20):

Said he, "Every one has a partner, yet I have none": Thus, **"But for Adam no fitting helper was found"** (Gen. 2: 20). And why did He not create her for him at the beginning? Because the Holy One, blessed be He, foresaw that [Adam] would bring charges against her, therefore He did not create her until he expressly demanded her. But as soon as he did, forthwith **"So the Lord God cast a deep sleep upon the man, and while he slept, He took one of his ribs and closed up the flesh at that spot"** (Gen. 2:21).

In this account, even divine foreknowledge of future female failings cannot produce an improved product. Rather God simply delays the inevitable. The rabbinic conundrum is explicit: Women are essential for human survival and for human completeness, yet it was clear from the start that their potential for upsetting the cosmos would be a perpetual concern.

The theory of a simultaneous creation of separate male and female entities is, nonetheless, considered in other rabbinic texts attempting to resolve the apparent contradiction between the creation of male and female in Genesis 1:27 and the subsequent events of Genesis 2:22, where Eve is formed from Adam's rib. This issue was clearly a source of debate among the rabbis, since it is raised in at least three tractates of the Babylonian Talmud. B. Berakhot 61a picks up the theme of the androgynous Adam, where *Genesis Rabbah* stops, in a discussion of the meanings of **"The Lord God formed man from the dust of the earth"** (Gen. 2:7):

R. Nahman b. R. Hisda expounded: What is meant by the text, **"The Lord God formed (*vayyitzer*) man"**? *Vayyitzer* is written with two *yods* in order to show that God created two inclinations, one good and the other evil. . . . Or again, as explained by R. Jeremiah b. Eleazar, for R. Jeremiah b. Eleazar said: God created two faces in the first human being, as it is says, "You have formed me before and behind" (Ps. 139:5).[6]

But if, in fact, the first being incorporated both male and female "faces," this talmudic passage immediately asks, how can one account for the creation of woman from a rib alluded to in "And the Lord God built the rib that He had taken from the man into a woman" (Gen. 2:22)? One proposed solution is simply to understand the word *tzel'a*, usually translated "rib" as meaning "face." In this case there would be no contradiction. At the moment referred to in Genesis 2:22, God simply built the female "face" of the original human creation into an autonomous woman. However, if *tzel'a* refers to a different part of Adam's anatomy, for instance his actual rib, or an appendage of some kind, then there is a contradiction. The solution proposed to this dilemma depends on accepting variabililty in God's intentions. "Male and female He created them" (Gen. 1:27b) is said to indicate that initially God certainly intended to create two separate beings, a male and a female. However, before creation actually ensued, the divine intention changed and only a single being, a male, was actually created, as can be seen from "And God created *'adam in His image*" (Gen. 1:27a). Only later was the female formed from the man's rib. While numerous arguments on both side of the debate are now offered, no final resolution is reached in this passage.

This dispute over whether the initial human creation comprised only one man or the creation of a being with both male and female characteristics also appears in B. 'Eruvin 18a, where many of the same arguments found in B. Berakhot 61a also appear. Here the discussion begins with the citation of R. Jeremiah b. Eleazar's saying that the first man had two full faces, based on "You have formed me before and behind" (Ps. 139:5). Other sages are then invoked who interpret the verse as referring to the order in which Adam was created: "R. Ammi said: [Adam was] *behind* [last] in the work of the creation and *before* [the other creatures] for retribution." Further contentions, also raised in B. Berakhot 61a, are now put forward and refuted, including the fact that the unexpected two *yods* in *vayyitzer*, "And the Lord God formed" (Gen. 2:7), refers to the creation of two entities in one body. Ultimately, however, here, too, no final closure on the question is achieved.

A resolution to the vexing question of whether man was created alone or whether man and woman were created together (in one androgynous entity) is reached in B. Ketubbot 8a in the context of a discussion of the appropriate number of benedictions to be recited at a wedding feast. The Talmud text relates that R. Levi came to the wedding feast of Rabbi's son R. Simeon and recited five benedictions, while his fellow

guest R. Assi recited six benedictions. The sages assume that the benediction omitted by R. Levi was the second, "Blessed are you O Lord,
Creator of man," and that it was omitted because R. Levi believed it
was redundant, since a subsequent blessing also refers to the creation of
human beings. The discussion continues as follow:

> Does it mean to say that they differ in this: that one [R. Levi] holds that there
> was one formation [of man, and woman was formed from him subsequently],
> and therefore the third benediction: "Blessed are You . . . who has created man
> in His image, in the image of the likeness of His form, and has prepared for
> him from his very own person an eternal building"[7] [is therefore sufficient,] and
> the other [R. Assi] holds there were two [separate] formations [in which man
> and woman were initially created in one entity and a second formation in which
> a female being was separated from the male and therefore he recited both ben-
> edictions]?
> No. The whole world agrees that there was only one formation [and it was
> of man alone], [but they differ in that] one holds that we go according to the
> [divine] intention [which had been simultaneously to create one entity both, man
> and woman] and the other holds that we go according to the fact [only man
> was created and woman was later created out of him]. [This is the import] of
> that statement of Rab Judah [who] asked: It is written, **"And God created man
> in his own image"** (Gen. 1:27), and it is written **"Male and female He created
> them"** (Gen. 5:2). How is this [to be understood?] [In this way]: In the beginning
> it was the intention [of God] to create two [human beings in the divine image],
> and in the end [only] one was created.

This crucial passage affirms as definitive the view, cited as a possibility
in both B. Berakhot 61a and B. 'Eruvin 18a, that God's original intention
to create both a male and female human being simultaneously was aban-
doned and only a male was ultimately created. Thus, this text supports
the evidence from *Genesis Rabbah* 8 that the predominant view among
the rabbinic sages was that man alone was created in the divine image
and only later was a woman built from his body. The possibility that
God simultaneously created two independent entities, a man and a
woman, is never directly addressed in rabbinic exegesis.

Delineating the nature of the first human creation was important because of what was at stake. Essentially, the theoretical basis for rabbinic
Judaism's conviction that men shared in the divine image in ways that
women did not and that men should therefore be privileged in ways that
women were not rested on the belief in the initial creation of a single
man. This version of events maintained the primacy of the male and
made clear that only men were created in God's likeness with all the
implications of potency, dominance, and generativity which followed
from this analogy. Conversely, the secondary nature of woman's creation
from man's rib affirmed her subordinate position in marriage, in reproduction, and in the public aspects of rabbinic society.

Iterations of male dominance appear frequently in aggadic midrash. B. Niddah 31b, for example, asks :

And why does the man lie face downwards [during sexual intercourse] and the woman face upwards towards the man? He [faces the elements] from which he was created and she [faces the man] from whom she was created.[8]

In a discussion of the "exegetical politics of gender" following the expulsion from Eden, Reuven Kimelman suggests that this sexual domination by the male seems to follow from Eve's disobedience:

The new connubial situation raises questions about whether conjugality is potentially a stage for aggression. It also raises the issue of whether inequality is an erotic necessity. If so, the intimacy of two bodies fitting so perfectly together to exchange life could double as a form of conquest. Once being on top is seen as an expression of dominance, becoming one flesh, according to [this] reading, can spark memories of origins, with man looking down at earth and woman looking up at man.[9]

For rabbinic exegetes, however, male sexual dominance over the female is not a consequence of the human fall from grace. Dominance is inscribed from the instant of woman's formation and is understood to have been ordained by divine plan. It is explicit in such rabbinic readings of Genesis 1:28 as **"Be fertile and increase, fill the earth and master her,"** with all the verbs understood as masculine singular forms and "her," the feminine singular object of *master*, a reference to Eve.[10]

These concerns over sexual politics are also implicit in the discussions in B. Berakhot 61a and B. 'Eruvin 18b concerning the nature of human creation. These parallel passages raise the following question: If, in fact, the original human was a single entity with male and female "faces," which of the two faces—the male or the female—would have looked forward?

R. Nahman b. Isaac answered: It is reasonable to suppose that the man's face went in front, since it has been taught: A man should not walk behind a woman on the road [to avoid unchaste thoughts], and even if his wife happens to be in front of him on a bridge he should let her pass on one side, and whoever crosses a river behind a woman will have no portion in the future world [because the woman in crossing will naturally lift up her skirts]. Our rabbis taught: If a man counts out money from his hand into the hand of a woman so as to have the opportunity of gazing at her, even if he can vie in Torah and good deeds with Moses our teacher, he shall not escape the punishment of Gehenna, as it says **"Hand to hand, the evil man will not escape"** (Prov. 11:21).[11]

As these texts reveal, privileging male precedence and control were major concerns in constructing an acceptable narrative of human origins. Even a simultaneous formation of male and female features in one body could imply a gender equality profoundly disturbing to rabbinic sexual politics.

Moreover, in their betrayal of considerable sexual anxiety over the possibility of independent women walking in front of men, these passages reflect and support the asymmetric gender relationships based on male dominance which were seen as desirable in rabbinic social life. They reveal, as well, rabbinic Judaism's characteristic association of women with uncontrolled sexuality and all its dangers.

The first creation story is utilized in other ways to reinforce the secondary status of women vis-à-vis men. The meanings of human mastery are explored in the interpretation in *Genesis Rabbah* 8:12 of "**God blessed them and God said to them, 'Be fertile and increase, fill the earth and master it;**[12] **and rule the fish of the sea, the birds of the sky, and all the living things that creep on earth'** " (Gen. 1:28). Here, R. Leazar speaking in the name of R. Jose b. Zimra, observed that while the commands "**Be fertile and increase**" in the first part of Genesis 1:28 are written in the second person plural, the last verb in the next set of commands, "**and master it,**" could be read as a second person masculine singular. Extrapolating by analogy that the three previous verbs should also be read as masculine singular forms, R. Leazar derived from this verse the normative halakhic ruling that "man is commanded concerning procreation, but not woman."[13] R. Johanan b. Beroqah refuted this view, citing the evidence of the text: "Concerning both man and woman it says, "**And God blessed *them*, and God said to *them* . . .**" (Gen. 1: 28). His opinion, however, which also appears in M. Yevamot 6:7, remained a minority view.

The next comment in *Genesis Rabbah* 8:12 accepts that the verbal component in this form, "**and master it,**" is indeed a second personal masculine singular. The focus now shifts to the third person feminine singular suffix completing the form, which is usually read as "it," referring to the earth:

"**And master *her*"** is written: the man must master his wife, that she go not out into the marketplace, for every woman who goes out into the marketplace will eventually come to grief. Whence do we know it? From Dinah, as it is written, "And Dinah . . . went out . . ." (Gen. 34:1).

Genesis Rabbah 8:12 deliberately undercuts the biblical evidence in Genesis 1 that the first woman was as empowered as the first man in regard to fertility as well as in stewardship over the earth. By absolving women from both the obligation to procreate and an equal share in overseeing the natural world, rabbinic social policy diminished women's legal status and reduced them to dependence on male control.

The final reference in this midrash justifies male authority on the grounds of women's inherent sexual unreliability. This is an allusion to the biblical Dinah, Jacob's daughter, who went out on her own to visit the daughters of Canaan. Assaulted and raped, her misfortune instigates an inter-tribal incident in which her family emerges with victory but without credit. Generally, midrashic tradition blames all that ensued on Dinah's forwardness in "going out," presumably against her father's wishes. This mention of her story reinforces the preferences within rabbinic Judaism for strong paternal jurisdiction over a minor and vulnerable daughter, as well as the desirability of confining one's wife to the home as much as possible.[14]

Rabbinic Judaism located the origins of a woman's essential inferiority at the moment of her creation. Her many openly recognized social disadvantages, discussed in detail in chapter 3, were explained as consequences of inherent defects. These essential flaws account, as well, for her inevitable moral deficiencies. It is never definitively determined whether woman is irredeemably flawed because she was formed from the man, himself a created and therefore imperfect entity, or if there was something fundamental about the female in general which accounted for her failings. What is clear is that as a secondary and subordinate conception, woman was essentially and unalterably different from man and, moreover, at a further remove from the divine.

Certainly, Adam and the men descended from him were not portrayed as flawless. According to *Genesis Rabbah* 8:4, God was aware in creating Adam that some of his descendants would act wickedly. However, foreknowledge of the positive potentialities of righteous men overcame divine scruples as to the failings of Adam's iniquitous descendants, as this *aggadah* relates:

R. Berekhiah said: When the Holy One, blessed be He, came to create Adam, He saw righteous and wicked arising from him. Said He: "If I create him, wicked men will spring from him; if I do not create him, how are the righteous to spring from him?" What then did the Lord do? He removed the way of the wicked out of His sight and associated the quality of Mercy with Himself and created him, as it written, "For the Lord cherishes the way of the righteous, / but the way of the wicked is doomed (*tobed*)" (Ps. 1:6). What does *tobed* mean? He destroyed it (*ibbedah*) from before His sight and associated the quality of Mercy with Himself and created him. R. Hanina did not say thus, but [he said that] when He came to create Adam He took counsel with the ministering angels, saying to them, "Let us make man." "What shall his character be?" they asked. "Righteous men shall spring from him," He answered, as it is written, "For the Lord cherishes (*yode'a*) the way of the righteous" (Ps. 1:6), which means that the Lord made known (*hodi'a*) the way of the righteous to the ministering angels; "But the way of the wicked is doomed" (Ps. 1:6): He destroyed [hid] it from them. He revealed to them that righteous men would arise from him, but He did not reveal to them that the iniquitous men would spring from him; [had He done so] the quality of Justice would not have permitted [Adam] to be created.

Genesis Rabbah 8:5 also records a dispute among the ministering angels as to whether Adam should be created. This passage concludes as follows:

All our Rabbis say the following in the name of R. Hanina, while R. Phinehas and R. Hilkiah say it in the name of R. Simeon: *me'od* ("very") is identical with Adam,[15] as it is written, **"And God saw all that He had made, and found it very good (*tov me'od*)"** (Gen. 1:31). [This means] And behold Adam was good. R. Huna the Elder of Sepphoris, said: While the ministering angels were arguing with each other and disputing with each other, the Holy One, blessed be He, created him. Said He to them: "What can you do about it? Man has already been made!"[16]

The first woman, on the contrary, received no such special pleading. In an extended midrashic excursus on the second version of creation, *Genesis Rabbah* 18:2 meditates on women's inherent weaknesses. According to this midrash, as in *Genesis Rabbah* 17:4, cited above, the first woman is imagined as inevitably flawed even before she came into being.

R. Joshua of Siknin said in R. Levi's name: *vayyiven* (**"And He built"** [Gen. 2: 22]) is written, signifying that He considered well (*hitbonnen*) from what part to create her. Said He: "I will not create her from [Adam's] head, lest she be swelled-headed; nor from the eye, lest she be a coquette; nor from the ear, lest she be an eavesdropper; nor from the mouth, lest she be a gossip; nor from the heart, lest she be prone to jealousy; nor from the hand, lest she be light-fingered; nor from the foot, lest she be a gadabout; but from the modest part of man, for even when he stands naked, that part is covered." And as He created each limb He ordered her, "Be a modest woman." Yet in spite of all this **"You spurned all my advice, / And would not hear my rebuke"** (Prov. 1:25). I did not create her from the head, yet she is swelled-headed, as it is written, **"Because the daughters of Zion / Are so vain / And walk with heads thrown back"** (Isa. 3:16); nor from the eye, yet she is a coquette: **"With roving eyes"** (Isa. 3:16); nor from the ear, yet she is an eavesdropper: **"Sarah was listening at the entrance of the tent"** (Gen. 18:10); nor from the heart, yet she is prone to jealousy: **"Rachel became envious of her sister"** (Gen. 30:1); nor from the hand yet she is light-fingered: **"And Rachel stole her father's household gods"** (Gen. 31:19); nor from the foot, yet she is a gadabout: **"Now Dinah . . . went out to visit the daughters of the land"** (Gen. 34:1).

In this literal excursus on the construction of the female body, God is described as attempting to build a woman who would personify what the framers of rabbinic Judaism believed to be ideal female qualities of humility, sexual modesty, domesticity, discretion, and passivity. However, despite the best divine intentions, woman, once built, possessed a profusion of undesirable characteristics. Apparently, something inherent in the very essence of the feminine prohibited the elimination of undesirable traits.[17]

Tirzah Meacham has observed that the negative portrayals of the founding mothers of the Jewish people in *Genesis Rabbah* 18:2 represent a deliberate effort to denigrate female achievements and to justify limiting women's roles in an ideal rabbinic society. She points out that biblical instances could have been found in which each of the women cited in this midrash used her limbs and senses in positive ways.[18] This tendency to diminish women's intellectual abilities and qualities is present throughout rabbinic literature in biblical exegeses, general comments, and personal anecdotes, despite biblical examples of vigorous and resourceful women, and in the face of admirable and active women in rabbinic times.

As in *Genesis Rabbah* 18:2, where the mothers of humanity and of the Jewish people are disparaged, so midrashic versions of the stories of such estimable biblical women as Miriam, Deborah, Rahab, Tamar, and Yael tend to criticize their protagonists' pride and presumption. The biblical judge, Deborah is likened to a wasp, and the prophetess Huldah to a weasel. Other biblical heroines are similarly disparaged, and women who display unusual sagacity often meet early deaths.[19] Women do utter words of wisdom in rabbinic stories, but generally such stories are related in a tone of surprise. These are the exceptions that prove the rule. Often the woman's wit serves either to confirm a rabbinic belief about female character, such as women's higher degree of compassion for others, or it delivers a rebuke to someone in need of chastisement. To be bested by a woman is humiliation indeed.[20] This ambiguity attaches to virtually all named women who appear in rabbinic texts.[21] Such characterizations betray a rabbinic anxiety to designate females as essentially different from males and as deficient in what are seen as admirable male qualities, particularly wisdom, stored up knowledge, and analytical abilities.

This is not to say that females are seen as lacking in positive characteristics and usefulness. Woman's nurturing attributes, as well as her physical characteristics, are seen as essential to her most important functions as mother and wife. *Genesis Rabbah* 18:3 explains "**And the Lord God built (*vayyiven*) the rib that he had taken from the man into a woman**" (Gen. 2:22) as follows. "R. Hisda said: He built more chambers in her than in man, fashioning her broad below and narrow at the top, so that she could receive child." Moreover, honoring the wifely role, this aggadic comment concludes:

"**And he brought her to the man**" (Gen. 2:22). R. Abin observed: "Happy the citizen for whom the king is best man!"

Marriage is not only the necessary condition for human survival, but also offers the best chance for human happiness and the closest human model to the intimacy that can exist between man and God. None of this would be possible without women.[22]

Sometimes women are credited with having a few desirable traits deficient in men. *Genesis Rabbah* 18:1 cites the view that **"And the Lord God built (*vayyiven*) the rib"** (Gen. 2:22) means that woman was created with more instinctual understanding and common sense (*binah*) than man, pointing out that a young woman is considered an adult at the age of twelve while a boy only reaches legal maturity at thirteen. As Judith Romney Wegner has written, however:

the Midrash can equally be interpreted as making an invidious distinction between male cognition-by-intellect (*hokhmah*) and female cognition-by-instinct (*binah*), with the latter as more of an animal attribute than a human one, as is clear from the commencement of traditional morning prayers with a blessing that praises God for giving the rooster sufficient *binah* to distinguish night from day.[23]

Moreover, *Genesis Rabbah* 18:1 immediately goes on to offer an opposing opinion even to this ambiguous compliment for women to the effect that "Some reverse the opinion [that women have more *binah* than men], because a woman generally stays at home, whereas a man goes out into the streets and learns understanding from people." In this counter-tradition, the dominant rabbinic effort to diminish any positive female attribute, even a virtue of dubious value, is again triumphant.

Genesis Rabbah 18:2, then, is in the mainstream of rabbinic discourse when it imagines that the divine efforts to create a virtuous woman went awry at the very moment of creation and cites the failings of the matriarchs to prove this contention. As Meacham remarks, a midrash might have ennumerated the recorded flaws of the patriarchs in a similar way. Instead, the nearest parallel passage dealing with a male protagonist is overwhelmingly positive:

When God was about to put a soul into Adam's God-like body, He said: At which point shall I breathe the soul into him? Into his mouth? Nay, for he will use it to speak ill of his fellow man. Into his eyes? With them he will wink lustfully. Into the ears? They will hearken to slander and blasphemy. I will breathe her into his nostrils; as they discern the unclean and reject it, and take in the fragrant, so the pious will shun sin, and will cleave to the words of the Torah.[24]

Meacham notes that succeeding *aggadot* describe the perfections of Adam's soul, how God revealed the future to him, his generosity, and his wisdom. She asks why "the possibilities for imperfections in males and in females are parallel but only the positive aspects of male creation were expanded upon," despite numerous biblical examples of men indulging in slander, lust, and blasphemy.[25] She concludes that for the rabbis passivity was the most desirable female quality, writing: "The ideal woman, according to the sages' view, should lower her head in subjugation, shut her eyes and block her ears to outside stimulation, deaden her curiosity, and bear up cheerfully when her one sphere of power, fertility, does not manifest itself."[26] Many rabbinic voices would agree that women's apparently innate inability to conform to this desirable model without strong social strictures is the cause of much of the disorder in human life.

The inherent unreliability and harmful propensities of unregulated women are examined in an extensive midrash, *Genesis Rabbah* 17:3, based on "I will make him a help against him [literal translation of *k'negdo*]" (Gen. 2:18). This excursus, discussed in more detail in chapter 4, begins with the comment, "If he is fortunate, she is a help; if not, she is against him," and proceeds to tell the cautionary tale of the "bad wife" of R. Jose the Galilean.[27] *Genesis Rabbah* 17:6, in a comment on "He took one of her ribs and closed up the flesh at that spot" (Gen. 2: 21), goes further, connecting the creation of woman with the introduction of disorder and turmoil into the cosmos.

R. Hanina, son of R. Adda, said: From the beginning of the Book [Genesis] until here no *samekh* [Hebrew letter beginning the word *vayisgor* "closed up"] is written, but as soon as she [Eve] was created, Satan was created with her."[28]

This farfetched effort to associate Satan, usually corresponding in rabbinic literature to human evil inclinations, with the creation of the first female is indicative of extreme rabbinic threads of ambivalence about women, especially given the fact that Satan is usually spelled with the initial Hebrew letter *sin*, not *samekh* at all. Such negative, indeed misogynistic, views of women and their injurious propensities may be, as Daniel Boyarin has argued, rare indeed in rabbinic literature,[29] but their inclusion in a text which is grappling directly with the nature and meaning of female creation provides support for what appears to be the preferred rabbinic view, that women's flawed and dangerous natures require their subordination to their fathers or husbands.

The First Eve

The apparent contradictions in the biblical creation narratives as to the origins of the first female also elicited another explanation in rabbinic literature. This is the view, expressed obliquely rather than directly, that a different woman is referred to in each account. Obscure references to this legend of the "first Eve" appear in several rabbinic sources. Thus, *Genesis Rabbah* 18:4 offers the following interpretation for "And the man said: This one *at last* / Is bone of my bones / And flesh of my flesh" (Gen. 2:23):

R. Judah b. Rabbi said: At first He created her for him and he saw her full of discharge and blood [and was disgusted]; thereupon He removed her from him and recreated her a second time." This is why he said "**This instance at last** (*zot hapa'am*) / **Is bone of my bones**" (Gen. 2:23). This is she of the previous occasion; this is she who is destined to strike the bell and to speak [in strife] against me, as you read, **A golden bell** (*pa'amon*) (Ex. 28:34); it is she who troubled me (*me-fa'amtani*) all night.[30] All these remarks showed his amazement.

Resh Lakish was asked: Why do not all other dreams exhaust a man, yet this [a dream that intimacy takes place] does exhaust a man. Because from the very beginning of her creation she was but in a dream, replied he.

These two rather cryptic aggadic comments suggest several reasons why the "first Eve," created simultaneously with Adam, was unacceptable to him. One interpretation relates that when Adam saw the first woman in the process of creation, he found her repulsive. This explanation is expanded upon in *Genesis Rabbah* 17:7, where a certain Matrona asked R. Jose why Eve was created while Adam was asleep. The lady accepts R. Jose's explanation that Eve was formed while Adam slept so that he would not be repelled from accepting her as his wife by seeing the messy process of creation. She corroborates it as follows: "It had been arranged that I should be married to my mother's brother, but because I was brought up with him in the same house I became plain in his eyes and he went and married another woman, who is not as beautiful as I." This anecdote supports the view that the first Eve was unacceptable because she held no erotic mystery for her husband.[31]

Conversely, however, this comment may also imply that the "first Eve" was rejected not because she was too familiar to Adam, but because she was too different and sexually disturbing. In this passage, the mysterious "first Eve" is seen as instigating male sexual fantasies and causing nocturnal emissions. Another reference to the disruptive qualities of the "first Eve" appears in *Genesis Rabbah* 22:7 in a discussion of the source of the dispute between Cain and Abel:

"**Cain set upon his brother Abel**" (Gen. 4:8). Judah b. Rabbi said: Their quarrel was about the first Eve. Said R. Abihu: The first Eve had returned to dust.

This discussion is part of a rabbinic effort to establish, in the absence of biblical information, not only the basis for the enmity between the brothers but also the identification of Cain's wife who is mentioned in Genesis 4:17 ("**And Cain knew his wife, and she conceived and bore Enoch**"). The first Eve must have seemed a likely prospect. However *Genesis Rabbah* 22:7, having rejected her, offers another scenario:

Then what was their quarrel about? Said R. Huna: An additional twin was born with Abel, and each claimed her. The one claimed: "I will have her, because I am the firstborn"; while the other maintained: "I must have her, because she was born with me."[32]

While the legend of a "first Eve" is not developed much further in extant rabbinic literature, in the early Middle Ages it was combined with longstanding legends about Lilith, a major figure in Jewish demonology with roots in ancient Near Eastern folklore. Mentioned in Isaiah 34:14 among the "beasts of prey and the spirits that will lay waste the land on the day of vengeance," Lilith appears in the Talmud as a female night spirit with a woman's face, long hair, and wings.[33] One legend, referred to in parallel passages in *Genesis Rabbah* 20:11 and 24:6, implies that all demons, both male and female, are descendants of "**Adam's line**"(Gen. 5:1). The version in *Genesis Rabbah* 24:6 interprets the biblical phrase, "**This is the record of Adam's line**" (Gen. 5:1), as follows:

These are descendants, but the earlier ones were not [human] descendants. What were they? Demons. For R. Simon said: Throughout the entire one hundred and thirty years during which Adam held aloof from Eve [as an act of repentance following their expulsion from the Garden of Eden] the male demons were made ardent by her and she bore, while the female demons were inflamed by Adam and they bore.

In a similar passage in B. 'Eruvin 18b, Adam alone begets demonic descendants, which are said to include the female night spirits (*lilitot*) who fill the world.[34]

A conflation of all these legends appears in an anecdote in the medieval *Alphabet of Ben Sira,* an anonymous midrashic work, probably composed in a Muslim country during the Geonic period (possibly as early as the eighth century),[35] that identifies Lilith with the "first Eve." In this rather mysterious text, which seems to be an anthology of bawdy and often misogynistic parodies of midrashic traditions, the roots of Lilith's disobedience are attributed to her equal creation with Adam. Her story appears in the context of a discussion about the efficacy of amulets in curing a sick child:

Soon afterward the young son of the king took ill. Said Nebuchadnezzar, "Heal my son. If you don't, I will kill you." Ben Sira immediately sat down and wrote an amulet with the Holy Name, and he inscribed on it the angels in charge of medicine by their names, forms, and images and by their wings, hands, and feet. Nebuchadnezzar looked at the amulet. "Who are these?" "The angels who are in charge of medicine: Snvi, Snsvi, and Smnglof. After God created Adam, who was alone, He said, 'It is not good for the man to be alone' (Gen. 2:18). He then created a woman for Adam, from the earth, as He had created Adam himself, and called her Lilith. Adam and Lilith immediately began to fight. She said, 'I will not lie below,' and he said, 'I will not lie beneath you, but only on top. For you are fit only to be in the bottom position, while I am to be in the superior one.' Lilith responded, 'We are equal to each other inasmuch as we were both created from the earth.' But they would not listen to one another. When Lilith saw this, she pronounced the Ineffable Name and flew away into the air. Adam stood in prayer before his Creator: 'Sovereign of the universe!' he said, 'the woman you gave me has run away.' At once, the Holy One, blessed be He, sent these three angels to bring her back.

Said the Holy One to Adam, 'If she agrees to come back, fine. If not, she must permit one hundred of her children to die every day.' The angels left God and pursued Lilith, whom they overtook in the midst of the sea, in the mighty waters wherein the Egyptians were destined to drown. They told her God's words, but she did not wish to return. The angels said, 'We shall drown you in the sea.' 'Leave me!' she said. 'I was created only to cause sickness to infants. If the infant is male, I have dominion over him for eight days after his birth, and if female, for twenty days.'

When the angels heard Lilith's words, they insisted she go back. But she swore to them by the name of the living and eternal God:'Whenever I see you or your names or your forms in an amulet, I will have no power over that infant.' She also agreed to have one hundred of her children die every day. Accordingly, every day one hundred demons perish, and for the same reason, we write the angels' names on the amulets of very young children. When Lilith sees the names, she remembers her oath, and the child recovers."[36]

This extended *aggadah* assumes that both Lilith and Adam were created by God from the earth as autonomous entities. As a result, Lilith is unwilling to forgo her equal status with Adam. This narrative reflects rabbinic tradition in its certainty that mutuality cannot work in marital relations; the husband must be dominant. It is no accident that the author of the *Alphabet* presents the cause of the final separation between Adam and Lilith as an argument over who would assume the superior position in sexual intercourse. While this may have been meant on one level to amuse and titillate the readers of this racy and subversive satirical work, it also draws upon the strong rabbinic statement noted above that defends the male dominant position in intercourse, as in married life, as a perquisite of man's primacy in creation.

Male sexual anxiety, particularly over the mystery of nocturnal emissions, is also a significant theme in rabbinic speculation about the "other Eve." Jewish folklore in rabbinic times interpreted nocturnal emissions as a consequence of sexual contact with female night demons who set upon sleeping men. By the early medieval period, as evidenced by the *Alphabet of Ben Sira*, these demons were identified with Lilith who was said to give birth to an infinite number of offspring from her sexual forays among human beings. Similarly, the vindictive Lilith was linked with fears connected with maternal deaths in childbirth and infant mortality, frequent and terrifying events in most periods of human history. The *Alphabet* addresses this trepidation directly and offers recourse through the use of amulets bearing the names of angels.

The connections between Lilith and the demonic in the *Alphabet of*

Ben Sira have played a significant role in Jewish mystical writings, including *The Zohar*, where Lilith became a major character in kabbalistic demonology."[37] As Joseph Dan has shown, a later edition of *The Alphabet of Ben Sira*, which became prevalent in medieval Europe, inserted an addition into the story of Lilith. In this subsequent version, Lilith refuses to accompany the angels who have come to take her back to Adam on the grounds that she has subsequently married someone else, the Great Demon. Dan notes that as a result of this new material, Jewish mystical writings, beginning with those of R. Isaac ben Jacob ha-Kohen in thirteenth century Spain, transformed Lilith from the first Eve into the spouse of Samael, the central satanic figure in Jewish folklore. This evil couple, who were now said to have come into being simultaneously with the creation of Adam and Eve, are deemed responsible for all evil in the cosmos. As Dan points out, "Even the creation of Samael and Lilith is a parallel to the creation of Adam and Eve. Rabbi Isaac did not hesitate to depart radically from the content of his sources in order to achieve this, as he did in this last detail, forsaking the myth of Lilith as Adam's first wife in order to be able to present a complete parallel between the two pairs."[38]

While it is impossible to delineate the full outlines of rabbinic folklore about the "first Eve" from the scanty extant references in rabbinic literature, it is clear—both from what does survive and from the afterlife of Lilith in Jewish folklore, demonology, and mysticism—that the very notion of an autonomous woman, co-existent with the first man and dangerous to submissive women and their children, was a source of significant social, spiritual, and sexual anxiety to the collective rabbinic psyche.

The First Couple as Androgyne

Several rabbinic sources, referred to at the beginning of this chapter, attempted to explain the discrepancies between the two biblical creation stories by imagining that the first human being was created with both male and female characteristics. Only afterwards was a female entity separated from this essentially male being. However, this appealing solution to the conundrum of the two creation narratives remained very much a minority view. With the sole exception of *Genesis Rabbah* 8:1, cited above, the rest of *Genesis Rabbah* echoes the Talmud's rejection of a concurrent origin of man and woman, insisting that Genesis 1:27, which appears on the literal level to depict a simultaneous creation of male and female human beings in the divine image, refers only to the creation of a single male from whom woman would later be formed. Equally striking is the fact that when it is suggested that the divine commandments in Genesis 1:28 written in the plural imperative, concerning procreation and human authority over the natural world, also refer to women, rabbinic interpreters devote considerable energy to diminishing female legal rights in these areas, while stressing the scriptural mandate for husbands to control their wives' activities. The claim for the androgynous initial human being in *Genesis Rabbah* 8:1, attributed to R. Leazar, used as its prooftext, **"Male and female He created them, and He called their name Adam"** (Gen. 5:2). Yet this midrash is wholly missing from direct exegesis of Genesis 5:2 in *Genesis Rabbah* 24:6, although other remarks about the creation of Adam that appeared in *Genesis Rabbah* 8 are repeated there.

It is extremely telling, as well, that when *Genesis Rabbah* 8:11 offers commentary on **"Male and female He created them"** (Gen. 1:27), the only tradition cited, apparently with approval, is the observation that "This is one of the things which they altered for King Ptolemy, [emending the verse as] 'Male *with his apertures* He created them.' " In this modification of Genesis 1:27, "them" is said to refer to the "apertures" of the male body, not to "male and female" human beings. According to this aggadic tradition, those who translated the Hebrew Bible into the Greek Septuagint in the third century B.C.E. were so disturbed by the notion of a simultaneous creation of man and woman in the divine image that they altered the scriptural text. It seems likely that this emendation, which does not in fact appear in the Septuagint, is a projection of the rabbis' own uneasiness with this verse that appears to include women within the divine image.[39]

Indeed, this suspicion is confirmed by *Genesis Rabbah* 8:11 itself, which continues its discussion of Adam's creation as follows:

R. Joshua b. R. Nehemiah said in the name of R. Hanina b. R. Isaac, and the Rabbis in the name of R. Leazar said: He created him with four attributes of the higher beings [i.e. angels] and four attributes of the lower beings [i.e., beasts]. [The four attributes of] the higher beings are: he stands upright, like the ministering angels; and sees, like the ministering angels. Yet does not a dumb animal see! But this one [man] can see from the side. He has four attributes of the lower being: he eats and drinks, like an animal; procreates, like an animal; excretes, like an animal; and dies, like an animal. R. Tifdai said in R. Aha's name: The celestial beings were created in the image and likeness [of God] and do not procreate, while the terrestrial creatures [dumb animals] procreate but were not created in [His] image and likeness. Said the Holy One, blessed be He: "Behold, I will create him [man] in [My] image and likeness, [so that he will partake] of the [character of the] celestial beings, while he will procreate, [after the nature] of the terrestrial beings." R. Tifdai said in R. Aha's name: The Holy One, blessed be He, said: "If I create him of the celestial elements, he will live [forever] and not die, and if I create him of the terrestrial elements, he will die and not live [in a future life]. Therefore I will create him of the upper and of the lower elements: if he sins he will die while if he does not sin, he will live."

In this midrash, the moral implications of creation in the likeness of God are manifest. The human drama is to be the struggle between the higher and lower elements in man's makeup. He who triumphs over the lower impulses will be rewarded with life in the world to come. Here, human sexual differentiation and human procreation are both explicitly denied as reflecting the divine image. However, given the reality of human mortality, both are essential for human continuity, despite the difficulties which are bound to ensue. As Jeremy Cohen has written, "Within such a framework, sexual reproduction denotes not only an attribute of the lower world, but also—along with the divine image—the essence of the singular perfection that allows humans, and humans alone, to choose between life and death."[40] The role that women will play in this moral struggle, however, remains ambiguous at best.

Given the privileged place accorded male creation in rabbinic cosmology, one might ask why the midrash of the original androgyne was preserved at all. I would argue that the primary reason was its homiletical benefits in teaching that only when the male and female are united are they truly 'adam, that is truly human. Certainly, the idea that the first human being was androgynous was not unique to Jewish literature and such stories would have been widely current in the environments in which rabbinic literature was formed. However, while parallels to this rabbinic tradition in other cultural traditions have long been noted,[41] the legend of the primordial androgyne seems to be uniquely utilized in rabbinic writings to stress the foreordained role of marriage in human life.

A significant body of aggadic homiletical material, discussed in more detail in chapter 4, is devoted to the theme of marriage as the prerequisite for achieving fully human status for both males and females. The connection of marriage with human creation is a major theme in this discourse, including many traditions that do not invoke the notion of a simultaneous creation of male and female. Thus, parallel comments in *Genesis Rabbah* 8:9 and 22:2 maintain the precedence of man in human creation while stressing the crucial role of marriage and procreation in human life: "In the past, Adam was created from the ground, and Eve from Adam; but henceforth [with the birth of offspring to the first couple] it shall be, '**In our image, after our likeness**' (Gen. 1:26): Neither man without woman nor woman without man, nor both of them without the Shekhinah." This invocation of the Shekhinah, the indwelling nurturing aspect of the divine which is designated by a feminine noun, indicates that the female does share in the divine image in some measure when she is joined to man in a fruitful marriage.

Similarly, *Genesis Rabbah* 8:12 comments as follows on **"God blessed them"** (Gen. 1:28):

R. Abbahu said: The Holy One, blessed be He, took a cup of blessing and blessed them. R. Judah b. R. Simon said: Michael and Gabriel were Adam's "best men." R. Simlai said: We find that the Holy One, blessed be He, blesses bridegrooms, adorns brides, visits the sick, buries the dead, and recites the blessing for mourners. He blesses bridegrooms, as it is written, **"And God blessed them"**; He adorns brides, as it is written, **"And the Lord God fashioned the rib that he had taken from the man into a woman"** (Gen. 2:22).

However, neither of these groups of homilies is as powerful as the notion that man and woman were initially created as one entity, an entity to which they return when they become **"one flesh"** (Gen. 2:24) in marriage.

Several scholars have suggested that the endorsement of marriage implied in the rabbinic legend of the first androgyne is an implicit rejection of some of the attitudes towards human sexuality current in late antiquity. The first century Greek Jewish writer Philo of Alexandria, who was strongly influenced in his biblical exegesis by Greek philosophical writings, resolved the contradiction between the two creation narratives with the aid of Platonic imagery, writing:

There is a vast difference between the man thus formed [at Genesis 2:7] and the man that came into existence earlier [at Gen. 1:27] after the image of God; for the man so formed [i.e., at Gen. 2:7] is an object of sense-perception . . . , consisting of body and soul, man or woman, by nature mortal, while he that was after the (Divine) image was an idea or type or seal, an object of thought (only), incorporeal, neither male nor female . . . [42]

Thus, Philo holds that it is the human intellect and not the body which was created in the divine image in Genesis 1.

Genesis Rabbah 8:1, conversely, insists that the first human creation was an actual physical entity displaying both male and female sexual characteristics. Daniel Boyarin writes that for Philo and those who shared similar views, "the return to the original state of humankind involves a putting off of the body and sexuality and returning to a purely spiritual androgyny."[43] He notes that the rabbis were most likely to have encountered the myth of the primal androgyne in this spiritual form and suggests that the rabbinic conviction that the "physical union of man and wife restores the image of the original whole human being" may be seen as a rabbinic reversal and rejection of a commonplace of Hellenistic and Hellenistic Jewish culture.[44] While I disagree with Boyarin's contention that the opinion that "Eve and Adam (or at any rate, their genitals) were both contained physically in the first human being" was the "more common rabbinic view," there is no arguing with his conclusion that midrashic statements such as these explicitly ground "the Rabbis' ideology of marriage in their interpretation of the creation stories of Genesis."[45]

As Gary Anderson has pointed out, the primal marriage, as all marriages, has strong eschatological implications in rabbinic thought. The joy of the bride and bridegroom were foreshadowings of the joyful restorations which would take place in the days of the Messiah. As he writes, "On the one hand, Eden represents a concentrated locus of divine blessing—a blessing that actualizes itself in sexual fertility. On the other hand, Eden is a mythic topos for the anticipated joy of the eschaton. Just as marital bliss shall characterize the *Endzeit*, so marital bliss characterized the *Urzeit*."[46] Indeed, these themes are dominant in the marriage benedictions preserved in B. Ketubbot 8a that link the joy of marriage to the hoped-for gladness of the end of days. For rabbinic Judaism, then, the conjoining of male and female corporeality and difference represented in the myth of the first human creature was of central importance, since it pointed towards the final fulfilment of the divine plan for human creation and human destiny.

Creation as Destiny

Praise for a woman's necessary role in marriage does not constitute advocacy for her social equality in that or any other human institution. The preponderance of voices supporting a version of female creation that was subsequent, secondary, and inherently inferior to the creation of man reveals that most rabbinic sages were prepared to rationalize a social vision that disadvantaged women in numerous ways.[47] As chapter 3 demonstrates, midrashic expositors shifted the blame for their own constructions of women as lesser beings to a higher authority by explaining female handicaps as a natural consequence of their mode of creation, and, indeed, as a result of their inherent deficiencies.

❧ 3 ❧

EVE'S CURSES:
FEMALE DISADVANTAGES AND
THEIR JUSTIFICATIONS

Most voices within rabbinic literature agreed that women were best kept separate from centers of communal governance, holiness, and learning. The men who formulated these strictures were well aware of the dichotomy they had established between male privilege and female disempowerment, and it is worthy of note that some felt compelled to explain and justify the exclusion of women from the activities and prestige available to their own sex. This chapter explores rabbinic texts detailing the various disadvantages which were seen as part of the female condition and demonstrates how a significant number of rabbinic voices insisted that these handicaps were a consequence of women's inherent physical, emotional, and intellectual deficiencies. Nor were any exceptions to this vision of divine providence allowed. Rabbinic tradition overwhelmingly barred any semblance of equal standing, even to those women endowed with unusual intellectual gifts, significant economic resources, or access to political power.

Delineating Women's Disempowerment

The formulators and editors of aggadic literature recognized and attempted to rationalize what they saw as the numerous disadvantages which made women's lives manifestly inferior to their own. Two sets of texts in particular, *Genesis Rabbah* 17:8 and a very similar passage in *Avot de-Rabbi Nathan* B 9, and B. 'Eruvin 100b detail and explain a series of perceived female handicaps.

Genesis Rabbah 17:8, expanding on "So the Lord God cast a deep sleep upon the man; and, while he slept, He took one of his ribs and closed up the flesh at that spot" (Gen. 2:21), attributed the source of woman's inherent inadequacies both to the nature of her creation from the man's body and to her subsequent acts:

R. Joshua was asked: "Why does a man come forth [at birth] with his face downward, while a woman comes forth with her face turned upwards?" [He answered,] "The man looks towards the place of his creation [the earth], while the woman looks towards the place of her creation [the rib]." "And why must a woman use perfume, while a man does not need perfume?" "Man was created from earth," he answered, "and earth never putrefies, but Eve was created from a bone. For example: if you leave meat three days unsalted, it immediately goes putrid." "And why has a woman a penetrating voice, but not a man?" "I will give you an illustration," he replied. "If you fill a pot with meat it does not make any sound, but when you put a bone into it, the sound [of sizzling] spreads immediately." "And why is a man easily appeased, but not a woman?" "Man was created from the earth," he answered, "and when you pour a drop of water on it, it immediately absorbs it; but Eve was created from a bone, which even if you soak it many days in water does not become saturated." "And why does the man make [sexual] demands upon the woman, whereas the woman does not make demands upon the man?" "This may be compared to a man who loses something," he replied; "he seeks what he lost, but the lost article does not seek him." "And why does a man deposit sperm within a woman while a woman does not deposit sperm within a man?" "It is like a man who has an article in his hand and seeks a trustworthy person with whom he may deposit it." "Why does a man go out bareheaded while a woman goes out with her head covered?" "She is like one who has done wrong and is ashamed of people; therefore she goes out with her head covered." "Why do [women] walk in front of the corpse [at a funeral]?" "Because they brought death into the world, they therefore walk in front of the corpse [as it is written], 'He is brought to the grave . . . and all men follow behind him,/Innumerable are those [women] who precede him' (Job 21:32–33)." "And why was the precept of menstruation given to her?" "Because she shed the blood of Adam [by causing his death], therefore was the precept of menstruation given to her." "And why was the precept of dough (hallah) given to her?" "Because she corrupted Adam, who was the dough of the world, therefore was the precept of dough given to her." "And why was the precept of the Sabbath lights given to her?" "Because she extinguished the soul of Adam, therefore was the precept of the Sabbath lights given to her."

The disadvantages enumerated here, and discussed in detail below, are said to result first and foremost from woman's secondary formation from the man's rib. As the previous chapter demonstrated, rabbinic tradition was virtually united on upholding the second biblical creation story of an initial male creation followed by the formation of the female from his body, while discounting the narrative of human origins recounted in Genesis 1. By concluding that woman was essentially other than man because of her secondary formation from a created entity, and by linking the inferior nature of female creation with woman's responsibility for death, Genesis Rabbah 17:8 defends rabbinic sexual politics and the male/female status quo by portraying woman's numerous faults and disadvantages as divinely ordained and as deserved due to her inherent moral weaknesses. The very similar passage in *Avot de-Rabbi Nathan* B 9 will be cited as well in the discussion that follows.

Genesis Rabbah 17:8 begins by reinforcing both the inferior nature of female creation and woman's dependence upon and subordination to man with the argument that males are born looking down to the place of their origin, the earth, while females are born facing upwards towards the rib from which they were formed. This farfetched remark has no basis in reality. *Avot de-Rabbi Nathan* B 9 preserves the aggadic tradition discussed in chapters 1 and 2 that the male takes the superior position in sexual intercourse because he looks at the material from which he was created, the earth, while the woman looks at the man from whose bone she was formed.[1] *Genesis Rabbah* 17: 8 goes on to attribute several unpleasant characteristics to women in general; these are portrayed as consequences of female creation from a bone. The supposed results of woman's secondary and inferior origins include not only her subordination to her husband, but also her unpleasant odor which must be masked by perfume, her shrillness, and her unappeasable nature. This initial passage is similar in many ways to *Genesis Rabbah* 18:2, discussed in chapter 2, which also suggested that a number of negative characteristics were inherent in woman from the moment of her creation, despite the best divine efforts to prevent them.[2]

Women are also deemed less fortunate than men in *Genesis Rabbah* 17:8 because they are compelled to be sexually passive while men may actively seek out women for sexual relations. The aggadah explains that this is because the man is seeking his lost rib; he is complete only when he is joined in sexual congress with the woman whose formation he made possible. The woman, objectified as the "missing rib," must wait to be found since "lost articles" do not seek their owners. While female sexual passivity was seen as absolutely essential for the smooth functioning of rabbinic society, the rabbis perceived the requirement of female loyalty to one sexual partner as an inconvenience from which men, who could enjoy sexual relations with more than one woman, were exempt. Since a woman who bore a man's children had sexual contact only with him, women were constructed as trustworthy vessels for the deposit of sperm which it was hoped would develop into new life. The statement that women were disadvantaged in comparison to men because men had the possibility of additional spouses, or at least were permitted sexual access to more than one woman at a time, is also found in B. 'Eruvin 100b, discussed below. Such statements indicate that polygyny and concubinage, subjects little explored in rabbinic literature, were probably far more common than apologists have maintained.

While some sources indicate that polygyny was far more typical of Jewish life in the Babylonian milieu than in the Land of Israel, it is worth noting that *Genesis Rabbah*, where male sexual freedom is also seen as a male advantage, is a Palestinian document.[3]

Genesis Rabbah 17:8 cites the veiling of women as another disability and connects having to cover one's face in public with guilt and shame. *Avot de-Rabbi Nathan* B 9 adds the comment: "In the same way Eve disgraced herself and caused her daughters to cover their heads." From the point of view of a male, who could travel freely and openly, a woman's need to conceal herself must have seemed unpleasant, confining, and even furtive. M. Sotah 3:8 cites this difference in answering the question, "How does man differ from a woman? He may go with hair unbound and with garment rent, but she may not go with hair unbound and garments rent." A married woman's hair had to be covered because it was considered a sexual incitement (B. Berakhot 24a). Certainly it was customary for most women in the ancient Near East and in the Greco-Roman world to cover their hair when they went outside the home. Leila Leah Bronner has written that for married Jewish women, "hair covering was a sign not only of rabbinically enjoined modesty, but of a wife belonging to a particular man, and the veil had to be worn whenever she was in mixed company or went out in public."[4] B. Gittin 90a–b declared that a woman who went out with her hair unfastened and spun in the street with her armpits uncovered must be divorced for her immodesty, while in B. Ketubbot 65a, a widow who let her veil slip during a court proceeding was perceived by other women as making sexual advances to their husbands and was chased out of town.[5] In B. Yoma 47a, the mother of two men who served as high priests in one day attributed this signal honor to never uncovering her hair, even in the privacy of her home. Veiling, then, was an absolute necessity for women in a society so highly conscious of sexuality and its dangers; nevertheless, it was a personal imposition and restriction from which men were glad to be exempt.

Genesis Rabbah 17:8 connects the social institution of women's wearing veils with their guilt and shame over Eve's role in bringing death into the world.[6] This theme is also found in B. 'Eruvin 100b, discussed below, where women's curses include being "wrapped up like a mourner." Women are additionally linked with death in *Genesis Rabbah* 17:8 because of their roles at funerals where they walked in front of the corpse. *Avot de–Rabbi Nathan* B 9 comments at this point: "Why do women march first in front of the bier? What is it they say? We caused all the inhabitants of the world to come to this." Indeed, women's connection with keening and chanting dirges is an ancient one in the Middle

East.[7] Biblical texts indicate that both men and women participated in funeral laments, separately and perhaps also together in antiphonic style.[8] By rabbinic times, however, it appears that public keening had become an exclusively female role and one that was deemed essential to appropriate mourning. M. Ketubbot 4:4 quotes R. Judah as ruling that "even the poorest in Israel should hire not less than two flutes and one wailing woman" for his wife's funeral. As Meir Bar Ilan writes, "The only social ceremony in which the Jewish woman participated was the funeral—only there was she permitted to appear in public and express herself, not only in wailing and heart-rending sobbing, but also in the literary composition of elegies chanted aloud." Composition of funeral dirges was apparently the one area of rabbinic life in which women could publicly display their literary creativity. Bar Ilan also notes that the collection of eight elegies in B. Mo'ed Qatan 28b attributed to the women of Shoken-Zeb in Babylon is probably the most extensive quotation of women's words in the Talmud.[9]

Galit Hasan-Rokem has suggested that female figures appear frequently in the midrash collection, *Lamentations Rabbah*, because mourning is the central theme of that text. She writes that *Lamentations Rabbah* stresses the experiences of women as widows and bereaved mothers, "due to the cultural and traditional link between lamentation as a genre and women as its performers." She believes that public mourning was gendered in rabbinic society and seen as appropriate for women because "[t]he traditional male roles, which are linked to leadership, combat, and various forms of control, including self-control, restrain the cultural license to express sensitivities and feelings with the heightened intensity of the lament."[10]

While rabbinic strictures against hearing a woman's voice in public were relaxed in the case of funerals, women, who usually walked in front of the funeral bier, always remained strictly separate from the men.[11] Nevertheless, the statement in *Genesis Rabbah* 17:8 that women walk in front of the corpse because they brought death into the world is clear evidence that significant male ambivalence about women's roles in mourning remained. Some of the sexual anxiety generated by their very visible and audible presence in funeral processions is expressed in B. Qiddushin 80b, commenting on the mishnaic ruling (M. Qiddushin 4:12) that a man may not be alone with two women. In response to the opinion of Abba Saul that a deceased child may be buried by one man and two women, on the grounds that "in the time of grief one's passions are subdued," the rabbis disagreed and supported the view of R. Isaac who said: " **'Of what shall a living man mourn? / Each one of his own sins!'** (Lam. 3:39)—even in a man's grief, his lusts prevail against him."

B. Qiddushin 80b then goes on to discuss cases of adultery conducted at cemeteries or under the pretexts of a funeral and warns of the dangers to even the most respectable men of walking behind a woman on the road.

In B. Berakhot 51a Joshua b. Levi cautions that funeral processions, so profoundly tied in the imagination to sex and death, constitute a liminal moment of great peril for men:

> Three things were told me by the Angel of Death. Do not take your shirt from your attendant when dressing in the morning, and do not let water be poured on your hands by one who has not washed his own hands, and do not stand in front of women when they are returning from the presence of a dead person, because I go leaping in front of them with my sword in my hand and I have permission to harm. If one should happen to meet them what is his remedy?— Let him turn aside four cubits; if there is a river, let him cross it, and if there is another road let him take it, and if there is a wall, let him stand behind it; and if he cannot do any of these things, let him turn his face away and say, "**And the Lord said to Satan, 'The Lord rebuke you, O Satan; may the Lord who has chosen Jerusalem rebuke you! For this is a brand plucked from the fire' "** (Zech. 3:2).

This passage, which incorporates numerous elements of popular folk-lore, is wholly centered on how men can protect themselves from contact with the Angel of Death. Not only is there no concern for how women might protect themselves from similar peril, but in some fundamental way the women who lament at a funeral are seen as in league with the Angel of Death because of their responsibility for human mortality.

Genesis Rabbah 17:8 connects women's supposed role in bringing death into the world with women's ritual obligations. Although few details survive, Jewish women in ancient and late antique times did participate in their own religious observances in the private domain, including abstention from work on Rosh Hodesh, the new moon (J. Ta'anit 1:6, 64c). The details of most such rituals particular to women, many of which would have taken place in the private domain, are now mainly lost to us. Carol Meyers has written about women's domestic religion in biblical times, a subject on which biblical texts are also generally uninformative. She suggests that references to girls' puberty rites in Judges 11:39–40, harvest dances in Judges 21:20–21, and childbirth rituals in Leviticus 12:6–8 give fleeting illumination to exclusively female ceremonies which were not of interest to male biblical writers and editors—and therefore were not recorded in any detail. While these and similar female customs may have persisted well into rabbinic times, they are not preserved in rabbinic literature, perhaps because they had no direct relevance to male religious obligations.[12]

The female ritual responsibilities of concern to rabbinic Judaism were all connected with the home, including preparation and serving of food according to rabbinic dietary laws (*kashrut*). As Ross Shephard Kraemer has written, these commandments were binding on both men and women. However, M. Ketubbot 5:5 and 5:9 specify that women were in charge of ensuring that "the food eaten, the methods by which it was prepared, the pots in which it was cooked, and the jars in which it was stored were all in accord with rabbinic interpretations of *kashrut*."[13] The three religious obligations that rabbinic Judaism considered to be specific to a woman were her observance of limitations on marital contact during the prescribed period of menstrual impurity (*niddah*); the separation and burning in the oven of a piece of the dough used in making Sabbath bread (*hallah*), a reminder of Temple sacrifice; and kindling of Sabbath lights (*hadlaqah*). In fact, men could fulfil either of the last two commandments if no woman was present. Her observance of the first was purely for the benefit of her husband to preserve him from ritual impurity.

It is likely that observing these rituals provided many women with satisfying spiritual avenues for sanctification of aspects of daily life. Yet, as indicated in *Genesis Rabbah* 17:8, at least some strands of rabbinic tradition did not regard women's performance of these ordinances as *mitzvot*, that is, as divine commandments whose observance enhanced the religious life of the observer and assured divine favor. Instead, these rituals were constructed as eternal punishments or atonements brought upon woman to remind her of Eve's responsibility in the death of Adam and therefore in all human mortality.[14] *Avot de-Rabbi Nathan* B 9 goes even further:

Why were the commandments of menstrual purity given to woman and not to man? Because Adam was the blood of the Holy One, blessed be He; Eve came and spilled it. Consequently, the commandments of menstrual purity were given to her so that the blood which she spilled might be atoned for.[15]

In this formulation '*adam*, the first human being, is connected with *dam* (blood), and Adam himself is said to be the blood of God. There is a strong implication here that Adam, created in the divine image, was originally intended to live forever. It is Eve who is responsible for his death and thus for the mortality of all humanity.

According to M. Shabbat 2:6, disregard of these three commandments brings dire consequences: "For these transgressions do women die in childbirth: for heedlessness of the laws concerning their menstruation, the dough offering, and the lighting of the Sabbath lamp." This statement is also found in *Avot de-Rabbi Nathan* B 9. In the adumbration of M. Shabbat 2:6 in J. Shabbat 2:6, 8b, virtually the same midrash about Eve's responsibility for human mortality is repeated as justification for women's having to fulfil these precepts. Interestingly, this tradition about the culpability of Eve does not appear in the discussion of M. Shabbat 2: 6 in B. Shabbat 31b–34a. There, women's risk for death, if they fail in these three specific areas, is cited in the context of a long discussion about the causes of various human misfortunes for individuals in general, with virtually every ill and catastrophe justified as the consequences of a specific human disobedience. In this passage, the major question on the punishment women receive for transgressing the commandments of *niddah*, *hallah*, and *hadlaqah* is whether their disobedience leads to death in childbirth specifically (the opinion of the rabbis), or becomes the cause for any premature death (the opinion of R. Eleazar cited at B. Shabbat 32a). That dire consequences will follow on their neglect is not disputed.[16]

It is difficult to fathom what lies behind this formulation connecting these specific commandments with Eve's supposed responsibility for death. Certainly it is repeated often enough to merit description as a mainstream rabbinic view. Kraemer suggests that the severity of these statements may reveal a rabbinic effort to remove external non-Jewish associations from female rituals that had parallels in the "religious observances of women in the various forms of paganism with which Jewish women were likely to come into contact."[17]

A complementary explanation may be that such dire pronouncements are part of a rabbinic polemic against widespread non-compliance with these precepts, perhaps particularly in regard to non-observance of *niddah* regulations. As Kraemer has pointed out, "except for the prescriptions of the rabbis themselves, we have no evidence for women separating dough, baking Sabbath bread, lighting Sabbath candles, or observing *kashrut* or *niddah*, the laws of menstrual purity."[18] Significant evidence suggests that observance of ritual prohibitions outside of rabbinic circles was often weak, both in the rabbinic period and later in Jewish history.[19] Threats of early death may have been one rabbinic strategem to ensure higher degrees of compliance to what were seen as defining rituals for women that also had consequences for men, particularly in the area of ritual purity. Certainly the anxiety one can discern in rabbinic literature to control women's activities may reflect the dissonance between what many women actually did and what the rabbinic sages preferred them to do.

A closer look at these texts also makes clear that they belong to a larger body of rabbinic theological speculation which attempts to demonstrate that divine justice is fully operative in the world. All misfortunes and human suffering have a cause and often, if not always, this cause can be identified and forestalled by changes in human behavior. Women were demonstrably at great risk of death in childbirth, a tragedy unique to their gender. It is not surprising that rabbinic expositors found an explanation for this frequent misfortune in failure to observe these commandments. At the same time, causes were found for calamities affecting men as well. B. Shabbat 32a teaches that women's righteousness is examined at childbirth, a liminal moment of crisis, but then goes on to discuss extensively the parallel moments at which men are examined. Similarly, Daniel Boyarin points out that in *Ecclesiastes Rabbah* 3:3, a document that was probably redacted in the Land of Israel, the text, "For three things women die in childbirth," is accompanied by the parallel construction, "and for three things men die."[20] Rabbinic theodicy may have eschewed ultimate certainty on all of the causes of specific human misfortunes, but that there were causes could not be denied without calling into question the reality of divine justice.

But finally, one must wonder if the rabbis believed that women were blessed with three empowering commandments, or cursed with three eternal punishments, or at best three modes of atonement. Did women view these obligations as special opportunities for sanctity or as deserved reminders of Eve's sin? These questions cannot be answered. The polyphonic complexity of rabbinic literature renders its formulations as irreducible as they are ultimately mysterious. Meanwhile, women's voices are entirely absent. Although one may agree with Boyarin that "these [commandments] are particularly given to women because they belong particularly to woman's sphere as understood by rabbinic culture, to her body, cooking, and the comfort of the house, just as other commandments, which belong to the 'male' spheres of public life and worship are restricted to men,"[21] it is nevertheless the case that we do not see a similar construction of male obligations as burdens or punishments rather than as avenues to righteousness. It seems no accident that all three of these commandments/punishments specifically directed at women have to do with separation. All three may be read as symbolizing the chasm between the sacred and the profane, the holy and the secular, the pure and the impure, the realm of men who obey commandments and that of women who suffer disadvantages, and ultimately between the realms of life and death themselves. As such, they epitomize the profound disparity between the lives and experiences of men and women, which significant voices within rabbinic Judaism recognized and wished to maintain.

Women's Ten Curses

The detriments to being female are also pursued in B. 'Eruvin 100b.[22] The context is a discussion of inappropriate and appropriate modes of marital sexuality, including the impermissibility of coercing a wife to have sexual relations. The recounting of women's "curses" in this talmudic passage is prompted by a citation of the tradition that "A woman who solicits her husband to the [marital] obligation will have children the like of whom did not even exist in the generation of Moses." This apparent praise of direct expressions of female sexuality is challenged on the following grounds, built in part around an exegesis of Genesis 3: 16 **"And to the woman He said, 'I will greatly multiply / Your pangs in childbearing; / In pain shall you bear children. / Yet your urge shall be for your husband, / And he shall rule over you' "**

R. Isaac b. Abdimi stated: Eve was cursed with ten curses, since it is written: **"And to the woman He said, 'I will greatly multiply' "** (Gen. 3:16), which refers to the two drops of blood, one being that of menstruation and the other to that of virginity, **"Your pangs"** refers to the pain of bringing up children, **"And your travail in childbearing"** refers to the pain of conception; **"In pain shall you bear children"** is to be understood in its literal meaning. **"Yet your urge shall be for your husband"** teaches that a woman yearns for her husband when he is about to set out on a journey; **"And he shall rule over you"** teaches that while the wife solicits with her heart the husband does so with his mouth, this being a fine trait of character among women. What was meant is that she ingratiates herself with him.

But are not these only seven? When R. Dimi came he explained: She is wrapped up like a mourner, banished from the company of all men, and confined within a prison. What is meant by "banished from the company of all men?" If it be suggested: That she is forbidden to meet a man in privacy, is not the man also forbidden to meet a woman in privacy? The meaning rather is that she is forbidden to marry two men. In a *baraita* it was taught: She grows long hair like a *lilith*, sits when making water like a beast, and serves as a bolster for her husband. And the other? [How do these three differ from R. Dimi's suggestions?] These [three qualities] he holds are rather complimentary to her, R. Hiyya having made the following statement: What is meant by the biblical text, **"Who gives us knowledge from the beasts of the earth / Makes us wise by the birds of the sky?"** (Job 35:11)[23] **"Who gives us knowledge from the beasts of the earth"** refers to the mule which kneels when it makes water, and **"Makes us wise by the birds of the sky"** refers to the cock which first coaxes and then mates.

In this passage, the first seven divinely ordained afflictions for women are based on a sequential exegesis of Genesis 3:16. True to the rabbinic principle that scripture contains no repetitions, this talmudic passage demonstrates that each component of this verse has a separate meaning. Thus, the biblical phrase **"I will greatly multiply"** (*harbah 'arbeh*), in which forms of the Hebrew verb "to multiply" appear twice for emphasis, is understood to refer to two female flows of blood: the blood shed at menstruation and the blood shed at the loss of virginity. "Your pangs" is said to refer specifically to the pain of bringing up children, and "your travail" to the pain suffered during pregnancy, while **"In pain** shall you bear children" refers to the discomforts of labor and delivery. "Yet your urge shall be for your husband" is said to refer to a woman's desire for her husband when he is away on a journey and she has no sexual partner. The seventh curse, based on the end of Genesis 3:16, "And he shall rule over you," is said to mean that a woman may not address her husband sexually with words, but must ingratiate herself with him by her actions when she is desirous of sexual attention. It is this statement that answers the question that prompted this entire excursus. A woman may solicit her husband sexually, but must do so indirectly. Having to express her needs covertly is indicative of the sexual passivity imposed on women, certainly an undesirable condition from the male vantage point, and hence one of Eve's curses.

Four of these supposed woes are directly related to what men saw as undesirable and distasteful features of women's bodies and their biological functions which result in blood flow and in physical pain. The other three drawbacks—the pains of bringing up children, a woman's frustrated sexual desires when her husband is absent, and her enforced sexual passivity—are due to female dependence on male mastery. Yet for none of these disadvantages were men in any way culpable. All were considered either ordained by God at the outset of the human drama or were part of women's punishment for disobeying God. Of the debilities enumerated so far, menstruation and sexual passivity correspond to female burdens cited in *Genesis Rabbah* 17:8.

At this point, the discussion turns to the three remaining banes which are said to make women's lot so much less appealing than that apportioned to men. According to R. Dimi, the final three curses are: "She is wrapped up like a mourner, banished from the company of all men, and confined within a prison." Here is a strong descriptive statement, indeed, of the consequences for women of their separation from participation in the major activities of Jewish communal life, as well as evidence that men were fully aware of the ramifications of that deprivation. "Wrapped up like a mourner" evokes the connections drawn between women and death in parallel texts such as *Genesis Rabbah* 17:8 and B. Berakhot 51a, discussed above. Even if it is understood as a straightforward reference to women having to veil themselves when they appear in public, the comparison of woman's ordinary public state to that of a mourner is a telling and disturbing remark which also evokes the blame and guilt attached to women in *Genesis Rabbah* 17:8.

B. 'Eruvin 100b then debates the meaning of "banished from the company of all men." This curse had to be distinguished from "confined within a prison," the disability which immediately follows, in order to eliminate any possibility of repetition. What differentiated these two conditions for the rabbinic expositors was that "banished from the company of all men" was said to refer to the fact that a woman is forbidden to be married to two men at the same time. "Confined within a prison," on the other hand, meant that a woman was best kept occupied at home. Again, we see an acknowledgement in this passsage, as in *Genesis Rabbah* 17:8, of the male's relative freedom which allowed him sexual access to more than one woman at a time, while patriarchal norms demanded that a wife's fidelity be assured. The frequent references to women's lack of access to a variety of sexual partners as a disadvantage strongly implies that polygyny and/or frequent resort to women outside of marriage were accepted features of men's lives in the various times and places in which rabbinic literature was composed.[24]

The ninth affliction suffered by women, according to B. 'Eruvin 100b, was their enforced absence from most public domain activities. Rabbinic social policy apportioned separate spheres and responsibilities to women and men, making every effort in its blueprint for an ideal society to confine women and their activities to the private realms of the family and its particular concerns, including home-based economic activities which would benefit the household.[25] That men would characterize the consequences of this social pattern for women as "confinement in a prison" is reminiscent of *Genesis Rabbah* 18:1, cited in chapter 2,[26] which suggested that women's inherent potential for common sense and understanding atrophied because they were isolated from the rest of the world.

In her confinement from the public realms of Jewish life, women's situation was analogous to that of other excluded and disadvantaged classes of human beings, including minors, disabled men, male slaves, and male gentiles. In a court of law, for example, the testimony of a woman was generally unacceptable, since like slaves and children who are also subject to someone else's authority, her reliability was suspect (M. Shevuot 4:1).

Similarly, she was among those exempt from most public religious rituals. M. Hagigah 1:1 rules, for example: "All are subject to the command to appear before the Lord [at the Temple] excepting a deaf-mute, an imbecile, a child, one of doubtful sex, . . . women, slaves that have not been freed, a man that is lame, or blind, or sick, or aged, and one that cannot go up to Jerusalem on his feet."[27] Here women were associated with men perceived as lacking or damaged in some way or those, like minors and slaves, who were subject to a master's will. Such incomplete individuals could not function in the ways available to the unblemished, free, Jewish male who shared fully in the covenantal relationship between God and Israel. The three-fold prayer, discussed earlier in this volume, in which a Jewish adult male expressed gratitude for not being created a gentile, a slave, or a woman maintains these distinctions between completeness and deficiency.[28] Moreover, the exclusion of women goes further. Presumably a male Jewish slave who was freed could assume the rights and privileges of any other free Jewish male. Similarly, a male gentile could convert, undergo circumcision, and also join the covenant community as a spiritual equal. Jewish males who were minors became adults. A woman, however, was condemned by the essential qualities and characteristics of her gender to permanent restriction from fully sharing the privileges and responsibilities of male-defined covenantal Judaism, particularly the highly valued communal pursuits of worship, study, and governance.

As this passage illustrates, women were disempowered in the public realm of rabbinic society. These and similar remarks strongly support the contention that the roots of the exclusion of women from participation in group worship, literary culture, and the communal life of their community, and their relegation to domestic, enabling roles, were deeply embedded in rabbinic Judaism's profound consciousness of corporeality and its consequences. They also indicate that men were perfectly aware of women's subordinate and segregated position in their society and felt some obligation to justify it.

Most of women's curses as described in B. 'Eruvin 100b resulted from their physical differences from men. Indeed, B. 'Eruvin 100b concludes its discussion of women's less desirable lot with three alternate curses derived from a *baraita*; two of these stress aspects of woman's physical otherness, while the third is simply a bald acknowledgement of the unpleasant nature of a woman's enabling role from a male perspective. These burdens are as follows: "She grows long hair like a *lilith*,[29] sits when making water like a beast, and serves as a bolster for her husband." But are these curses or benefits? R. Dimi is cited as saying that these three qualities are compliments to women. Perhaps from a male point of view they were. Women's long hair can be attractive; making water in a sitting position bespeaks modesty; and serving as a support for her husband is certainly desirable, at least from R. Dimi's point of view.

R. Dimi's statement facilitates a segue into an apparently unrelated midrashic discourse which both concludes the larger talmudic passage and offers a last word on rabbinic understandings of the relative roles and capacities of women and men. The mention of the inconvenience of women's need to sit while urinating evoked an exegesis of Job 35:11 explaining what humans can learn from the animals and yielded the following remarks:

R. Johanan observed: If the Torah had not been given we could have learned modesty from the cat, honesty from the ant, chastity from the dove, and good manners from the cock who first coaxes and then mates. And how does he coax his wife? Rab Judah citing Rab replied, "He tells her this: 'I will buy you a cloak that will reach to your feet" [an interpretation of the spreading of the rooster's wings and the bending of their tips towards the ground prior to mating]. After the event he tells her, 'May the cat tear off my crest if I don't buy you one when I have any money.' "

This praise of the rooster in B. 'Eruvin 100b who seduces his mate rather than coercing her, fittingly completes the entire *sugya* in which the delineation of Eve's curses is embedded. This text, which begins with the statement "A man is forbidden to compel his wife to the [marital] obligation," ends appropriately with a commendation of gentle seduction. The final depiction of women as easily persuaded, credulous, and likely to be deceived, moreover, could only reinforce male satisfaction at not being created female.

In another exploration of the consequences of the primal drama in the Garden of Eden, *Avot de-Rabbi Nathan* B 42 relates that ten decrees were passed with regard to Adam, ten with regard to Eve, ten for the serpent, and the ten for the earth. The ten decrees passed against Eve are listed as follows:

The first is menstruation, when she is driven from her house and banned from her husband. The second is that she gives birth after nine months. The third is that she nurses for two years. The fourth is that her husband rules over her. The fifth is that he is jealous of her if she speaks with any other man. The sixth is that she ages quickly. The seventh is that she ceases to give birth while men never cease being able to beget children. The eighth is that she stays in the house and does not show herself in public like a man. The ninth is that when she goes out to the marketplace her head has to be covered like a mourner. That is why women precede the bier, saying, "We have brought death upon all the inhabitants of the world." The tenth is that if she was upright, her husband buries her. For we find that this was the case with our ancestors: our father Abraham buried Sarah our mother. Isaac buried Rebecca our mother. Jacob buried Rachel and Leah.

These pronouncements for women occur in the context of the consequences suffered by the other participants in the original act of human disobedience. Thus, Adam, among other things, is stripped of precious garments, condemned to live through toil, and ultimately to die. Finally, he is destined to stand in judgement, as Scripture says, **"O youth, enjoy yourself while you are young! Let your heart lead you to enjoyment in days of your youth. Follow the desires of your heart and the glances of your eyes—but know well that God will call you to account for all such things"** (Ecc. 11:9). Similarly, the serpent has lost its hands and feet and the ability to speak, eats dust, is the enemy of man, and remains always cursed, while the earth was altered from a watered garden to a rocky and thorny place that will ultimately be depleted.

Six of Eve's punishments in this conceptualization are disagreeable functions of her body. They include menstruation, nine months of pregnancy, nursing each child for two years, aging rapidly, losing her fertility, and likely death before her husband. The other disabilities have to do with her subordinate status. As stated in previous enumerations, she is subordinate to her husband, cannot speak to any other men, is confined within her home, and can only go out into the marketplace covered like a mourner. Although *Avot de-Rabbi Nathan* B 42 delineates decrees against four entities, it is telling that it concludes with a reiteration of woman's guilt in fomenting all the trouble. The final segment of the chapter begins, "Adam was the blood of the world" and goes on to detail the connection between female culpability for bringing death into the world and the three female commandments. The passage ends, "From this our sages, blessed be their memory, said: For three offenses women die when they are giving birth: For carelessness in regard to menstrual purity, the dough offering, and lighting the Sabbath lamp."

Fencing Women Off: The Realms of Prayer and Study

As is evident from the passages just discussed, rabbinic Judaism not only deliberately limited women's spiritual and intellectual possibilities in the communal realm, but justified these restrictions on the basis of women's deservedly inferior capacities. Since women were exempted from most regular religious group obligations, especially those bound to be performed in the synagogue at specified times, they were excluded from full inclusion in many religious activities and from those endeavors, particularly intellectual and leadership pursuits, which conferred social and religious status. This is not to say, however, that women were granted no spiritual roles. Women were responsible for obeying all of Judaism's negative commandments, and for observing the Sabbath and all of the festivals and holidays of the Jewish calendar, though male and female obligations on these days often differed. And, although women were exempt from participation in communal prayers which were to be recited at specific times, they were not released from the obligation to pray. B. Berakhot 20b, comments on the nature of female prayers in an explication of M. Berakhot 3:3, "Women, slaves and minors are exempt from reciting the *Sh'ma* and from putting on *tefillin* but they are subject to the obligations of *tefillah* (prayer) and *mezuzah* and grace after meals":

Because this [prayer] is a [supplication for divine] mercy. You might [however] think that because it is written in connection with **"Evening and morning and at noonday,"**(Ps. 55:18), therefore it is like a positive precept for which there is a fixed time [from which women are exempt]. Therefore we are told [that this is not so and that they are obligated].

Although there are some rabbinic references to both biblical and con-temporaneous women praying, the rabbis have little to say about the content of women's prayers. One exception to this is the exegetical ad-ditions to the biblical Hannah's prayer of 1 Samuel 1 in B. Berakhot 31b. One of these adumbrations builds on the biblical language to link Hannah to the defining female commandments.

"If You will look upon the affliction of Your maidservant and will remember me and and not forget Your maidservant, and if you will grant Your maidservant a male child . . . " (1 Samuel 1:11). R. Jose son of R. Hanina said: "Why these three [repetitions of] **'maidservant'**? Hannah said before the Holy One, blessed be He: Sovereign of the Universe, 'You have created in woman three criteria of death (some say three vulnerable points for death), namely, *niddah, hallah,* and the kindling of the light [on Sabbath]. Have I transgressed in any of them?' "

For later Jewish tradition, Hannah's spontaneous prayer from the heart became the model for women's prayers and was also said to be instruc-tive for men.[30]

It is often suggested that women were relieved from time-bound com-mandments such as communal prayer, because of their family respon-sibilities and obligations which might prevent their regularly fulfilling them. Saul Berman, for example, has suggested that many of the social and legal disabilities women suffer in rabbinic Judaism are accidental by-products of the system's insistence on her confinement to the duties of the domestic sphere. He suggests "The exemption from communal presence seems to be a central element of women's status in Jewish law, necessary to ensure that no mandated or preferred act conflict with the selection of the protected role."[31] However, I would argue that women's exclusion from communal worship and related activities cannot be ra-tionalized solely on the grounds of women's domestic duties. Women were not required to participate in communal worship even at those times in their lives when they were independent of the authority or de-mands of others, for example, as childless adults, or widows with grown children.

Judith Hauptman believes that woman's exemption from performing ritual acts at specific times was emblematic not only of her household responsibilities but of her primary allegiance to her husband: "Once married, she would not have the opportunity to fulfil religious obliga-tions unless her husband allowed her to do so." Moreover, she suggests that women were exempt from the essential ritual acts of Judaism because of their subordinate status, since "only people of the highest social standing, according to the rabbis, does God consider most fit to honor or worship Him in this important way."[32] Similarly, Judith Romney Wegner has written that rabbinic Judaism is based on "a legal presumption that men, as heads of households, perform cultic precepts on behalf of wives, children, slaves, and all within their jurisdiction."[33]

However, while male children and slaves have the potential to join the covenant community as spiritual equals when their circumstances change, a woman is always a woman; her presence is inappropriate in the central communal domains of prayer and study, regardless of whether or not her attendance would interfere with her domestic functions. Nor does her status change when she is no longer under male authority as a widow or divorcée. One cannot escape the conclusion that women are encouraged to be absent from the public domains of rabbinic religious life because the male formers of the tradition wanted it that way.

Rabbinic discourse on whether or not women should learn Torah raises similar issues.[34] The major nexus of debate is the dispute between Rabbi Eliezer and Ben-Azzai, cited in M. Sotah 3:4. The context of the discussion is the ordeal prescribed for a woman accused of adultery:

Hardly has she finished drinking before her face turns yellow and her eyes bulge and her veins swell, and they say, "Take her away! Take her away! That the Temple Court be not made unclean!" But if she had any merit this holds her punishment in suspense. Certain merits may delay punishment for one year, others for two years, and others for three years; hence Ben Azzai says: A man ought to give his daughter a knowledge of the Law so that if she [is guilty and] drinks [the bitter water] she may know that the merit [that she had acquired] will delay her punishment [but not prevent it]. R. Eliezer says: If any man gives his daughter a knowledge of the Law it is as though he taught her lasciviousness. R. Joshua says: A woman has more pleasure in one measure [of material wealth] with lasciviousness than in nine measures with modesty.

There are several ambiguities in Ben Azzai's statement. Does he mean that knowledge of Torah itself is the merit that mitigates the penalty? Or is Torah study important so that the daughter will know that her punishment has only been delayed by her other merits and will not assume that heavenly judgment is faulty? Regardless, Ben Azzai is immediately countered by R. Eliezer's view that teaching Torah to women is not to be countenanced since it would encourage their lascivious inclinations.

Rabbi Eliezer's opposition to teaching Torah to girls and women became the dominant outlook in the Babylonian Talmud and in later Jewish tradition. Indeed, the Babylonian Talmud's discussion of M. Sotah

3:4 just excises Ben Azzai's opinion altogether. Daniel Boyarin points out that by choosing not to take notice of Ben Azzai's statement, the compilers of the Babylonian Talmud all but ensured that his point of view would be significantly marginalized. As he writes, "It seems, therefore, that our Babylonian texts [as opposed to the Palestinian Talmud] were at much greater pains to simply eliminate the possibility that women would be considered candidates for study of Torah.[35] Certainly the received consensus until recent times remained that such learning was inappropriate for females.

Nevertheless, numerous rabbis were aware of the intelligent and acute women they encountered in their daily lives and some must have wondered why such apparently able minds should be prevented from undertaking serious study. Some traditions, discussed in previous chapters, stressed women's essential unsuitability for such endeavors on the grounds that their secondary mode of creation had resulted in physical deficiencies and mental unfitness of various kinds. Still, it remains clear that uneasiness about excluding women from Judaism's ultimate cultural enterprise remained.

The most illustrative indications of rabbinic anxiety when confronted with intellectually able females are the traditions associated with R. Meir's learned wife, Beruriah. In a number of rabbinic passages, a woman named Beruriah is portrayed as demonstrating a profound knowledge of biblical interpretation, an admirable ability to handle traditional texts, and a quick wit. Yet aggadic praises of Beruriah's supposed halakhic skills have something of an illusory quality. Beyond one very early reference in the Tosefta which is repeated nowhere else, no actual legal rulings are ever attributed to her.[36] Moreover, even Beruriah's reputed scholarly expertise became a problem for rabbinic Judaism. In a medieval reference, which may reflect earlier sources, she is shown to reap the tragic consequences of the "light mindedness" inherent in women. The eleventh century French commentator Shlomo ben Isaac (Rashi) relates a tradition in his commentary on B. 'Avodah Zarah 18b that Beruriah was seduced by one of her husband's students and subsequently committed suicide.

Recent scholarship has shown that the Beruriah who appears in the Babylonian Talmud is a literary construct with little historical reality. Nor can any credence be given to Rashi's account of her ignominious downfall.[37] However, Tal Ilan has convincingly argued that the early Tannaitic Tosefta ruling attributed to someone named Beruriah must be taken as historical, and that in many ways the rabbis of the Amoraic period were as amazed by this citation as modern readers. She suggests that the composition and preservation of the later Beruriah traditions in the Babylonian Talmud, built around the faint historical memory of an actual woman capable of making subtle legal distinctions, articulate the rabbis' astonishment at such a "wonder-woman."[38] These literary constructions may also attest to the existence of "counter-hegemonic voices that recognize the reality of *some* women's intellectual and spiritual accomplishment."[39] Certainly, they constitute additional evidence of a degree of rabbinic doubt about the justice of women's enforced role of intellectual passivity vis-à-vis male cultural endeavors.

Rachel Adler has suggested that the Beruriah narratives express rabbinic ambivalence about where a woman might possibly fit in a wholly male scholarly world of "teachers and students and study partners," a locus in which her sexuality was bound to be a source of havoc.[40] Similarly, Daniel Boyarin writes that for the Amoraic sages of the Babylonian Talmud, Beruriah served as proof of "R. Eliezer's statement that 'anyone who teaches his daughter Torah, teaches her lasciviousness' (M. Sotah 3:4)." For Boyarin, Rashi's tale of Beruriah's fall into sexual licentiousness, which may have had its origins in longstanding extra-talmudic legends, must be understood as the necessary consequence of any woman studying Torah.[41]

The dissociation of Beruriah from the halakhic regulation which was her original claim to renown, then, is not so surprising. As Ilan writes:

When the editors of the Mishnah had to decide what to do with Beruriah's ruling, they decided it was too valuable to lose, but at the same time the finished product of the editorial activity—the Mishnah—was designed to uphold the ideal world of learning in which women had no place. Beruriah was therefore edited out."[42]

Rabbinic society, in its effort to reflect an imagined divine plan for human society, insisted on sharply defined and controlled categories of being in which each gender had a particular set of roles and obligations. As Boyarin observes of rabbinic culture, "The Torah and the wife are structural allomorphs and separated realms . . . both normatively to be highly valued but also to be kept separate."[43]

Fencing Women Off: Stories about Yalta

Recently, some scholars, including Judith Hauptman, have attempted to show that not all rabbinic authorities were agreed on the isolation of women from learning and communal prayer. They argue that some minority strands more supportive of women's intellectual and spiritual abilities and needs also weave through the tradition, particularly from

sources in the land of Israel.[44] Boyarin, too, suggests that while the dominant discourse in both the Babylonian and Palestinian Talmuds sup-
presses women's participation in study and communal worship, in Palestine a dissenting voice was tolerated while in Babylonia "this issue
seems to have been so threatening that even a minority voice had to be
entirely expunged." As he notes, however, "The historical effect of the
Babylonian text . . . which was hegemonic for later European Jewish culture, was to suppress quite thoroughly the possibilities for women to
study Torah until modern times."[45]

Rabbinic resolve to erect and maintain separations between men and
women in the communal realm, including serious study, must be seen
as a deliberate choice since this was not the only Jewish model available
to the framers of rabbinic Judaism, at least for those who lived within
the boundaries of the Roman Empire. Various literary and archeological
data, discussed in more detail in chapter 1 of this volume, suggest that,
during the centuries of rabbinic Judaism's formation, there were Jewish
women who acted in independent ways in the public domains of the law
court and the synagogue. Some such women, even while married, exercised legal options independently through litigation, successfully man-
aged complicated financial affairs, and served in positions of religious
leadership and patronage.[46] Thus, rabbinic efforts to confine women's
activities to the domestic domain may have been as much a reaction to
unwelcome alternative patterns in the Jewish milieu as to concerns about
the negative impact of the non-Jewish world encountered in the public
marketplace.[47]

This determination to undercut traditions of female autonomy is visible throughout rabbinic literary traditions. One cardinal example is
texts about Yalta, portrayed as an aristocratic woman of notable learning who exercised significant communal authority in the Jewish community in Babylon. Yalta, one of the very few named women in rabbinic
literature, figures in seven aggadic narratives in the Babylonian Talmud.
While virtually no historicity can be applied to any of the details of these
stories,[48] their general themes are quite clear. The rabbis were aware of
women whose strong personalities, control of significant financial resources, and/or aristocratic lineage afforded them far more communal
respect, and even power, than ordinary women could imagine. While
several of the seven extant stories about Yalta report her ability to act
independently against Jewish rabbinic and political authority when necessary, two Yalta stories, B. Qiddushin 70a–b and B. Berakhot 51b,
demonstrate a rabbinic desire to curtail such instances of female pretensions to independence and power.

It is significant that the Yalta stories take place in Babylonia, which was almost certainly a far more conservative social environment vis-à-vis social segregation of women than the Land of Israel or the Greco-Roman Diaspora. In several of these narratives, Yalta is said to have been the daughter of the *Rosh Galut* or Exilarch, the descendant of King David who was the political head of the Jewish community in Babylonia. In some of the stories, Yalta appears to have a close relationship to R. Nahman. Although later tradition assumed she was his wife, there is no real evidence for this. Rather she seems to have been closely associated with this Babylonian sage, perhaps as a patron of his activities.

In return for her influence, and possibly her financial support, her protégé was prepared to rule flexibly on various legal issues on her behalf in very specific instances, including the combination of milk and meat and riding on the Sabbath. That Yalta is not intimidated by rabbinic authority is particularly evident in the narrative in B. Niddah 20b, in which she seeks a second rabbinic opinion on the ritual status of a blood stain when she believes the first rabbinic judgement is incorrect.[49] Her intrepid actions are cited with approval and are said to demonstrate that women are to be believed in such circumstances.

It is evident, however, that such a figure, or even the idea of such a figure, caused extreme discomfort to a social policy predicated on the dominance of men. The following narrative in B. Berakhot 51b demonstrates the rabbinic effort to show that even a woman of influence like Yalta is eliminated from any special privileges in the area of religious ritual, regardless of her circumstances, lineage, or abilities, simply on the grounds of gender. The context is a discussion of the necessary requirements of the cup of wine used for grace after meals and whether these include sending it around to the members of the household "so that his wife may be blessed":

'Ulla was once at the house of R. Nahman. They had a meal and he said grace, and handed the cup of benediction to R. Nahman. R. Nahman said to him: "Please send the cup of benediction to Yalta."[50] ['Ulla refused to do so and] said to him: "R. Johanan said: The fruit of a woman's body is blessed only from the fruit of a man's body, since it says, **'He will also bless the fruit of your body'** (Deut. 7:13). It does not say the fruit of *her* body, but the fruit of *your* body. . . ." Meanwhile Yalta heard, and she got up in a passion and went to the wine cellar and broke four hundred jars of wine. R. Nahman said to him: "Let the Master send her another cup." He sent it to her with a message: "All that wine can be counted as a benediction." She answered: "Gossip comes from peddlers and vermin from rags."[51]

'Ulla, a sage from the Land of Israel who frequently visited Babylon to report on the work of Palestinian rabbinic leaders, is connected with strict interpretations of *halakhah*. It is also worth noting that it is 'Ulla who is credited with the statement, "Women are a separate people" (B.

Shabbat 62b). Thus, it is not surprising that he is said to have refused to show respect to Yalta by passing her the cup over which the *kiddush* (sanctification) had been recited on the grounds that women are already blessed through male participation in fulfilling this commandment, even though it was clearly customary to take note of certain women in this way. Moreover, he justified his refusal to honor Yalta on the grounds that *kiddush* celebrates fertility, a male obligation in which women simply serve as passive vessels. Yalta, who was accustomed to special recognition when she was present at communal events, was infuriated by 'Ulla's rudeness in excluding her and demonstrated both her wrath and her wealth by smashing the wine jars. As Rachel Adler has written about this passage:

> In 'Ulla's biological metaphor, male potency is conflated and fused both with spiritual blessing and with social dominance. By analogy, just as a woman cannot be fertile through any act of her own so too they cannot be blessed through any act of their own, but only through the agency of men acting for and upon them . . . Given the existence of other interpretations in texts which include women in the ceremony, we might ask why 'Ulla is bent upon reducing Yalta to a womb. Perhaps he is compensating for other disparities. Yalta, daughter of the fabulously wealthy leader of the Jews in Babylonia, is 'Ulla's superior both in affluence and lineage. The only thing that 'Ulla has which Yalta does not is the appendage around which he and his sources have been creating a satisfactory structure. Small wonder that Yalta heads for the wine storage to castrate 'Ulla symbolically four hundred times, shattering the containers and spilling out the sanctifiable liquid, whose blessing, according to 'Ulla, is a man's prerogative to dispense.[52]

As Adler has further noted, even 'Ulla's effort to placate Yalta with a second cup of wine is also essentially scornful of her pretensions to equality with men, since this second cup is of lesser holiness than the first: "Flinging his contempt for women back in his face, [Yalta] declares that it is 'Ulla himself who is disgusting. His offer of wine from the unsanctified pitcher is like a beggar offering his lice, a worthless and repulsive gift from a giver with nothing to give."[53]

One must agree that in preserving this narrative with its close and appreciative delineation of Yalta's anger and wit, the rabbinic redactors are expressing admiration for Yalta's penchant for appropriate gestures and learned repartée. However, Yalta's strength of character cannot alter the outcome. While feminist readers of this passage have praised Yalta for her feistiness and presence of mind, most have failed to emphasize the central message of this narrative. Yalta's response to 'Ulla changes nothing. Neither her wealth, nor her high social position, nor her asperity count for anything in this instance. She is still excluded from full participation in the *kiddush* because of her gender.[54] And if this is the case for Yalta, the influential daughter of the Exilarch, how much more so for an ordinary woman!

Conclusion

Rabbinic literature reveals a highly tuned consciousness and uneasiness about women's disadvantages. Moreover, the rabbinic construction of women as inherently less able and talented than men must have constantly been called into question by the women of high intelligence and eminence encountered by individual rabbis in their everyday lives. It is not surprising that narratives about exceptional women, including Beruriah and Yalta, have been preserved in rabbinic texts. Nevertheless, the realities of rabbinic social policy required that even these extraordinary women be distanced from the actual exercise of such male prerogatives as communal study, public rituals, and worship, or the formation of *halakhah*. Only by undermining and denigrating the capacity of all women for involvement in these primary endeavors could the rabbinic status quo of male empowerment be maintained. As chapter 4 will demonstrate, rabbinic Judaism was most comfortable with women when they supported male undertakings as compliant and enabling wives.

❦ 4 ❧

FRUITFUL VINES AND SILENT PARTNERS:
WOMEN AS WIVES
IN RABBINIC LITERATURE

Rabbinic Judaism considered marriage as foreordained and essential for all adults. Within the confines of marriage, procreation, a legal obligation for men, could take place and the lineage of children, a significant concern in rabbinic culture, could be assured. Marriage also served as a licit channel for sexual energies for both women and men, as well as a source of mutual companionship. And it provided the social mortar and division of labor on which rabbinic society depended. Moreover, in a system of theological imagery which envisioned human marriage as the closest approximation of the intimacy which could exist between human and divine, the relationship between wives and husbands also assumed sacred significance.[1] In rabbinic Judaism's vision of the ideal ordering of human society, however, marriage could not be a partnership between equals. As the earlier chapters of this volume have shown, special position and status-conferring obligations belonged to eligible males, while females were a less privileged and often problematic category of creation.

Rabbinic Judaism perceived the female body and female activities in domestic terms. Just as "house" or "household" becomes a euphemism for "wife" in rabbinic discourse, so rabbinic social policy preferred that all nubile women be married and that all married women be confined to supportive familial roles, where they could provide for their husband's needs and nurture children at the same time. Contact with other men was severely limited. When a woman crossed the boundary from the internal to the public realm she potentially endangered not only herself, but the entire structure of rabbinic sexual politics.[2] That the rabbis' idealized social blueprint was often more theoretical than actual only underscores the ambivalence implicit in contrasts between insistence on the wife's subordinate status within the halakhic parameters of marriage and aggadic portrayals of matrimony and its discontents.

Marriage as Legal Transaction

The Mishnah, the foundation document of rabbinic *halakhah*, views marriage as a legal undertaking initiated when a man acquires a wife in one of three ways, "by money, by deed, or by intercourse," along with a statement of espousal (M. Qiddushin 1:1). This view of the woman as an object or commodity, with authority over her sexual function being transferred from male guardian to husband, is expressed by M. Ketubbot 4:5: "She continues within the control of her father until she enters the control of the husband at marriage."

As Judith Romney Wegner has noted, this impression of woman as chattel is heightened by the unilateral nature of the declaration in which the man states that the woman is "set apart" for him alone and to which the woman makes no reply.[3] Judith Hauptman has written that the rabbis' view that a man may acquire a wife from her male guardian and may also dismiss her at will is derived not only from biblical practice, but is also in consonance with social practices in the environments in which they lived. Since it was assumed that a husband would manage all household finances and could control his wife's activities—even to the extent of cancelling or annulling her vows, preventing her from talking to other men, or from leaving her own home—it is evident that in most aspects the mishnaic portrayal of marriage is far from a partnership of equals.[4]

Over time, the formal mechanics of marriage became more complex. Elaborating on the mishnaic framework, the Babylonian Talmud (Ketubbot 57a) presents an ordered progression of the union between a man and a woman in which, following a period of engagement (*shiddukhin*), marriage required a two-part process: betrothal (*'erusin\qiddushin*) and consummation (*nissu'in*). Betrothal, which constituted a legally binding marriage, was achieved by the reading of the marriage contract (*ketubbah*), which specified the groom's obligations, financial and otherwise, toward the bride and the presentation of an object of value by the groom to the bride in the presence of two witnesses. While the Mishnah speaks of betrothal and marriage in the language of purchase, other rabbinic sources including the Babylonian Talmud imply that a woman must agree to her betrothal and in some cases might even negotiate her own marriage.[5] The marriage was finalized through *nissu'in* (literally "elevation," also known as *huppah*) when the bride was escorted to her husband's home and benedictions were recited. *Nissu'in* often did not take place until a year after the betrothal in order to enable both families to make the necessary preparations for married life. These innovations are indicative of the ways in which the social dynamics of marriage changed in rabbinic times, generally in directions with positive consequences for women and their status.

The most significant aspect of these modifications was the ratification of marriage through a written contract, *ketubbah* (B. Qiddushin. 2a). The *ketubbah* imposed rights and obligations on both sides. Marriage remained an unequal power relationship but the *ketubbah* transformed a wife from an acquired object into a subject in a shared enterprise who received specific benefits in return for her domestic and sexual services. As Judith Hauptman has written of the importance of this innovation:

The patriarchal construction of marriage, although certainly not dismantled with the development of the *ketubbah*, was significantly altered. Marriage became a relationship into which two people entered.[6]

The rabbinic *ketubbah* enumerated ten obligations of the husband towards the wife. These included a husband's providing his wife with food, appropriate clothing (M. Ketubbot 5:8), and conjugal rights.[7] He is to ransom her, provide for her support after his death, and guarantee that her property would pass from him to her heirs, an important provision in a polygynous society. He also pledged to give her sufficient money to cover her minor expenses; if he did not, the wife could keep the proceeds of her work in wool which normally belonged to her husband (M. Ketubbot 5:9). Should a man take more than one wife, as he was permitted to do, he was required to fulfil his obligations to each wife in an equitable way. Even if no written *ketubbah* existed, these responsibilities incumbent upon the husband became widely accepted and would be enforced by a court.[8]

Hauptman is clearly correct that the most important provision of the *ketubbah* was the arrangement for a wife's financial protection should the marriage end in either death or divorce. This *ketubbah* payment, the only economic benefit the wife would receive from her husband's estate, consisted not only of any dowry she brought into the marriage, but also a stipulated amount from the husband's resources, set aside at the time of the marriage, and payable in case of divorce or the husband's death.[9]

In the marriage agreement entered into by both parties, a wife still kept certain degrees of independence, particularly in the economic sphere. She retained title to property she brought into her marriage, although her husband was entitled to any profit it yielded. She also had the power to sell the property, and her husband could not sell it against her will (M. Gittin 5:6). From these and other similar provisions, it is clear that the wife was expected to be a significant part of the family economic unit, contributing not only investment revenues but also her earnings from the making of cloth and needlework. Her commercial transactions were considered to be activities belonging to the *house*, the domestic/private realm in which she functioned. In certain situations, in fact, a wife might undertake to support her husband financially or to take full economic responsibility for her household in her husband's absence.[10]

The duties incumbent upon the wife are not enumerated in the *ketubah*, since they are assumed by her agreement to enter into marriage. They are listed in M. Ketubbot 5:5:

The following are the kinds of work which a woman must perform for her husband: grinding corn, baking bread, washing clothes, cooking, suckling her child, making ready his bed and working in wool. If she brought him one bondwoman she need not do any grinding or baking or washing. If she brought two bondwomen, she need not even cook or suckle her child. If three, she need neither make ready his bed nor work in wool. If four, she may lounge in an easy chair.

The same *mishnah* goes on to note, however, that R. Eliezer objected to this easy life for the wealthy woman, insisting:

[E]ven if she brought him a hundred bondwomen he may compel her to work in wool; for idleness leads to unchastity. And she should nevertheless fill her husband's cup, make ready his bed and wash his face, hands and feet.

Rabban Simeon b. Gamliel concurred, noting that idleness leads to boredom. In its explication of this passage at B. Ketubbot 61a–b, the Talmud states that the *halakhah* is in agreement with R. Eliezer: No matter the extent of her wealth, a woman must engage in worthwhile activities and must fulfil her husband's personal needs. One might note here, as well, the rabbinic conviction of fundamental female unreliability in the face of sexual temptation and the need to keep women occupied in useful ways.

In some situations a wife could petition the court to compel her husband to divorce her for specified causes (M. Ketubbot 7:1–5, 10),[11] but she had no power to unilaterally end her marriage. This was the right of the husband alone, and the sources make clear that he might divorce his wife for any reason (M. Gittin 9:10), provided that he return the monetary settlement specified by her *ketubbah*. Indeed, this requirement of financial restitution, from his means as well as hers, offered women a degree of protection. Raising the funds needed to pay the contracted *ketubbah* amount could constitute a strong financial disincentive to a rash husband who might then step back from ending his marriage. When divorce did occur, the payment of the *ketubbah* provided a crucial economic base on which a second marriage or the possibility of an independent livelihood might be built for a cast-off wife.[12] In this way, the institution of the *ketubbah* not only enhanced women's rights and status, but played a positive part in rabbinic social policy, both by preventing ill-considered divorces and by limiting the numbers of indigent widows and divorcées dependent on community support.

While the *ketubbah* afforded protection to cast-off wives, the rabbinic decision to enforce unilateral divorce went against previous Jewish practice. The biblical statement on divorce in Deuteronomy 24:1–4 indicated that a man might divorce a wife if he was unhappy with her and prohibited a man's remarrying the wife he had divorced after she had been married to someone else. It did not say that divorce could only be initiated by a man, nor did it prohibit a woman from beginning divorce proceedings. Surviving evidence indicates that Jewish women did initiate divorces prior to and during rabbinic times. As Mayer Gruber has written:

Moreover, there is significant testimony that in both Second Temple times and in the Tannaitic era Jewish women still had the right to initiate divorce. In fact, as demonstrated by Mordechai Friedman, for a millennium after the dawn of the Rabbinic period, Jewish women throughout the Middle East continued to take advantage of the age-old pre-nuptial guarantee of their rights as persons.[13]

Thus, limiting of the right to initiate divorce to men only, as stated in M. Yevamot 14:1, "A women may be divorced willingly or unwillingly, but a man divorces only willingly," may be seen as a rabbinic innovation deliberately intended to limit women's options in the realm of personal status issues. As with other rabbinic acts of female disempowerment, eliminating the right to initiate a divorce would have had the desired effect of removing women from the public domains of worship, study, and communal jurisprudence while further anchoring them to the realm of the domestic.[14]

Determining the legal status of the wife in the *halakhah* is complex. Some aspects of rabbinic legislation endowed a wife with a high degree of personhood. Her legal rights as a property holder were protected and she was assigned rights and privileges denied to the non-Israelite male. On the other hand, she also remained her husband's possession, at least in terms of her sexuality. The case of the wife suspected of adultery offers an example of the legal duality implicit in the wife's ambiguous role. As a sexual chattel, a suspected wife (*sotah*) could be put through a humiliating ordeal without evidentiary proof, but as the owner of a valuable marriage settlement, she could not be deprived of her property without due process. Similarly the rabbinic acceptance that, in certain cases, a wife is morally entitled to a divorce reveals an analogous paradox. As Wegner has pointed out, the notion of a wife's legitimate right to a divorce recognized her as a person, yet the formalities of actually being divorced required her husband to use a procedure that treated her like a piece of property.[15]

Moreover, the protection offered to women by the *ketubbah* did not hold in all situations. A wife could be divorced without her marriage settlement if she violated Jewish law or ritual or refused conjugal relations with her spouse. Offences punished in this way include both violations of the "law of Moses," such as preparing untithed food, not separating *hallah*, breaking the rules of menstrual separation, not keeping a vow, and transgressions against Jewish custom, including behavior construed as immodest or offensive (M. Ketubbot 7:6–7).[16] A wife had no recourse if her husband violated any of these prohibitions. If she were to transgress the rules of menstrual separation by engaging in sexual relations with her husband without telling him she was in a state of *niddah*, her husband could cast her out penniless, since she was expected to behave responsibly and not to transmit ritual impurity to him.[17] However, rabbinic tradition, accepting the private nature of sexual relations, knew that a husband could choose to have sexual relations with his wife during her period of *niddah*:

> When one's wife menstruates, she is alone with him at home. If he wishes to, he has intercourse with her; if he does not wish, he does not have intercourse with her. Does anyone see him or does anyone know so that they might say anything to him? He fears only [God] who has commanded concerning menstruation. (*Avot de-Rabbi Natan* A, ch. 2)

As David Biale has remarked about this passage, the rabbis recognized the limitations on their enforcement powers in the face of patriarchal prerogatives. When a woman was the object of male action in this instance and knowledge of the forbidden contact remained between the two of them, no social penalties could be exacted of either spouse.[18] Since the husband alone was liable for ritual contamination, he might elect to incur it; the status of the *niddah* herself was unaffected by engaging in sexual intercourse.

This ambiguity is present in other areas of conjugal relations where the married woman is a person with rights as well as obligations and concurrently a sexual object. A husband's sexual obligation towards his wife is a good example. The Mishnah legislated that a woman possesses the absolute right to sexual intercourse with her husband. This is based on an interpretation of the difficult biblical term *'onah* (Ex. 21:10) to mean that a husband must provide his wife with regular conjugal visits, in addition to providing her with food and clothing. In fact, the Mishnah provides detailed guidelines for fulfillment of this matrimonial duty, based on the husband's occupation and the amount of time he spends at home (M. Ketubbot 5:6).[19]

As Michael Satlow has pointed out, however, the motivations behind this insistence on the woman's right to 'onah are unclear. Are her marital rights important because the wife is entitled to sexual pleasure or are they important because she is entitled to the opportunity to bear children? Satlow suggests that for rabbis in the Land of Israel, where procreation was seen as the primary goal of sex within marriage, a woman's entitlement to sexual relations is best understood as a "right" to have the opportunity to bear children. Her sexual pleasure is not an issue.[20] As chapter 5 of this volume demonstrates, the childless wife lacked both protection and status in rabbinic times and childlessness was seen as grounds on which a wife could petition for divorce. Satlow believes that the rabbinic community in Babylon, which was more accepting of non-marital and non-procreative expressions of sexuality than the rabbis in the Land of Israel, did link a woman's sexual desire and her conjugal rights. In their view 'onah meant that men were obligated to attend sexually to their wives, not only for procreative purposes, but because it gave their wives pleasure.[21]

Regardless of the purposes of sexual intimacy, the husband's legal duty to have intercourse with his wife was matched by her corresponding obligation to consent. Although such an obligation by the woman was never explicitly expressed, it was assumed as one of the concomitants of marriage. When claims were made to a rabbinic court against a spouse for non-compliance, daily financial penalties were exacted. The penalty for a rebellious wife (*moredet*), which was deducted from her marriage settlement, was more than twice as heavy as that imposed on a recalcitrant husband (M. Ketubbot 5:7). The wife who refused intercourse with her husband risked exhausting the funds in both her dowry and her husband's set aside marriage payment and could ultimately be divorced penniless. Michael Satlow suggests that the penalty was double for the wife because in general the sages believed that male sexual needs were stronger than women's. This notion is expressed in the following *aggadah* in B. Ketubbot 64b:

R. Hiyya bar Yosef said to Samuel: What is the difference between the rebellious man and the rebellious woman? He said to him: Go and learn from the market of prostitutes. Who hires whom?[22]

That men are the ones who have recourse to prostitutes when their sexual demands are not being met was understood to prove that men's sexual needs were more importunate than those of women and that women who refused to submit sexually to their husbands did more harm to their spouses than the other way around.

In fact, men were privileged both in terms of obtaining satisfaction of their own sexual desire within marriage and in neglecting their sexual obligation towards their wives when they chose to do so. Wegner's suggestion that "in penalizing the rebellious wife more severely, the Sages value the woman's rights below those of a man"[23] is supported by the reality among the rabbinic elite in Babylon, where many men would leave their wives—sometimes for years at a time—to study away from home without any legal penalty. In this instance, the value of learning Torah was deemed superior to responsibility towards wife and family.[24] This tension between the human rights of the wife as an independent subject who is a party in a legal contract and the wife as an object of a particular man's sexual control remains unresolved in the rabbinic *halakhah* and is a central theme in the midrashic discourse on marriage discussed below.

Marriage as Social Mortar

A number of aggadic texts considered marriage essential for the achievement of full human status. Although the subject of most of these homiletical remarks is the man, nevertheless it is his connection with a woman that is deemed crucial. Thus, the interconnectedness of spouses is expressed in the maxim that "any man who has no wife is no proper man" (B. Yevamot 62b), based on an interpretation of Genesis 5:2: **"Male and female He created them and He called their name Adam."** Underlying this statement is the rabbinic midrash in *Genesis Rabbah* 8:1, already mentioned in chapter 2, that the first human being created by God was both male and female at once:

When the Holy One, blessed be He, created the first *'adam*, He created it androgynous, as it is written, **"Male and female He created them, and He called their name Adam."** Rabbi Samuel b. Nahmani said, "When the Holy One, blessed be He, created the first *'adam*, He created him with two faces, then split him and made him two backs—a back for each side."

As this strong endorsement of marriage implies, only when male and female are rejoined through marriage are they both fully human and only in their union is there the potential for the propagation of new life.

Similar comments are found in *Genesis Rabbah* 17:2 on Genesis 2: 18, **"It is not good for man to be alone"**:

It was taught: He who has no wife dwells without good, without help, without joy, without blessing, and without atonement. Without good: **"It is not good for man to be alone"** (Gen. 2:18). Without help: **"I will make a fitting helper for him"** (Gen 2:18). Without joy: **"And you shall feast there, in the presence of the Lord your God, and rejoice with your household"** (Deut. 14:26).[25]

Without a blessing: "You shall further give the first of the yield of your baking to the priest, that a blessing may rest upon your house" (Ezek. 44:30). Without atonement: "Aaron shall then offer his bull of sin offering, to make atonement for himself and his household" (Lev. 16:11). R. Simeon said in the name of R. Joshua b. Levi: Without peace too, for it is said: "Peace to you and your household" (1 Sam. 25:6). R. Joshua of Siknin said in the name of R. Levi: Without life too, for it is said, "Enjoy life with a woman you love" (Ecc. 9:9). R. Hiyya b. Gomdi said: He is also incomplete, for it is written, "And He blessed them and called them humanity" (Gen. 5:2) [thus, only together are they fully human]. Some say: He [who does not marry] even impairs the Divine likeness: thus it is written, "For in His image / Did God make humanity" (Gen. 9:6), which is followed by "Be fertile, then, and increase" (Gen. 9:7).

The final statement in this midrash suggests that a man attains to the divine image only when joined in marriage to a woman with whom he will father children. Procreation is the overwhelming value to be achieved in marriage since what makes man like God is his ability to generate new life in the body of his wife. This is the nearest parallel to divine creativity that a human being can achieve and of such importance that all men are legally obligated to procreate. It is no accident that many of the biblical verses cited as proof texts refer to a man and his "house" or "household" (bayit). For the rabbis, a man's wife is his "house," a construction built from his body to bear his children and fulfil his sexual and domestic needs.

Rabbinic folklore underscores the personal and societal value of matrimony in its vision of marriages as foreordained; so crucial is this conviction that several aggadot describe matchmaking as God's principal occupation since the completion of creation.[26] Other traditions, too, emphasize that when it comes to marriage nothing is left to chance. According to B. Sotah 2a, Rabbah b. Bar Hanah is said to have related in the name of R. Johanan: "It is as difficult [for God] to pair [a woman with a man] as was the division of the Red Sea, as it is said, "God restores the lonely to their houses, sets free the imprisoned, safe and sound" (Ps. 68:7). Similarly, B. Sotah 2a and B. Sanhedrin 22a relate that forty days before the embryo is formed, a heavenly voice goes forth and "proclaims the unborn child's intended spouse."[27]

Nevertheless, certain strands within rabbinic literature preserve a deep-seated ambivalence about the benefits of marriage, particularly for scholars who might prefer to devote all their energies to study of the divine word, despite the legal imperative to reproduce. In B. Yevamot 62b, the sage Ben Azzai defends not being married on the grounds that his soul desired only the Torah. Daniel Boyarin has described how energetically the rabbis opposed the appeal of remaining a bachelor:

Extravagant praise of the married state, which occurs over and over in rabbinic texts, is a marker not of how happily married the Rabbis were but of how much pressure against marrying there was in their world. Celibacy provided an attractive "out" from the world's pain, and moreover, the life of the purely spiritual seeker of wisdom was the ideal of much of the circumambient culture, both Jewish and non-Jewish.[28]

Many of these issues are raised in a lengthy discussion of the boons and woes of matrimony in B. Yevamot 61b–64a, prompted by the mishnaic ruling that a man may not abstain from the duty of procreation (M. Yevamot 6:6). In a portion of this long passage, B. Yevamot 62b defends marriage by inquiring into the ways a wife helps her spouse:

R. Jose met Elijah and asked him: "It is written, 'I will make a fitting helper for him' (Gen. 2:18); how does a woman help a man?" The other replied: "If a man brings wheat, does he chew the wheat? If flax, does he put on the flax? Does she not, then, bring light to his eyes and put him on his feet?"

Elijah's response is quite literal. A wife helps her husband through the essential domestic services she performs. By turning wheat into flour and flour into bread, she feeds her husband and household. By turning flax into linen and linen into garments, she clothes her husband and children. Without food or clothing, the life of the mind and spirit is not possible. Thus, the wife's practical endeavors sustain her husband and enable him to function in the wider world of study and learning.

In B. Yevamot 63a, R. Hama b. Hanina is said to have stated, "As soon as a man takes a wife his sins are buried; for it is said in the book of Proverbs, 'He who finds a wife has found happiness / And has won the favor of the Lord' (Prov. 18:22)." "Sins" here refers to the licit sexual outlet a woman provides for her husband; this is also an allusion to a man's obligation to procreate which is to be fulfilled through the generation of offspring in marriage. Such aggadic endorsements emphasize that matrimony is not only a required step in life for every man, but an advance with positive ramifications. B. Yevamot 62b teaches that a man who loves and honors his wife will reap many rewards:

Our Rabbis taught: Concerning a man who loves his wife as himself, who honors her more than himself, who guides his sons and daughters in the right path and arranges for them to be married near the period of their puberty, Scripture says, "You will know that all is well in your tent" (Job 5:24). Concerning him who loves his neighbors, who befriends his relatives, marries his sister's daughter, [63a] and lends a *sel'a* to a poor man in the hour of his need, Scripture says, "Then, when you call, the Lord will answer / When you cry, He will say, 'Here I am' " (Isa. 58:9).[29]

Similar admonitions about treating one's wife with love and compassion include B. Bava Metzi'a 59a, where Rav is quoted as saying, "One should always be heedful of wronging his wife, for since her tears are frequent she is quickly hurt." R. Helbo is said to have taught, "One must always observe the honor due to his wife, because blessings rest on a man's home only on account of his wife, for it is written, 'And because of her, it went well with Abram' (Gen. 12:16)."

Rabbinic testimonials to marriage are unabashedly androcentric: They detail why marriage is a good thing for men and advise how men might best comport themselves within a marital relationship. The advantages of marriage for woman are generally assumed, rather than voiced. Certainly in a patriarchal society in which unprotected women were at risk, where childless women faced a perilous future, and where there also may have been a shortage of males, it is not surprising that marriage was seen as crucial for a woman's well being. As B. Yevamot 113a puts it, "More than the man desires to marry does the woman desire to be taken in marriage." B. Ketubbot 75a declares:

A woman is satisfied with any sort [of husband] as Resh Laqish said. For Resh Laqish stated: It is preferable to live in grief, that is, with a bad husband, than to dwell in widowhood. Abaye said: With a husband [of the size of an] ant [i.e., of low status] her seat is placed among the great. R. Pappa said: Though her husband be a carder [i.e., of a humble profession] she calls him to the threshold and sits down [at his side]. R. Ashi said: Even if her husband is ugly she requires no lentils for her pot. A Tanna taught: But all such women play the harlot and attribute the consequences to their husbands.

This view of women as sexually motivated in their requirements for marriage is also expressed in the preamble to a parallel passage in B. Yevamot 118b which suggests that a woman might wish to remain in a difficult and quarrelsome marriage, rather than accept a divorce, "since the gratification of bodily desires is possibly preferred by her."

As Michael Satlow has demonstrated, women are portrayed not only as more sexually avid than men, but, unlike men, are assumed to be incapable of controlling their overwhelming desires.[30] This light mindedness inherent in women is why B. Qiddushin 80b ruled that a man cannot be alone with two women, while a woman may be alone with two men since one man's presence will restrain the other. Similarly, M. Sotah 3:4, the passage about how a woman accused of adultery is forced to drink a bitter potion, discussed in chapter 3, attributed the following opinion to R. Joshua: "A woman prefers one measure [of material comfort] and lasciviousness to nine measures [of material comfort] and celibacy."[31] This rabbinic conviction of female sexual voraciousness and the sexual unreliability of women is expressed in the recognition that not all wives find their spouses appealing. According to B. Ketubbot 75a, a woman married to an insignificant or unattractive husband will probably despise him; she will be likely to share her favors with other men, and give birth to children of uncertain lineage.

Marriage As Metaphor

While marriage is deemed essential for both men and women, the relationship between husband and wife is not a connection between equals. According to B. Sanhedrin 22b, Samuel b. Unya is said to have taught, "Before marriage a woman is a shapeless lump. It is her husband who transforms her into a useful vessel." In fact, the parallel is drawn that, just as God formed the character of the people of Israel, so does a husband shape the personality of his wife. "**For He who made you will espouse you—His name is the Lord of Hosts**" (Isa. 54:5)." Nor is the divine metaphor unusual; in the Hebrew Bible and throughout later Jewish literature, the relationship between a man and a woman is often understood metaphorically as signifying the intimate bonds between God and human beings. Traditional rabbinic interpretation of the Song of Songs, for example, has always assumed that the biblical book's love poetry between a man and a woman is an allegory detailing the passion between God and the male community of Israel. Ironically, the consequence of this formulation is that women are erased from the equation. Thus, *Song of Songs Rabbah* 7.11 §1 explicates "**I am my beloved's, and his desire is for me**" (Song of Songs 7:11), as follows:

There are three yearnings: The yearning of the community of Israel is only for their Father who is in heaven, as it is said, "**I am my beloved's, and his desire is for me.**" The yearning of a woman is only for her husband: "**And your desire shall be for your husband**" (Gen 3:16). The yearning of the Evil Impulse is only for Cain and his ilk: "**To you is its desire**" (Gen 4:7).

In this passage, the male *Knesset Israel*, the congregation of Israel, is constructed as the female beloved. In the relationship between God, who is characterized as masculine, and the male covenant community of Israel, characterized as feminine, there is no place for woman. At best, women direct their yearnings towards their husbands and share by reflected glory in their husband's communion with the divine. As Jacob Neusner has observed about the feminization of Israel in *Song of Songs Rabbah*, as a wife must submit faithfully to her husband, and follow him wherever he leads with perfect faith in his wisdom and judgment, so the male *Knesset Israel* must direct full devotion and faith to God and wait patiently for God's redemption. "Implicit in this representation of the right relationship, of course, is the promise that the feminine Israel will evoke from the masculine God the response of commitment and intervention: God will intervene to save Israel, when Israel makes herself into the perfect wife of God."[32]

However, if the male Jew was to cleave fully to God as a wife must cleave to her husband, then what of his relationship to his actual wife? Total devotion to the divine could have the effect of displacing a wife in her husband's affections and devaluing the human marital relationship. If love between husband and wife served simply as a metaphor of the infinitely more important relationship between God and *Knesset Israel*, then at some level the human connection would always be secondary, just as women were subordinate and disadvantaged in other aspects of daily and marital life.[33]

Good Wives

Since rabbinic tradition asserts that women have a general propensity to be flighty, sexually motivated, and of questionable fidelity, one must ask whether the rabbis believed it possible to find a good wife. Certainly, an ongoing rabbinic discourse considers traits which distinguish good and bad wives. Conversely, negative qualities in husbands are not a particular matter of concern. Thus, R. Hiyya is said to hold that "A wife should be taken mainly for the sake of her beauty; and mainly for the sake of children" (B. Ketubbot 59b). The implication appears to be that a wife must not be treated as a bondwoman doing heavy work like grinding which would impair her beauty or adversely affect her pregnancies; rather she should work in wool in return for the maintenance her husband allows her. Elsewhere, R. Hiyya is credited with the view: "It is sufficient for us that they rear up our children and deliver us from sin [by bearing children and providing a sexual outlet]" (B. Yevamot 63a).

There is little sense in rabbinic writings of companionate marriage. Women by their nature are distractions to men and discussion with all women should be avoided since it may lead men into undesirable behavior (B. Nedarim 20b). While wives who fulfil marital obligations must be indulged within their domestic boundaries, no man should assume that his spouse is an intellectual partner with whom he can communicate in any substantive way.

In B. Yevamot 62b, R. Pappa is said to have advised that one should be quick in buying land, but deliberate in taking a wife: "Come down a step in choosing your wife; go up a step in choosing your best man." Here, too, the social dynamics of marriage in rabbinic times are evident:

By marrying below himself a man is sure of a grateful and subservient wife at home; by using the opportunity of his marriage to make friends above himself he strengthens his position in the male community of the public domain. The most desirable qualities in a wife are delineated in a passage in B. Shabbat 25a, in response to the query, "Who is rich?" In R. Meir's view, it is he who has pleasure in his wealth. R. Tarfon said: "He who possesses a hundred vineyards, a hundred fields and a hundred slaves working in them." But R. Aqiva is said to have responded: "He who has a wife comely in deeds." In this statement, referring back to the description of the ideal wife of Prov. 31:15 ("**And let her deeds praise her in the gates**"), the rabbinic vision of the wife whose domestic undertakings enable her husband's activities for the sake of heaven is incarnated.

Indeed, the classic "good wife" story in rabbinic literature is that of R. Aqiva's wife who becomes a paradigm of female loyalty and devotion. Born into a wealthy household, Rachel, as she is named in only one of the narratives about her, is said to have forfeited a rich dowry from her father in order to marry R. Aqiva when he was a destitute and illiterate shepherd. This story, versions of which appear in six places in rabbinic writings, encapsulates what many strands of tradition within rabbinic Judaism must have seen as the virtues of the model wife.

According to the account in B. Nedarim 50a, R. Aqiva's wife, unnamed in this source, sent her uneducated husband away to study for twelve years and then another twelve, despite great personal suffering. When he returned with thousands of students, he lauded her before them, declaring that all his learning rightly belonged to his wife. In rabbinic terms, Rachel is exemplary because of her willingness to erase herself from her husband's daily life; she serves as a paradigm of what is expected of the wife of the scholar whose studies may take him far away for long periods of time. Such a wife garners cultural esteem through enabling the men of her family to pursue their studies, even though this may mean enduring economic deprivation and a husband's absence for long periods of time. Indeed, according to sources, including B. Berakhot 17a and B. Sotah 21a, this is precisely how wives earn merit: "By sending their sons to learn [Torah] in the synagogue, and their husbands to study in the schools of the rabbis, and by waiting for their husbands until they return from the schools of the rabbis."

B. Nedarim 50a relates that R. Aqiva's wife expresses satisfaction with her choices; having sacrificed the status of wealth for love of a poor but talented man, she puts aside her own needs for many years in order that her husband may earn higher position for both of them as a result of his learning. In the end, she also regains the approbation of the father

she had defied. We cannot know the authenticity of this story. Tal Ilan
has demonstrated in her detailed analysis of these traditions that two
common themes present in each account, that R. Aqiva's wife helped
her husband during his years of study and that R. Aqiva subsequently
bought his wife an expensive gold headdress, probably have some historical veracity.[34] It is certain that this popular story expresses sentiments
approved and validated by significant circles of the Babylonian rabbinic
class.

The story of R. Aqiva's wife illuminates the degree to which rabbinic
leaders were torn over the conflict between devotion to Torah study and
the legal obligations to procreate and attend to one's wife. Although the
option of an ascetic and celibate life entirely devoted to the divine was
always deemed impermissible, the very preservation of a minority strand
in favor of a spiritual life without intimate contact with women speaks to
the strains inherent in the rabbinic enterprise between family obligations
and complete dedication to God.

As Stephen Fraade has written, "Rabbinic culture . . . is beleaguered
with a constant unresolved tension—almost an antimony—between the
obligation to marry and the equal obligation to devote oneself entirely to
the life of Torah-study."[35] Such ascetic yearnings, heightened by the hom-
osocial milieu of the study house, contributed, as well, to some of the very
negative constructions of women and their bodies which are found
throughout rabbinic writings. Moreover, in rabbinic traditions that emphasized the primacy of learning, the personal bond between teacher and
student could be more highly valued than the ties between father and son.
Thus, M. Bava Metzi'a 2:11 ordains that, unless his father is also a sage,
the student's first obligation is to his teacher in cases of returning lost
property, relieving someone of a burden, and ransoming a captive. This is
because "his father brought him into this world but his teacher has taught
him the wisdom that will bring him into the world to come." In this
hierarchy of relationships the natural order is overturned: All familial
responsibilities are rendered secondary, if not antithetical, to Torah study.[36]

David Biale has analyzed the rabbinic ambivalence about sexuality, even
within marriage, noting that the rabbis were aware of the Greco-Roman
view that "sexuality was a thoroughly secular, material activity that con-
flicted with the life of the spirit." Biale writes that in the culture of late
antiquity, the competition between holy abstinence and the duty to produce children created a deep anxiety to which the rabbis were not immune.
Like the Stoics, the rabbis embraced the virtue of study as equal to and, in
some cases, greater than procreation. "The same ambiguous and dialectical
passion was thought to drive both."[37]

Daniel Boyarin points out that Palestinian Judaism dealt with the con-

flict between devotion to study and the imperative to reproduce by defer-
ring marriage until after an extended period of learning following a Hellenistic philosophical model. However, in the Babylonian community,
cultural imperatives insisted that young men be married as early as possible. This produced the untenable situation of husbands abandoning wives
and families for extended sojourns at far distant places of study, resulting
in the creation of a class of "married monks." [38]

A long passage in B. Ketubbot 62b–63a preserves a number of anecdotes
about men who studied away from home. These appear in the context of
an adumbration of M. Ketubbot 5:6, a *mishnah* ordaining the frequency
with which men should perform their conjugal duty depending on their
profession. B. Ketubbot 62b rules that the scholar is to perform his marital
obligation once a week, ideally on the Sabbath eve. However, B. Ketubbot
62b also preserves the determination, attributed to "the sages," that "students may go away to study Torah without the permission [of their wives
even for] two or three years." The ambivalence the rabbis felt over these
two contradictory approaches to marital responsibility is reflected in the
statement of Rava, the leading Babylonian rabbinic authority of the fourth
century, to the effect that the rabbis accepted the ruling that students might
leave their wives for long periods of time, even though they put their lives
at risk by doing so. Two anecdotes are then recounted in which rabbis
neglected to return home when expected, because they were distracted by
their studies. In one instance, disappointed anticipation caused a waiting
wife such grief that she began to weep. At that exact moment, the roof on
which her husband was sitting collapsed and he was killed. The rabbi in
the second story also meet an untimely end, because he put study before his
duty to his wife. These warnings that death may be the penalty for the
husband who neglects his obligations to nurture his family provides a
strong ethical counterweight to the wholesale permission to abandon home
for immersion in Torah.

B. Ketubbot 62b continues with contiguous narratives about fathers
who were away so long that when they returned they did not recognize
their own children, as in the following example:

R. Hananiah b. Hakinai spent twelve years at the academy. By the time he
returned the streets of the town were altered and he was unable to find the way
to his home. Going down to the river bank and sitting down he heard a girl
being addressed: "Daughter of Hakinai, O daughter of Hakinai, fill up your
pitcher and let us go!" It is obvious, he thought, that the girl is ours, and he
followed her. When they reached the house his wife was sitting and sifting flour.
She lifted up her eyes and seeing him, was so overcome with joy that her spirit
fled, and life left her. "O, Lord of the Universe," he prayed to Him, "This poor
soul, is this her reward?" And so he prayed for mercy to be shown to her, and
she revived.

It is interesting that in this story it is the wife who dies, rather like the noble wife in Euripides' play *Alcestis* who sacrifices herself to save her culpable husband. And, as in *Alcestis,* divine intervention on behalf of the husband permits the wife to return to life.[39] A preceding story in B. Ketubbot 62b tells of a wife who lost the ability to bear children during her husband's long absence. Ordinarily an infertile wife would have been divorced, but in this case her father-in-law pitied what she had endured while her husband was away. He prayed for mercy and she recovered. Boyarin suggests that these miraculous interventions are essentially unsuccessful attempts to provide resolutions "to the enormous moral and halakhic contradictions" occasioned by the family separations Babylonian rabbinic culture tended to condone.[40]

B. Ketubbot 62b–63a responds to these *aggadot* about negligent husbands and fathers with a rendition of the story of R. Aqiva's wife who gladly sacrificed her youth in order that her husband might achieve greatness in scholarship. R. Aqiva's wife's model is emulated by her daughter who is said to have married Ben Azzai, the sage who is more often represented as refusing to marry because of his devotion to the Torah:

The daughter of R. Aqiva acted in a similar way towards Ben Azzai. This is indeed an illustration of the proverb, "Ewe follows ewe; a daughter's acts are like those of her mother."[41]

The final anecdote in this passage is indicative of the irredeemable conflict the Babylonian rabbis perceived over the values of family responsibility and devotion to the explication of the divine word:

R. Joseph the son of Rava [was] sent [by] his father to the academy under R. Joseph, and they arranged for him [to stay there for] six years. Having been there three years and the eve of the Day of Atonement approaching, he said, "I would go and see my family". When his father heard [of his premature arrival] he took up a weapon and went out to meet him, [declaring] "You have remembered your harlot (*zontekha*)." Another version: He said to him, "You have remembered your dove (*yontekha*)."[42] They got involved in a quarrel and neither ate the final meal before the fast.

The father in this disturbing aggadic tradition is Rava, the rabbinic leader who was quoted earlier in this passage (B. Ketubbot 62b) as endorsing the practice of study away from home despite the known risks. Michael Satlow suggests that by terming his daughter-in-law a whore the father is really directing his wrath at his son's lack of sexual control. Satlow points out that while the larger *sugya* in B. Ketubbot 62b–63a began with concern over a wife's right to sexual attention, it ends by valuing male abstinence and devotion to Torah.[43]

I am not convinced that the resolution of the passage is so unambiguous. Rava is portrayed as enraged by the human frailty that led his son to elevate desire for wife and family over devotion to the divine word to the point that he and his son quarrel until the very onset of the most sacred Day of Atonement. This is far from admirable behavior. The confusion expressed here over the appropriate valuations of two conflicting obligations is palpable. In this distressing narrative, which is the final word in this lengthy *sugya*, no resolution emerges; on some fundamental level both men are right. Meanwhile wives remain passive nonentities. When they are depicted as active, it is always in support of enabling their husband's selection of study over family.

Marital Sexuality

Whatever can be derived from rabbinic writings on sexuality, Michael Satlow observes, is "sexuality as discussed and recorded by a small elite group of male religious leaders." And as Satlow writes, "The inaccessibility of women in these texts is frustrating, for discussion of women's sexuality is primarily confined to strategies of control of women's sexuality."[44] Moreover, it is impossible to know to what degree rabbinic legislation governing sexual relations between husband and wife reflected realities in any particular time or place[45] and to what extent it represents idealized rhetorical expressions of how Jewish family life ought to be regulated. What does seem evident is that marriage is privileged as the central arena for the expression of human intimacy.

Yet conjugal relations were constrained. Marital sexuality was highly controlled through the imposition of *niddah* regulations which effectively separated husband and wife for up to two weeks of each month.[46] That this separation was regarded as onerous is evident in the following aggadic comment from *Midrash on Psalms* 146:4 about the benefits of the world to come, commenting on **"He sets free the bound"** (Psalm 146:4).

Although nothing is more strongly forbidden than intercourse with a menstruant . . . in the time-to-come, God will permit such intercourse. As Scripture says, **"In that day, too—declares the Lord of Hosts— . . . I will also make the 'prophets' and the unclean spirit vanish from the land"** (Zech. 13:2); the "unclean" clearly refers to a menstruant, and of such it is said, **"Do not come near a woman during her period of uncleanness to uncover her nakedness"** (Lev. 18:19).

Warnings of the dire consequences that will result to men from even the most accidental contact with a *niddah* and to women who do not observe their period of *niddah* strictly, discussed in chapters 1 and 3, reflect

rabbinic efforts to enforce by fear a most unpopular series of stipula-
tions.[47]

Within the parameters of permitted sexual contact, rabbinic Judaism
endorsed harmonious sexual relations as an ethical ideal, as described
in the following midrash:

> When husband and wife meet each other in holiness, God gives them righteous
> children. We find that Hannah acted thus, when she said, **"For this child have
> I prayed and God granted my prayer"**(1 Sam. 1:27). Because Samuel was be-
> gotten and conceived in holiness, he was as saintly as Moses, for it says, **"Moses
> and Aaron among His priests, and Samuel among them that call upon His name"**
> (Ps. 99:6).[48]

Still mutuality only went so far. Dominant strands within rabbinic tradition took for granted that the husband's desires would direct a married
couple's sex life.

Many of these themes are discussed in a *sugya* in B. Nedarim 20a–b.
Although at least one voice within this passage objects to sexual practices not directly specifically towards procreation, it is made clear that
the *halakhah* allows for a wide latitude of sexual behavior. The discussion has its origins in deliberations about actions worthy people should
avoid, beginning with making vows and quickly moving to a favorite
rabbinic theme, building behavioral fences between men and women in
order to avoid falling into sin:

> [D]o not converse much with women, as this will ultimately lead you to un-
> chastity. R. Aha of the school of R. Josiah said: He who gazes at a woman
> eventually comes to sin, and he who looks even at a woman's heel will beget
> degenerate children. R. Joseph said: This applies even to one's wife when she is
> a *niddah*. R. Simeon b. Laqish said: "Heel" refers to the unclean part, which is
> directly opposite the heel.
> . . . R. Johanan b. Dahabai said: The Ministering Angels told me four things:
> People are born lame because they [their parents] overturned their table; dumb,
> because they kiss "that place"; deaf, because they converse during cohabitation;
> blind because they look at "that place." But this contradicts the following: Imma
> Shalom[49] was asked: Why are [20b] your children so very beautiful? She replied:
> [Because] he [my husband] "converses" with me neither at the beginning nor
> the end of the night, but [only] at midnight; and when he "converses," he un-
> covers a handbreadth and covers a handbreath, and it is as though he were
> compelled by a demon. And when I asked him, What is the reason for this [for
> the speed of his lovemaking], he replied, So that I may not think of another
> woman, lest my children be as bastards. [The rabbis said] There is no difficulty
> here [with the husband and wife conversing since] this refers to conjugal matters;
> the other [admonition against too much conversing with a woman] refers to
> other matters.
> R. Johanan said: The above [tradition about the Ministering Angels] is the
> view of R. Johanan b. Dahabai; but our Sages said: the *halakhah* is not according
> to R. Johanan b. Dahabai. Rather, a man may do whatever he pleases with his

wife, just as meat from the butcher shop may be eaten salted, roasted, cooked or seethed, and so with fish from the fishmonger.

Several different points of view on sexual activity are juxtaposed in this passage. While R. Johanan b. Dahabai represents an ascetic strand which is extremely negative about erotic creativity as a component of marital sexuality, his stance is ruled a minority opinion. The *halakhah* supports non-procreative as well as procreative activities as part of conjugal intimacy and allows for a wide range of sexual practices.[50] As is often the case in rabbinic literature, references to food and food preparation are used metaphorically for sexual behaviors. Ideally, both husband and wife participate willingly in all aspects of marital sexuality. However, it is clear that the husband is in charge. A wife who feels reluctance concerning a particular practice has no judicial support for her objections, as B. Nedarim 20b demonstrates:

A woman once came before Rabbi and said, "Rabbi! I set a table before my husband, but he overturned it." Rabbi replied: "My daughter! the Torah has permitted you to him—what then can I do for you?" A woman once came before Rab and complained, "Rabbi! I set a table before my husband, but he overturned it." Rab replied: "Wherein does it differ from a fish?"

In what appears a brutal metaphor to the modern reader, a wife is portrayed as her husband's sexual possession. Acquired on the marriage market, she must be compliant to her master's sexual demands, just as meat or fish purchased from the butcher or fishmonger is prepared according to the buyer's preference. The wife who appeals her husband's demands to the rabbinic court finds that in this instance she has no halakhic standing as a subject whose complaint will be considered. Rather, she is constructed as an object whose objections have no merit.

Conversely, women who attempt to initiate sexual alternatives to normal vaginal intercourse, perhaps in order to prevent conception in an era with few other reliable forms of birth control, are castigated for their effrontery, as in B. Yevamot 63b where the food/sex metaphor again comes into play:

How is one to understand the term a "bad wife"? Abaye said: One who prepares for him a tray and has her mouth also ready for him. Raba said: One who prepares for him the tray and turns her back upon him.

The issue at stake here is not sexual variety as much as the spousal balance of power. Husbands are in charge of bedroom matters, as they are in all other central issues connected with conjugal life.

Daniel Boyarin has suggested that these passages objectifying women go against a general talmudic tendency that sexual practice be only in accord with the wife's will and desire.[51] Certainly, the rest of the *sugya*

in B. Nedarim 20b appears to reinforce a rabbinic preference for harmonious intimacy between husband and wife during intercourse and
warns of consequences for husbands who do not respect their sexual
partners:

"So that you do not follow your heart and eyes in your lustful urge" (Num. 15:
39). [Deducing] from this Rabbi taught: One may not drink out of one goblet
and think of another. Rabina said: This is necessary only when both [women]
are his wives. "I will remove from you those who rebel and transgress against
Me" (Ezek. 20:38). R. Levi said: This refers to children belonging to the following nine categories: children of fear [conceived when a husband forces himself
upon his wife][52] of outrage [rape], of a hated wife, one under a ban, of a woman
mistaken for another, of strife, of intoxication [at the time of intercourse], of a
wife whose husband has already resolved to divorce her, of promiscuity, and of
a brazen woman [who demands her conjugal rights openly].

However, while Boyarin sees these texts as stressing the need for mutuality between husband and wife in sexual matters, I read them otherwise. These texts have little to say about female desire or female
agency. They offer ethical guidelines for a husband's sexual behavior
towards his wife that would transcend the minimal requirements of the
halakhah. A man who does not observe these amenities suffers the eu-
genic threat of rebellious children and violates desirable moral norms,
but he risks no judicial or social sanctions. Moreover, even in this context, there is significant ambivalence about prescribing a man's intimate
contact with his wife.

The discussion in B. Nedarim 20b, which ends the second chapter of
that tractate, concludes with consideration of the final category of undesirable sexual contacts, intercourse with a "brazen woman." In this
context, such a woman is understood as a wife who approaches her
husband sexually. There is some dispute over whether or not this is a
bad thing:

But that is not so: for did not R. Samuel b. Nahmani say in the name of R.
Jonathan: One who is summoned to his marital duty by his wife will beget
children such as were not to be found even in the generation of Moses? For it
is said, "Pick from each of your tribes men who are wise, discerning, and experienced, and I will appoint them as your heads" (Deut. 1:13), and it is written,
"So I took your tribal leaders, wise and experienced men" (Deut. 1:15), but
"discerning" [also specified in Deut. 1:13] is not mentioned. But it is also written, "Issachar is a strong-boned ass" (Gen. 49:14), while elsewhere it is written,
"Of the Issacharites, men who knew how to interpret the signs of the times" (1
Chron. 12:33). [It is virtuous] only when the wife ingratiates herself [but does
not solicit her husband for sex directly].

The final biblical proof texts cited here, condemning overt sexuality
on the part of a wife but approving her covert actions to initiate marital

intimacy, are references to the circumstances recounted in Genesis 30 that led to the birth of Jacob's son Issachar. In this narrative, Leah, Jacob's unloved wife, has mandrake plants, believed to increase female fertility, that her son Reuben found in the fields. She gives them to her sister Rachel, the favored spouse, in return for a night with Jacob. When Jacob comes home from the fields that evening, the biblical text relates:

> Leah went out to meet him and said, "You are to sleep with me, for I have hired you with my son's mandrakes." And he lay with her that night. God heeded Leah, and she conceived and bore him a fifth son. And Leah said, "God has given me my reward [*sekhari*] for having given my maid to my husband." So she named him Issachar (Gen. 30:16–18).

Issachar is cited in B. Nedarim 20b as an example of the type of extraordinary offspring who results when a wife solicits her husband sexually. This view, however, does not go unchallenged.

The idea of a woman taking the lead sexually was profoundly disquieting for a significant group of voices in rabbinic tradition. B. Nedarim 20b tempers the message by explaining that female assertion is acceptable only when the wife ingratiates herself, but does not request sex from her husband. And it is not surprising to find a more negative view of Leah's actions recorded in *Genesis Rabbah* 80:1, in a passage commenting on **"Now Dinah, the daughter whom Leah had borne to Jacob, went out to visit the daughters of the land"** (Gen. 34:1). In this midrash, Resh Laqish is said to ask a preacher the meaning of **"See, everyone who uses proverbs applies to you the proverb 'Like mother, like daughter' "** (Ezek. 16:44), and is answered as follows:

> "A cow does not gore unless her calf kicks; a woman is not immoral until her daughter is immoral," he replied. "If so," said he, "then our mother Leah was a harlot [since we find her daughter Dinah acting immorally]!" "Even so," he replied, "because it says, 'Leah went out to meet him' (Gen. 30:16), which means that she went out to meet him adorned like a harlot"; therefore **"Now Dinah, the daughter whom Leah had borne to Jacob, went out"** (Gen. 34:1).[53]

In this reading of the text, Dinah and her mother, Leah, are both condemned for their forwardness and likened to prostitutes. A "brazen woman," then, is a wife who attempts to assert control over sexual matters. If such behavior is overt, it affronts the dignity of her husband and is deemed unacceptable.

Bad Wife Tales

Rabbinic literature maintains an ongoing dialectic contrasting good and bad wives which is a covert debate on the benefits and evils of marriage as well as a strong endorsement of limiting a wife's prerogatives. Thus, B. Bava Metzi'a 59a quotes Rav as saying, "He who follows his wife's counsel will descend into Gehenna," but tempers this statement immediately with R. Pappa's objection: "But people say, If your wife is short, bend down and hear her whisper!" The resolution, as often in talmudic discourse, is that there is really no difficulty. One should not listen to one's wife's advice on general matters, but should certainly heed her words when it comes to household affairs. A second interpretation suggests that the first statement refers to religious matters, where a woman's advice would not be helpful, while the other refers to secular questions.

While these maxims might apply to married life in general, the rabbis were aware of the very individual nature of marital discord and the risks inherent in the formation of every new union. B. Bava Batra 145b relates:

R. Hanina said: "All the days of a poor man are wretched" (Prov. 15:15) refers [to him] who has a wicked wife; "But contentment is a feast without end" (ibid) refers [to him] who has a good wife. In the West, they used to ask a man who married, "found or find?" "Found," because it is written, "He who has found a wife has found happiness" (Prov. 18:22); "find," because it is written, "I find woman more bitter than death" (Ecc. 7:26).

Similarly, B. Shabbat 11a records: "Raba b. Mehasia also said in the name of R. Hama b. Goria in Rav's name: Rather any complaint, but not a complaint of the bowels; any pain, but not heart pain; any ache, but not headache; any evil, but not an evil wife!"

Rabbinic literature contains a number of what might be called "bad wife" stories which detail wifely conduct which is deemed unacceptable. Such anecdotes probably served the didactic purpose of warning women about the limits of provoking their husbands. The arenas in which a wife could rebel against her husband's authority or insult his dignity were exceedingly limited, and it is not surprising that most of these stories involve either food preparation or sexual behavior. As noted above, references to food and food preparation are often euphemistic metaphors for sexual practices.

In one such "bad wife" narrative in B. Yevamot 63a, Rav is said to have been constantly tormented by his wife. Her rebellions were on a small scale:

If he told her, "Prepare me lentils," she would prepare him small peas; and if he asked for small peas, she prepared him lentils. When his son Hiyya grew up he gave her [his father's instructions] in the reverse order. "Your mother," Rav once remarked to him, "has improved." "It was I," the other replied, "who reversed [your orders] to her." "This is what people say," the first said to him, "Your own offspring teaches you reason!"; however, you must not continue to do so, for it is said, "One man cheats the other, / They will not speak truth; / They have trained their tongues to speak falsely; / They wear themselves out working iniquity" (Jer. 9:4).

Rav was prepared to put up with such indignities; they were simply among the small annoyances which accompanied marriage. B. Yevamot 62b–63a also relates that when Rav's son Hiyya married, he too is said to have tolerated an unpleasant wife. Nevertheless, he brought her nice gifts. When his father reproached him, "But surely she is tormenting the master!" Hiyya replied, "It is sufficient for us that they rear up our children and deliver us from sin." Faced with such a utilitarian view of marriage, it is not surprising that some women fomented small disobediences.

Genesis Rabbah 17:3 comments on "**I will make a fitting helper for him**" (Gen. 2:18) with a more detailed account of wifely rebellion and its punishment.

If he is fortunate, she is a help; if not, she is against him. R. Joshua b. Nehemiah said: If a man is fortunate, she is like the wife of Hananiah b. Hakinai;[54] if not, she is like the wife of R. Jose the Galilean. R. Jose the Galilean had a bad wife; she was his sister's daughter, and used to put him to shame. His disciples said to him: "Master, divorce this woman, for she does not act as befits your honor." "Her dowry is too great for me, and I cannot afford to divorce her," was his reply. Now it happened once that he and R. Eleazar b. 'Azariah were sitting and studying, and when they finished, the latter asked him, "Sir, will you kindly permit that we go to your home together?" "Yes," replied he. As they entered, she cast down her gaze [in anger at the unexpected visitor] and was making her way out, when [her husband] looked at a pot standing on the pot-range and asked her, "Is there anything in the pot?" "There's a hash in it," she answered [perhaps to discourage the guest]. He went and uncovered it, and found in it some chickens. Now R. Eleazar b. 'Azariah knew what he had heard, and as they sat together and were eating he observed, "Sir, did she not say it was hash, yet we have found chickens" "A miracle has happened," replied he. When they finished he said to him: "Master, abandon this woman, for she does not treat you with proper respect." "Sir," he replied, "her dowry is too great for me and I cannot divorce her." "We [your students]," said the other, "will apportion her dowry among ourselves so you can divorce her." And they did so for him; they apportioned her dowry and had her divorced from him, and made him marry another and better wife.

The passage continues with the suffering which then befell the discarded wife as a consequence of "her sins." These included being married to a brutal husband who beat her in public; in her moment of deepest humiliation she was forced to accept the charity of her former husband, perhaps the cruelest punishment of all.[55]

Conversely, positive, if backhanded, testimony to a wife's influence on her husband appears in *Genesis Rabbah* 17:3:

There was once a pious man who was married to a pious woman; and they had no children. They said, "We are no profit to God." So they divorced one another. The man went and married a bad woman and she made him bad; the woman went and married a bad man, and she made him good. So all depends upon the woman.

More often, the wife is blamed for marital discord rather than the husband. B. Sotah 2a preserves a tradition which has a somewhat different implication:

R. Samuel b. R. Isaac said: When Resh Laqish began to expound [the subject of tractate] Sotah (the adulterous wife), he spoke thus: They only pair a woman with a man according to his deeds, as it is said, "For the scepter of the wicked shall never rest / upon the land alloted to the righteous" (Ps. 125:3). Rabbah b. Bar Hanah said in the name of R. Johanan: It is as difficult to pair them as was the division of the Red Sea; as it is said, "God sets the solitary in families; He brings out the prisoners into prosperity!" (Ps. 68:7). But it is not so; for Rav Judah has said in the name of Rav: Forty days before the creation of a child, a Bat Kol (a heavenly voice) issues forth and proclaims, "The daughter of A is for B." . . . There is no contradiction, the latter dictum refers to a first marriage and the former to a second marriage.

The suggestion attributed to Resh Laqish that men with unfaithful or otherwise bad wives deserve them because of their own evil actions is typical of a trend in rabbinic theology which attempts to explain misfortunes as justified punishment for human misdeeds. While this view is supported with allusions to the skill God demonstrates in the difficult task of matching men and women appropriately, it appears to be refuted by the tradition that couples are matched even before the creation of the embryo. If a marriage is preordained even before birth, how can a bad spouse be explained by an individual's inappropriate behavior? The compromise solution is that first marriages are foreordained, but that a bad wife in a second marriage is punishment for the husband's misdeeds.

Bad wives can be recognized by their immodesty in venturing into public places. As the midrash collection Tanhuma (Vayishlah 36, f. 55) puts it, commenting on "All glorious is the king's daughter within" (Ps. 45:13):

R. Jose says: When a woman keeps chastely within the house, she is fit to marry a High Priest and rear sons who shall be High Priests. On the same verse R. Phinehas bar Hama ha-Kohen says: This means, when she keeps chastely within the house. Just as the altar atones for the house, so does she atone for her house, as it says, "Your wife shall be like a fruitful vine within the sides of your house / Your sons, like olive saplings around your table" [the same word is used for "sides" here as in the sacrificial regulations with regard to the altar] (Ps. 128: 3). Where shall she be as a fruitful vine? When she is within the sides of your house. If she acts thus, then your children will be like olives; she will rear sons to be anointed with the olive oil of the High Priesthood.

This insistence that a woman should remain at home also reveals the rabbinic conviction that a wife's behavior reflects not only on her husband's status and piety, but also on the future fates of her sons.

The desirability of keeping women within the domestic circle is also the theme of a passage in B. Gittin 90a–b, where attitudes towards food consumption provide a convenient metaphor for different styles of marital control:

> R. Meir used to say: As men differ in their treatment of their food, so they differ in their treatment of their wives. Some men, if a fly falls into their cup, will put it aside and not drink it. This corresponds to the way of Pappus b. Judah. When he went out, he used to lock his wife indoors. Another man, if a fly falls into his cup, will throw away the fly and then drink from the cup. This corresponds to the way of most men who do not mind their wives talking with their brothers and relatives. Another man, again, if a fly falls into his soup, will squash it and eat it. This corresponds to the way of a bad man who sees his wife go out with her hair unfastened and spin cloth in the street with armpits uncovered and bathe with the men.

It is a religious duty, the rabbis continue, to divorce such a wife, and they warn that anyone who marries this wicked woman after her divorce courts death. Women require regulation, whether strict or moderate. According to this view, it is the uncontrolled woman who goes out into the public domain on her own who is a source of societal disruption and a danger to her husband.[56]

In its condemnation of the wanton wife who behaves immodestly, B. Gittin 90b reflects the language of M. Ketubbot 7:6, which describes "those who are divorced without their *ketubbah*." These include women who have transgressed the law of Moses and women who have violated Jewish custom. The latter are defined as follows:

> If she goes out with her head uncovered, or spins in the street, or she speaks with any man. Abba Saul says: "Also if she curses his parents in his presence." Rabbi Tarfon says: "Also [if she is] a vocal woman (*qolanit*) and regarded as a vocal woman. And who is deemed a vocal woman? Whosoever speaks inside her house so that her neighbors hear her voice."[57]

Many of these offences are associated with improper sexual behavior. A woman who revealed her hair, shoulders, or arms in public was understood to be issuing a sexual invitation. B. Ketubbot 72b associates both spinning in public and "speaking with any man" with prostitution. Cynthia Baker has argued that rabbinic anxieties associated with the brazen woman who ventures into the public domain of the marketplace or bath are part of "a complicated narrative about property, propriety, and female sexuality aimed at naming and securing broader cultural boundaries."[58] Not only do the rabbis view the immodest woman in the street as sexually untrustworthy and therefore as representing "a threat to property, honor, sexual purity, and genealogical continuity," but Baker also suggests that such a woman embodies for the rabbis their own discomfort with the cultural and ethnic diversity encountered in the marketplaces of the larger societies in which they lived. According to Baker:

> [T]he woman in the *shuq* (street or marketplace) conveys the sense that if only the female body (and all that it represents) is sufficiently controlled and bounded, perhaps that might serve as protection against the penetration and dissemination of an Other's culture into the closed Jewish society imagined by the rabbis. The enclosed female body, like the "fence around the Torah," may secure the "House of Israel" from Others within and without.[59]

She concludes that "the anxiety that surrounds the woman in the *shuq* is as much rabbinic anxiety about the creation and preservation of cultural identity and cultural boundaries as it is male anxiety about female sexuality and the limits of control."[60] While her analogy is provocative and not without merit, it is important to remember that the rabbinic polemic is not against all women who ventured beyond the domestic realm, since many did so in modest garb for acceptable purposes. Rather it is about women who flaunted their sexuality in public. Such a wife could not be tolerated.

Aggadic Views on Divorce

For many of the sages, the solution to a bad wife was obvious, as indicated in the following excerpts from an extended discussion of good and bad wives in B. Yevamot 63b:

> Rava said: [If one has] a bad wife it is a meritorious act to divorce her, for it is said, "Expel the scoffer, and contention departs, / Quarrel and contumely cease" (Prov. 22:10). Rava further stated: A bad wife, the amount of whose *ketubbah* is large, [should be given] a rival at her side, as people say, "By her partner rather than by a thorn" [i.e., a bad wife is more easily corrected by subjecting her to the unpleasantness of a rival than by chastising her with thorns]. Rava further stated: A bad wife is as troublesome as a very rainy day; for it is said, "An endless dripping on a rainy day / And a contentious wife are alike" (Prov. 27:15). . . . "I am going to bring upon them disaster, from which they will not be able to escape" (Jer. 11:11): R. Nahman said in the name of Rabbah b. Abbuha: This refers to a bad wife, the amount of whose *ketubbah* is large. "The Lord has delivered me into the hands of those I cannot withstand" (Lam. 1:14): R. Hisda said in the name of Mar 'Ukba b. Hiyya: This refers to a bad wife the amount of whose *ketubbah* is large. In the West it was said: This refers to one whose maintenance depends on his money.

In this text, the prevalence of bad wives seems to be agreed upon, as is the expense required in extricating oneself from an unhappy marriage through divorce. This is why Raba advises an unhappy husband to consider taking a second wife who might please him more and also humble the difficult first wife. This alternative had the disadvantage, however, of the significant costs involved in assuming the responsibility for another dependent and any children she might bear.

"Bad wives" are at a grave disadvantage and their rebellions are indicative of their limited arenas of influence. In fact, these "bad wife" stories are intended to be didactic. They delineate for men the boundaries of female freedom and they demonstrate to women potential penalties for their attempts to exceed them, particularly the risk of divorce which remained a ready expedient for men in unhappy marriages. Still, while divorce was legally easy to obtain (if sometimes financially painful), a number of sages harbored ethical qualms about the severing of marriage bonds. *Genesis Rabbah* 18:5 comments on **"Hence a man leaves his father and mother and clings to his wife, so that they become one flesh"** (Gen. 2:24), as follows:

Said R. Aha in the name of R. Hanina b. Papa: Throughout the book of Malachi **"The Lord of Hosts"** is used [in reference to God], whereas here [in reference to divorce] we have **"The God of Israel,"** as it says, **"For I detest divorce — said the Lord, the God of Israel"** (Mal. 2:16). It is as though one might say, His name has no bearing on divorce save in the case of Israel alone. R. Hanan said: When Nehemiah came up [to the land of Israel] from the land of Exile [he found that] the women's faces had been blackened by the sun, so that [their husbands] had gone and married strange wives, while these [rejected wives] would go around the altar weeping. Thus Malachi says, **"And this you do a second time"** (Mal. 2:13), you actually repeat [the sin committed] at Shittim![61] **"You cover the altar of the Lord with tears, weeping, and moaning, so that He refuses to regard the oblation any more and to accept what you offer"** (Mal. 2:13). The Holy One, blessed be He, said: "Who will accept weeping and sighing from them [the treacherous husbands]? Having robbed her, and deprived her of her beauty, you cast her away!"

This midrash makes clear that marriage, like the sacred relationship between God and the people of Israel on which it is modeled, must be cherished and preserved. Although the *halakhah* allows a man to divorce his wife, humane mandates of personal responsibility demand something higher—a sense of concern and responsibility towards a subordinate and dependent human being. This conflict between legal privilege and ethical responsibility is also closely argued in the conclusion of the talmudic tractate B. Gittin 90 a–b, following the halakhic ruling that a man is at liberty to divorce his wife for any reason:

"For a hateful one put away" (Mal. 2:16).[62] R. Judah said: [This means that] if you hate her you should put her away. R. Johanan says: It means, he that sends his wife away is hated. There is really no conflict between the two, since the one speaks of the first marriage and the other of the second, as R. Eleazar said: If a man divorces his first wife, even the altar sheds tears, as it says: "**And this you do as well: You cover the altar of the Lord with tears, weeping and moaning, so that He refuses to regard the oblation any more and to accept what you offer. But you ask, 'Because of what?' 'Because the Lord is a witness between you and the wife of your youth with whom you have broken faith, though she is your partner and covenanted spouse'** " (Mal. 2:13–14).

These admonitions to value the wife of one's youth should be seen in the context of a polygynous society which attached no reproach to a man's having more than one wife. Indeed, living in a polygynyous house-hold might have been seen by many women as preferable to divorce. For an older woman in an established marriage, the humiliation of be-coming a co-spouse was likely preferable to the shame and probable social and financial disaster of divorce.

It is difficult to gauge the prevalence of polygyny in rabbinic societies, whether in general or among the rabbinic sages in particular. As noted in chapter 3, the rabbis cited the impossibility of polygamy as one of the disadvantages inflicted upon women for their connection with Eve's sin, so certainly the possibility of having more than one spouse was seen as a benefit for men. Isaiah Gafni has pointed out the importance of external factors in the frequency of Jewish polygyny in rabbinic times, noting that Palestinian rabbinic sources appear to imply a predominantly monogamous Jewish society, perhaps under the influence of the monog-amous atmosphere of Roman society, together with a similar emphasis in Christian practice, while the situation in Sassanian Babylonia, where polygyny was generally common, was quite different.[63] A statement like the following, from the Palestinian midrash *Avot de-Rabbi Nathan* B, ch. 2, would seem to represent a tradition favoring monogamy:

Job said: "I have covenanted with my eyes / Not to gaze on a maiden" (Job 31: 1). R. Judah b. Batra said: Job was entitled to look upon an unmarried woman, since he could have married her himself, or given her as a wife to one of his sons or relations, but he said, "If it had been fitting for Adam to have been given ten wives, God would have given them to him, yet He gave him but one. So I, too, will be satisfied with one wife and my one portion."

Nevertheless, a strong tradition in favor of preservation of marriages, and in particular, of loyalty to one's first wife, need not be in conflict with polygyny. Indeed, it can be argued that polygyny is seen as cultur-ally preferable to divorcing one's first wife in order to take a new one. B. Sanhedrin 22a–22b provides an extended homily condemning divorce and meditating on the close links which exist between a man and his first wife, reinforcing this view:

R. Shiman b. Abba said: Come and see with what great reluctance is divorce granted; King David was permitted sexual intimacy with Abishag, yet not divorce [of one of his permitted limit of eighteen wives in order to marry her]. R. Eliezer said: For him who divorces the first wife, the very altar sheds tears. . . . R. Johanan also said: He whose first wife has died [is grieved as much] as if the destruction of the Temple had taken place in his days. . . . R. Alexandri said: The world is darkened for him whose wife has died in his days, as it is written, **"The lamp in his tent darkens; / His lamp fails him"** (Job 18:6). R. Jose b. Hanina said: His steps grow short, as it is said, **"His strides are hobbled"** (Job 18:7). R. Abbahu said: His wits collapse, as it is written, **"His schemes overthrow him"** (ibid). . . . R. Nahman said: All things can be replaced, except the wife of one's youth, as it is written, **"Can one cast off the wife of one's youth?"** (Isa. 54:6). Rav Judah taught his son R. Isaac: Only with one's first wife does one find pleasure, as it is said, **"Let your fountain be blessed / Find joy in the wife of your youth"** (Prov. 5:18). "Of what kind of woman do you speak?" he asked him. "Of such as your mother," was the reply. But is this true? Had not Rav Judah taught his son R. Isaac, the verse: **"Now, I find woman more bitter than death; she is all traps, her hands are fetters and heart is snares. He who is pleasing to God escapes her, and he who is displeasing is caught by her"** (Ecc. 7:26), and [the son] asked him, "What kind of woman?" He answered, "Such as your mother." True, she was a quick-tempered woman but nevertheless easily appeased with a word. . . . A Tanna taught: The death of a man is felt by none [so much as by] his wife; and that of a woman by her husband.

The emphasis in these teachings on "first" wife implies that a man may have a second and even a third wife, simultaneously, but that the relationship with the wife of one's youth is unique and to be valued. Whether such statements reflect a widely prevalent trend of divorcing older wives in favor of younger women is impossible to determine. But these traditions reveal that the rabbis were aware of the pain of rejected women. They not only instituted legislation to protect them by insisting on the return of the *ketubbah,* but spoke out against such practices in their homiletical teachings as well.

Conclusion

Suspended between *halakhah,* with its emphasis on the minimum legal requirements by which a person is bound in his or her relationships with others, and *aggadah,* which attempts to exhort the believer to a higher ethical standard, the rabbinic vision of women as wives is complicated and unresolved, as in any area where ideal norms collide with experienced reality. Rabbinic Judaism was determined to localize wives' activities in the domestic sphere of family and family-based economic activities where they could facilitate the more culturally valued religious, intellectual, and communal endeavors of their husbands. Nor did the sages hesitate to express their compassion, appreciation, and need for those significant women in their lives who fulfilled the expectations of their society and gracefully yielded to male dominance.

Yet, a hermeneutics of suspicion informed all rabbinic ruminations on their other halves; the supposed sexual unreliablity of women was never forgotten. Wives who chafed at remaining silent partners and attempted to expand their activities or assert their influence outside permissable boundaries, whether in the sphere of the domestic or beyond its limits, were severely chastised and risked the ultimate punitive sanctions of rejection and divorce. Moreover, rabbinic Judaism preserved an enduring ambivalence over the relative importance of study versus family obligations. Although halakhic prescription demanded procreation and proscribed celibacy, strong societal values privileged devotion to the divine word. Essential to childbearing and nurturing, but emotional and financial obstacles to extended study abroad, females were caught in the middle, with few sanctioned options beyond submission and silent self-sacrifice. Women who were unable to fulfil the expected conditions of the wifely role, particularly bearing children, were especially vulnerable to dismissal and penury, as revealed in chapter 5.

"WHY WERE THE MATRIARCHS BARREN?":
RESOLVING THE ANOMALY OF
FEMALE INFERTILITY

The barren wife presented a challenge to rabbinic Judaism's comfortable conceptualizations of women as expansive houses and fruitful vines. In a legal system which considered procreation to be a religious obligation for males, infertile unions for childless men were a significant problem. The recommended halakhic solution was divorce after ten years without issue, with both husband and wife encouraged to enter into a new marriage.[1] Aggadic texts, on the other hand, validated the intensity of deeply felt marital bonds and suggested that compassion and faith should prevail over dissolving a loving marriage. Moreover, rabbinic reflections on the anomaly of the barren woman also convey important insights into the dilemma of suffering and the efficacy of prayer, as well as examples of the ways in which biblical models could become paradigms and symbols of empowerment in women's lives.

Men, Women, and Procreation

Earlier chapters in this volume have shown the ways in which rabbinic Judaism constructed differing legal, religious, and social responsibilities and status for men and women, demonstrating how rabbinic social policy fostered women's reproductive functions and nurturing qualities, even as it placed them under the aegis of a dominant husband.[2] Yet, it is important to recognize that the majority of the rabbis distinguished between procreation as an active male role, as discussed in chapter 3, and bearing children as the female's designated passive purpose. This distinction is of key importance in the rabbinic ruling that only males are obligated to have children. Rabbinic texts variously based the biblical origins of this legal mandate to father children on four passages: Genesis 1:28, **"God blessed them and God said to them: 'Be fertile and increase,** fill the earth and master it; and rule the fish of the sea, the birds of the sky, and all the living things that creep on earth' "; Genesis 9:1., "God blessed Noah and his sons, and said to them, 'Be fertile and increase, and fill the earth' "; Genesis 9:7, "Be fertile, then and increase; abound on the earth and increase on it";[3] and particularly Genesis 35:11, where Jacob is commanded in the second person masculine singular to "Be fertile and increase."

The primary halakhic statement that only men are required to produce offspring is found in M. Yevamot 6:6 and is elaborated in B. Yevamot 65b–66a. M. Yevamot 6:6 rules as follows:

No man may abstain from keeping the law "Be fertile and increase" (Gen. 1: 28), unless he already has children: according to the School of Shammai, two sons; according to the School of Hillel, a son and a daughter, for it is written, "Male and female He created them" (Gen. 5:2). If he married a woman and lived with her ten years and she bore no child, it is not permitted him to abstain [from fulfilling this legal obligation]. If he divorced her she may be married to another and the second husband may live with her for ten years. If she had a miscarriage the space [of ten years] is measured from the time of the miscarriage. The duty to be fruitful and multiply falls on the man but not on the woman. R. Johanan b. Beroqah [dissents from this view and] says: Of them both it is written, "God blessed them and God said to them, Be fertile and increase" (Gen. 1: 28).

M. Yevamot 6:6 raises a number of unresolved questions connected with the commandment to reproduce, including the number of children required to fulfil the biblical imperative, the precise course a man is to follow if his marriage is not fruitful after ten years, and perhaps most centrally, why only men are obligated to procreate and not women. The commandments to reproduce in Genesis 1:28 are plural verb forms, definitely directed to both of the newly created human creatures. This mysterious limitation is accentuated at the end of the mishnah, by the citation of R. Johanan b. Beroqah's minority opinion that women are also required to be fruitful.[4]

B. Yevamot 65b records significant disagreement among the sages over this question while reiterating the majority view that the obligation to procreate is incumbent only upon males. The reasons put forward are diverse. An initial argument invokes the need for male control over female sexuality:

Whence is this derived [that only the man, and not the woman, is subject to the duty to procreate]? R. Ile'a replied in the name of R. Simeon: Scripture stated, "Be fertile and increase, fill the earth and master it" (Gen. 1:28); it is the nature of man to "master" but is not the nature of a woman to "master." On the contrary! [someone objected to R. Ile'a] "And master it" implies two! [since the verb is a plural imperative form] R. Nahman b. Isaac replied: [the verse] is written, "And master it."

The final verb form in Genesis 1:28, **"And master it,"** is usually read *v'khivshuhah,* a plural imperative form with a feminine singular direct object suffix (since "earth" is a feminine noun). However, the unvocalized letters of this verb form may also be read *v'khivshah,* with an initial masculine imperative singular verb. In B. Yevamot 65b, the rabbis reason by analogy: Since this final of three verb forms may be read as a masculine singular form, similarly the other two verbs in the chain (**"Be fertile and increase"**) may also be read as masculine singular forms. Therefore, it may be argued on linguistic grounds, particularly with the support of the masculine singular forms in Genesis 35:11, that the commands apply only to men.

"And master it," the final verb form, ends with a feminine singular direct object suffix, usually translated as "it" in English. In fact, this verb form may also be read: **"And you [masculine singular] master her."** In one of the interpretations of Genesis 1:28 preserved in *Genesis Rabbah* 8:12, the connection of male dominance over women and the male obligation to procreate is raised explicitly:

R. Leazar said in the name of R. Jose b. Zimra: **"And you [masculine plural] master it"** is to be read as, **"And you [masculine singular] master it"**: man is commanded concerning procreation, but not woman. R. Johanan b. Beroqah [in objection] said: Concerning both man and woman it says, **"God blessed them ..."** (Gen. 1:28). [This objection is refuted as follows:] **"And master *her*"** is written: the man must master his wife, that she not go out into the marketplace, for every woman who goes out into the marketplace will eventually come to grief. Whence do we know it? From Dinah, as it is written, **"And Dinah ... went out ..."** (Gen. 34:1).[5]

This transformation of the biblical text against its apparent literal meaning is itself subsequently defended in several different ways in succeeding segments of B. Yevamot 65b. Thus, it is argued that the biblical commandment had to be modified from a plural to a singular form on the grounds that obligating women to procreate, when they are incapable of doing so on their own, would be to teach them to scorn the law in general:

R. Ile'a further stated in the name of R. Eleazar son of R. Simeon: As one is commanded to say that which will be obeyed, so one is commanded not to say that which will not be obeyed. R. Abba stated: It is a duty; for it is said in Scripture, **"Do not rebuke a scoffer, for he will hate you; / Reprove a wise man and he will love you"** (Prov. 9:8).

The statement that women would be unable to fulfil the commandment appears to be an additional reference to rabbinic understandings of generation. Just as it is a man's role to assert sexual mastery over a woman, so it is his function to generate new life. Genesis 1:28, therefore, must be understood as referring only to the man, since he alone is capable of procreation in this sense.

The next justification for emending the biblical mandate to refer solely to men invokes the maxim, "One may modify a statement in the interests of peace." Several rationales for this claim are offered, including the following:

At the school of R. Ishmael it was taught: Great is the cause of peace, seeing that for its sake even the Holy One, blessed be He, modified a statement; for at first it is written "And Sarah laughed to herself, saying, "Now that I am withered, am I to have enjoyment—with my husband so old" (Gen. 18:12) [which could be seen as implying that Abraham was impotent], while afterwards it is written, "Then the Lord said to Abraham, "Why did Sarah laugh, saying, "Shall I in truth bear a child, old as I am?" (Gen. 18:13) [with no reference to Abraham's old age].

In this segment of the passage, God is said to have altered Sarah's declaration in reporting it to Abraham in order to spare Abraham a reference to his diminished powers. It seems no accident that the texts chosen to prove that changing a scriptural statement is permissible for the goal of advancing peace juxtapose the elimination of women from the divine commandment to procreate with the classic biblical instance of a barren woman's conception. Sarah conceived when she least expected such a thing could be possible. Her pregnancy is not a fulfilment of a legal obligation but a divine mark of grace. In separating the male's requirement to procreate and the divine role in opening the female's womb, important homiletical points are made about the varying roles of man and woman in the reproductive process. Moreover, the divine partnership in the formation of each embryo, discussed above in chapter 1,[6] is accentuated.

And how does emending Genesis 1:28 to refer only to men increase peace? It may be that the reference here is to the "first Eve," the rabbinic narrative about the initial woman created equally with Adam, discussed in chapter 2.[7] As the vestiges of legends about her disruptive effects reveal, when male dominance is not clearly established in human relationships and women insist on equal roles, chaos and commotion result. For rabbinic sexual politics, it is in the interests of peace to revise the record, both as far as who was created first and who was commanded to procreate.

The remainder of this *sugya* in B. Yevamot 65b–66a offers a number of anecdotes, apparently supporting R. Johanan b. Beroqah contention that women are also obligated regarding reproduction. Several, discussed in more detail below, have to do with women who ask the rabbinic court to compel their husbands to divorce them because of unfruitful marriages. The Gemara makes clear in each instance that the individual women's requests were granted, not because they were halakhically required to have children, but because they offered compelling pleas to be permitted to attempt pregnancy with another spouse based on their specific circumstances.

Another narrative has to do with a woman who suffered an extremely difficult pregnancy and an agonizing delivery of twins. Relying on her husband's ruling that a woman was not commanded to propagate, she drank a sterilizing potion without his knowledge and to his later regret. Thus, this discussion also teaches that a woman is permitted to chose to use contraceptive measures since she has no legal duty to bear offspring.

The entire discussion in B. Yevamot 65b–66a ends with a final story that seems to derive from everyday life:

But does not the commandment [to procreate] apply to women? Surely, R. Aha b. R. Kattina related in the name of R. Isaac: It once happened in the case of a woman who was half slave and half free, that her master was compelled to emancipate her! R. Nahman b. Isaac replied: People were taking liberties with her.

The story of the emancipated slave was cited to support the claim that women were required to reproduce themselves. As someone whose status was indeterminate, this woman could not marry either a slave or a free man. Apparently she petitioned the rabbinic court to compel her master to free her so that she might marry appropriately and have children. Rabbi Isaac's reasoning was that the court would only have compelled her emancipation, an expensive loss for her master, if she were religiously obligated to marry and procreate. However, R. Nahman b. Isaac's response indicates that, just as with the particular infertile women referred to earlier in the passage who successfully persuaded the court to coerce their husbands to divorce them, the court's ruling in this case was based on special circumstances. This nubile woman was liberated because she was subject to constant sexual harassment and marriage was her only protection. While this story is meant to prove the point that women are not commanded regarding procreation, it also provides a poignant indication of the dangerous situation of the single woman in rabbinic society and the potential for sexual predation to which her anomalous situation exposed her. Such figures provoked severe anxiety in rabbinic society and it is not surprising that the remedy of manumission and marriage were resolved upon in her case. However, the final word in B. Yevamot 66a insists that her emancipation was not to be understood as affirming her legal obligation to procreate.

The discourse preserved in B. Yevamot 65b–66a indicates substantial rabbinic debate over limiting the commandment of reproduction to men. Although the majority of rabbis were prepared to discount the clear mandate to both sexes of **"Be fertile and increase"** in Genesis 1:28, a significant minority were uneasy with such blatant modification of the biblical text. Several scholars have asked why the larger number of rabbinic voices believed that removing women from the obligation to procreate would advance peace and why these sages discounted the examples of such biblical women as Lot's daughters (Gen. 19:31–36), and Tamar (Gen. 38), who took their obligation to procreate seriously enough to flaunt social custom, or even Rachel, whose poignant cry, **"Give me children, or else I am dead"** (Gen. 30:1) became a standard rabbinic proof text for obligatory male propagation.[8]

Rachel Biale has attempted to account for women's lack of obligation by suggesting that the rabbis assumed women had a natural desire to bear children and, unlike men, did not need to have biological imperatives transformed into religious duty. She proposes, as well, that women were absolved from the responsibility to produce offspring so that they could employ contraceptive measures in some circumstances.[9] It seems likely, however, that her first explanation more accurately qualifies as an apologetic, while the second is a legal corollary, rather than a motivating principle: Since women were not obligated to procreate they were permitted to use contraception.[10] David M. Feldman cites the rather more convincing opinion of Julius Preuss, that if the commandment were put to the woman to fulfil, it might inspire a kind of well-motivated promiscuity.[11] Certainly, independent, aberrant, or disruptive sexual behavior by women, as epitomized by the well-intentioned Tamar, or the desperate daughters of Lot, would constitute a grave threat to the patriarchal social fabric.

Indeed, preventing such outrages was a major goal of the rabbis' social agenda. Concern about possible female attempts at reproductive independence, even for worthy purposes, is apparent in the discussion of Hannah's prayer (1 Sam. 1:11) in B. Berakhot 31a–b. According to Numbers 5:28, the wife falsely accused of adultery will be cleared and will subsequently conceive: **"But if the woman has not defiled herself and is pure, she shall be unharmed and able to retain seed."** Commenting on a portion of Hannah's supplication, **"If you will indeed look"** (I Sam. 1:11), R. Eleazar interpreted Hannah's motivation as follows:

Hannah said before the Holy One, blessed be He: Sovereign of the Universe, if You will look [upon my affliction], it is well, and if You will not look, I will go and shut myself up with another man in the knowledge of my husband Elkanah, and as I shall have been alone [with this other man in compromising circumstances] they will make me drink the water of the suspected wife, and You cannot falsify Your law, which says, **"She shall be unharmed and shall retain seed"** (Num. 5:28).

The problem now became one of interpreting Numbers 5:28, for if the verse literally guaranteed conception for the barren wife cleared of a charge of adultery, considerable social uproar would result from barren wives pretending to be adulterous in order to be cleared so that they would subsequently conceive. The likely disappointment of many of their hopes would also call the law of Heaven into question. Rather, B. Berakhot 31b reinterprets the Numbers passage as follows: "No, it teaches that if she formerly bore with pain she now bears with ease, if she bore short children she now bears tall ones, if she bore swarthy ones she now bears fair ones, if she was destined to bear one she will now bear two."[12] Thus, metaphorical exegesis of an inconvenient biblical reassurance obviated the potential anarchy that might be occasioned by women taking their sexual destinies into their own hands. How much more likely the potential chaos if women were legally obligated to produce children!

However, in explaining why procreation is a male requirement only, one must come back to the reasoning attributed to R. Ile'a, in the name of R. Eleazar son of R. Simeon, discussed above: "It is the nature of a man to master but it is not the nature of a woman to master." As Feldman observes, in rabbinic Judaism's male dominated world view, it is obvious "that the man, the more aggressive of the two [sexes] be responsible for the performance of the command."[13] A similar statement also endorsing male sexual dominance is recorded in B. Niddah 31b:

And why does the man lie face downwards [during sexual intercourse] and the woman face upwards towards the man? He [faces the elements] from which he was created and she [faces the man] from whom she was created.

Elsewhere in this book, I suggested, in connection with this passage, that a preponderance of voices in rabbinic literature accept that male sexual dominance over the female was inscribed from the instant of woman's formation and is understood to have been ordained by divine plan.[14] As I argued in chapters 1 and 2, rabbinic Judaism insists, also in the face of biblical evidence to the contrary, that only males are created in the divine image and that being created in God's image implies the ability to generate new life.

It seems clear that this insistence on male sexual supremacy in procreation also lies behind the emendation of Genesis 1:28 in B. Yevamot 65b and *Genesis Rabbah* 8:12 to a series of masculine singular commandments. For the rabbis, procreation is a masculine act of potency quite different from the feminine role of bearing and birthing the fruit of male seed. In B. Berakhot 51b, a passage discussed in more detail in chapter 3,[15] the Palestinian sage 'Ulla explained his refusal to allow a woman to participate in sharing the cup of benediction that concludes the recitation of grace after a meal on the grounds that the blessing did not apply to her because of her passive role in reproduction. His statement, attributed to R. Johanan, that "the fruit of a woman's body is blessed only from the fruit of a man's body," is another way of indicating that woman's role in the procreation process is subordinate, just as her very creation was of a secondary nature.

Dissolving Infertile Unions

M. Yevamot 6:6 ruled, "If a man took a wife and lived with her for ten years and she bore no child, he may not abstain [any longer from the duty of propagation"], although exactly how he is to proceed in this instance is not spelled out in the *mishnah*. T. Yevamot 8:5, however, explicitly states that a man in this situation must divorce his wife and return her marriage settlement to her "for perhaps he did not merit being built up through her." Since there is no proof that their infertility is the divorced wife's fault, the Tosefta at Yevamot 8:6 makes clear that the divorced wife may marry again, "for perhaps she did not merit being built up through this man."[16]

These measures are also recommended in B. Yevamot 65b, where the rabbis point out that while there is no definite scriptural justification for the practice of divorcing an infertile wife after ten years, an allusion to it may be drawn from **"So Sarai, Abram's wife, took her maid, Hagar the Egyptian—after Abram had dwelt in the land of Canaan ten years—and gave her to her husband Abram as a concubine"** (Gen. 16: 3).[17] The explicit editorial comment in this verse that it was only after ten years of living in the land of Canaan that Sarai accepted her infertility and surrogated her servant to bear a child on her behalf is evoked to support ten years as the term in which infertility had to be established before dissolving a marriage.[18] This passage goes on to say that "if the man or the woman was ill, or if both were in prison, [the years when they are separated] are not included in the number" of years after which a divorce is required. The assumption of infertility must follow ten years of normal marital relations.

M. Yevamot 6:6 goes on, "If he divorced her, she is allowed to marry another and the second husband may also live with her [no more than] ten years [without offspring]." If the woman does not become pregnant during those ten years of her second marriage, she is now presumed to be barren, and must, once again, be divorced. However, *B. Yevamot* 65a rules that she may marry a third time, under specific circumstances:

> Our rabbis taught: A woman who had been married to one husband and had no children and to a second husband and again had no children, may marry a third man only if he has children. If she married one who has had no children she must be divorced without receiving her *ketubbah*.

Since a woman is not obligated to procreate, her failure to produce offspring has no legal implications for herself. However, she cannot impede the fulfilment of this commandment by knowingly marrying a childless man.

Although the *halakhah* clearly mandated divorce so that both partners could try to procreate again in new relationships, there are indications that some men in childless marriages chose to take a second wife rather than divorce an apparently infertile spouse. Some of these men may have been happy with their first wives and reluctant to divorce them, despite their failure to give birth. Others may have preferred to maintain the economic basis on which their marriages rested rather than having to return a substantial *ketubbah*.[19] B. Yevamot 65a maintains an unresolved dispute over this issue:

> If the husband states that he intends taking another wife to test his potency, R. Ammi ruled: He must in this case also divorce [his present wife] and pay her the amount of her *ketubbah*; for I maintain that whosoever takes in addition to his present wife another one must divorce the former and pay her the amount of her *ketubbah*.
> Rava said: A man may marry wives in addition to his first wife provided only that he possesses the means to maintain them.

It seems likely that Rav's solution would have been chosen in a majority of cases. Certainly this was true in later periods of Jewish history where the evidence shows that even when offered the option of divorce, most women preferred to stay in their original marriages.[20] Since the woman was not legally obligated to procreate, there was no serious objection to her doing so. Nevertheless, it is important to emphasize that the *halakhah* appears to prefer that both spouses in an infertile marriage have the opportunity to begin anew.

In some infertile marriages, wives wished to divorce after ten years and their husbands did not. In such cases, a man may already have had children by an earlier marriage, or by another wife, or may simply have been loathe to surrender the *ketubbah* payment.[21] The only option for a childless woman in this situation was to petition the rabbinic court to compel her husband to divorce her. B. Yevamot 65b records two such successful instances:

Such a case once came before R. Johanan at the synagogue of Caesarea, and he decided that the husband must divorce her and also pay her the amount of her *ketubbah*. Now, if it be suggested that a woman is not subject to the commandment, how could she have any claim to a *ketubbah*? It is possible that this was a case where she submitted a special plea; as was the case with a certain woman who once came to R. Ammi and asked him to order the payment of her *ketubbah*. When he replied, "Go away, the commandment does not apply to you," she exclaimed, "What shall become of a woman like myself in her old age?" "In such a case," the Master said, "we certainly compel [the husband to divorce her and pay her *ketubbah*]."

A woman once came [with a similar plea] before R. Nahman. When he told her, "The commandment does not apply to you," she replied, "Does not a woman like myself require a staff in her hand and a hoe for digging her grave!" "In such a case," the Master said, "we certainly compel [the husband]."

These requests are granted, not because women are obligated to have children (they are not), but because these particular pleas based on fears of an impoverished widowhood and old age without the support of offspring are persuasive to the court. Here is an instance of the ways a woman could occasionally overcome the inability of a wife to divorce her husband, one of the major disabilities women suffered in rabbinic law.

Preserving Marital Ties

The extent to which divorce resulted from infertile marriages is impossible to determine. However, in general, divorce is deplored in rabbinic aggadic writings, even in cases of childless marriages.[22] Many passages in the *aggadah* presented the infertile marriage as a situation where human needs and feelings overruled legal prescriptions. In the case of a childless but otherwise happy couple, where significant human suffering would result from a drastic change in the marital situation, there is an acceptance that the obligation of procreation is neither enforceable nor paramount.

Uneasiness with obligatory divorce as solution to childlessness, combined with a paean to feminine virtues, characterizes this comment from *Genesis Rabbah* 17:7: "There was once a pious man who was married to a pious woman, and they had no children. They said, [w]e are no profit to God. So they divorced one another. The man went and married a bad woman, and she made him bad; the woman went and married a bad man and she made him good. So all depends upon the woman." A number of stories related to the infertility of the biblical matriarchs, discussed below, also express ambivalence about the option of divorce and stress the efficacy of prayer and the necessity of faith in God who may open the womb at any time, even after decades of marriage.

As the following homiletical tale, found in *Pesiqta de-Rab Kahana* 22:2, teaches, barrenness is never more than a presumption, nor should one despair of an answer to sincere supplication:

A man is under the obligation to fulfil the commandment, **"Be fertile and increase"** (Gen. 1:28) but a woman is under no such obligation. . . . In Sidon it happened that a man took a wife with whom he lived for ten years and she bore him no children. When they came to R. Simeon ben Yohai to be divorced, the man said to his wife: "Take any precious object I have in my house—take it and go back to your father's house." Thereupon, R. Simeon ben Yohai said: "Even as you were wed with food and drink [being served], so you are not to separate save with food and drink [being served]." What did the wife do? She prepared a great feast, gave her husband too much to drink [so that he fell asleep], then beckoned to her menservants and maidservants saying, "Take him to my father's house." At midnight he woke up from his sleep and asked, "Where am I?" She replied, "Did you not say, 'Whatever precious object I have in my house—take it and go back to your father's house?' I have no object more precious than you." When Simeon ben Yohai heard what the wife had done, he prayed on the couple's behalf, and they were remembered with children. For, even as the Holy One remembers barren women, righteous men also have the power to remember barren women.[23]

This moving story is found in the homiletical midrash collection *Pesiqta de-Rab Kahana*, an anthology of polished and revised versions of sermons delivered to popular audiences by renowned preachers. What is most striking about this very vivid tale is its anti-nomian slant and its subversive tendencies. The husband is only trying to obey the law that he is obligated to fulfil, even though that means dissolving a happy union. His wife, who is not so obligated, is free to maneuver events behind the scenes to preserve her marriage. She does so by using deceptive stratagems that succeed in convincing those around her that she is in the right. A great rabbi prays for the woman and her husband who are now reunited and they are ultimately blessed with children. Hope is offered to all who hear or read this story that infertility is never a certainty, that intercession is possible through prayer, and that devoted human relationships have a meaning that transcends halakhic demands. Through its psychological and sentimental appeal, this story provides reassurance to men and women caught in a painful religious and ethical dilemma. It also features as its protagonist a clever and loving woman who is able to undermine the rigid regulations of the male-oriented halakhah, a scenario which must have resonated with many ordinary Jews who harbored varying degrees of resentment over rabbinic prerogatives.

Both *Pesiqta de-Rab Kahana* 22:2 and a version of this aggadic tale found in *Song of Songs Rabbah* 1:4 §2 end the story with a consolation text offering future comfort to all who depend on God. The following is the conclusion found in *Song of Songs Rabbah*:

And is not the lesson clear: If a woman on saying to a mere mortal like herself, "There is nothing I care for more in the world than you," was visited, does it not stand to reason that Israel who wait for the salvation of God every day and say "We care for nothing in the world but You," will certainly be visited? Hence it is written: **"Let us delight and rejoice in Your love"** (Song of Songs 1:4).

Just as a barren woman may find her faith in God justified by conceiving and giving birth, how much more will Israel ultimately be vindicated for keeping faith with the divine covenant? The biblical and rabbinic personification of Israel/Zion as an infertile woman, whose patient hopes will ultimately be fulfilled, is discussed below.

The Grief of Childlessness

Childlessness is regarded as a grave misfortune for both men and women. A man's suffering is implicit in his inability to fulfil the commandment of propagation and leave pious offspring behind. Male failure to generate offspring, moreover, not only violated a legal obligation but also raised questions about his very status as a man. If being created in the divine image implies the ability to generate new life, then the "barren" man does not qualify for fully adult male status since his virility is questionable. According to B. Pesahim 113b, the childless man is reckoned as if *m'nuddeh*, "cut off" from all communion with God, like one who has deliberately disregarded divine commands. B. Nedarim 64b, together with a number of other texts, accounts him, based on Rachel's plaint in Genesis 30:1, as already dead, together with the pauper, the leper, and the blind.[24] B. Sanhedrin 36b ordains that the childless scholar is not eligible to sit on the Sanhedrin.

The barren woman suffers too, for even if she has no religious obligation to fulfil, she has failed to fulfil the primary expectation of her societal role, and as *Genesis Rabbah* 71:5 remarks in the name of R. Ammi, it is children who assure a woman's position in her home. The importance of children in securing a woman's status, as well as the divine role in fertility, is also elucidated in *Genesis Rabbah* 71:1:

"The Lord saw that Leah was unloved and He opened her womb" (Gen. 29: 31). **"For the Lord listens to the needy, and does not spurn His captives"** (Ps. 69:34). . . . **"And does not spurn His captives"** alludes to childless women who are as prisoners in their houses, but as soon as the Holy One, blessed be He, visits them with children, they become erect [with pride]. The proof is that Leah was unloved in her house, yet when God visited her she became erect; hence it is written, **"The Lord saw that Leah was unloved and he opened her womb."**

In a similar vein, *Genesis Rabbah* 71:2 interprets Genesis 29:31 as follows:

"The Lord supports all who stumble" (Ps. 145:14): This refers to childless women who fall [i.e. are disgraced] in their own homes; **"And makes all who are bent stand straight"** (Ps. 145:14): As soon as God visits them with children, they are raised up. The proof is that Leah was unloved in her house, yet when the Holy One, blessed be He, visited her, she was able to stand straight.[25]

As these passages compassionately delineate, the barren wife doubtless felt great shame and endured reproach for disappointing her husband at home and in the eyes of the world. That the rabbis were aware of her pain is evident in their exegeses of the biblical passages in which such women appear. *Genesis Rabbah* 45:4 recounts that Hagar accused Sarah as follows: "My mistress Sarah is not inwardly what she is outwardly: she appears to be a righteous woman, but she is not. For had she been a righteous woman, see how many years have passed without her conceiving, whereas I conceived in one night." *Pesiqta Rabbati* 42: 5 alludes to the "governors and governors' wives" who for so long jeered at Sarah, calling her "barren woman," and the same text at 43:8 describes the way the childless Hannah was mocked by her rival Peninah:

Peninah would vex Hannah with one provocation after another. What would Peninah do? According to R. Nahman bar Abba, Peninah would get up early and say to Hannah: "Why don't you rouse yourself and wash your children's faces, so they are fit to go to their schoolmaster?" And at twelve o'clock, she would say: "Why don't you rouse yourself and welcome your children who are about to return from school?" Such is the provocation referred to in the words, **"Moreover, her rival, to make her miserable, would taunt her that the Lord had closed her womb"** (1 Sam. 1:6).

Similarly, referring to the derision and sarcasm suffered by the childless wife as a present reality, *Genesis Rabbah* 73:5 interprets, **"Now God remembered Rachel; God heeded her and opened her womb. She conceived and bore a son, and said, 'God has taken away my disgrace' "** (Gen. 30:22–23) as follows: "R. Levi b. Zechariah said: Before a woman has given birth, any misdeed is attributed to her. 'Who ate this thing— your son? Who broke this article—your son?' " As these derisive jibes indicate, the position of the infertile wife was unenviable.

"Why were the Matriarchs Barren?"

Like all suffering, the suffering occasioned by childlessness is inexplicable. Still, the rabbis sought explanations. Some rabbinic comments attribute infertility to retribution for some misdeed of the childless father. B. Yevamot 64b points out, in a discussion of the childlessness of Sarah and Abraham, that "since she is not commanded to fulfil the duty of propagation, she is not so punished," implying the fault was his. An *aggadah* in B. Sanhedrin 21a, however, does attribute Michal's childlessness to her despising David in her heart (2 Sam. 6:16), and it seems likely, as in some of the *aggadot* cited below, that in the popular imagination childlessness for women was often seen as a divine punishment. On the whole, however, rabbinic literature shows compassion for the childless and hesitates to explain the divine dispensation in a facile manner.

Rabbinic exegetes were, of course, profoundly aware of the theme of apparent infertility in a number of biblical narratives about the matriarchs of the Jewish people and the mothers of great leaders such as Samuel. A strong exegetical tradition, intended to console as well as to explain, addressed the question, "Why were the matriarchs barren?" The most meaningful responses to this question stressed the efficacy of prayer and the value of suffering which leads to purification and brings people closer to God, as in this passage from *Genesis Rabbah* 45:4:

Why were the matriarchs barren? R. Levi said in R. Shila's name and R. Helbo in R. Johanan's names: Because the Holy One, blessed be He, yearns for their prayers and supplications. Thus it is written, **"O my dove, in the cranny of the rocks, / Hidden by the cliff"** (Song of Songs 2:14): Why did I make thee barren? In order that, **"Let Me see your face, / Let me hear your voice"** (Song of Songs 2:14).

Similarly, B. Yevamot 64b preserved the following response to the query, "Why were our ancestors [both male and female] barren?—Because the Holy One, blessed be He, longs to hear the prayer of the righteous."

Other reasons for the infertility of the matriarchs are offered in the remainder of *Genesis Rabbah* 45:4:

R. Azariah said in R. Hanina's name: So that they might lean on their husbands despite their beauty. R. Huna and R. Jeremiah in the name of R. Hiyya b. Abba said: So that they might pass the greater parts of their life untrammelled. R. Huna, R. Idi, and R. Abin in R. Meir's name said: So that their husbands might derive pleasure from them, for when a woman is with child she is disfigured and lacks grace. Thus, the whole ninety years that Sarah did not bear she was like a bride in her canopy.

Two of the explanations recorded in this text consider childlessness in terms of the mothers of Israel themselves. The first suggests that infertility was meant to humble the matriarchs who are imagined here as great beauties. Given women's propensity for vanity and frivolity, they might have behaved contemptuously to their husbands without the pain of childlessness to depress their spirits and render them dependent. The second explanation, conversely, explains childlessness as a benefit which allows a woman considerable freedom, since she is not subject to the constant needs and demands of her offspring. The matriarchs were spared such inconveniences until unusually late in their lives. *Genesis Rabbah* 45:4 concludes by suggesting that the matriarchs were infertile so that their husbands could enjoy their wives' beauty unimpaired by the ravages of pregnancies and child bearing. No doubt some comfort is intended here, for as B. Yevamot 63b notes, "A beautiful wife is a joy to her husband; the number of his days shall be [as if] double." A parallel passage in *Song of Songs Rabbah* 2:14 §8 adds at this point, "As soon as Sarah conceived, her good looks faded," as it is said, **"In sadness [at the loss of beauty] you shall bring forth children"** (Gen. 3:16). Thus, infertility as a punishment and infertility as a reward are juxtaposed here.

All of these inadequate explanations, however, are trivial responses to childlessness, which was most often a source of anguish and affliction. They constitute a powerful declaration of the futility of all human efforts in explaining the mysteries of suffering.

More convincing are rabbinic explanations that connect fertility to the operation of divine providence and the unfolding covenantal narrative of the relationship between God and Israel. Biblical and rabbinic sources are convinced that conception is granted by the grace of God and this presumption informs a number of rabbinic passages about the ultimate success of the matriarchs in conceiving and bearing children. Thus, B. Ta'anit 2a–b quotes R. Johanan as follows:

Three keys the Holy One, blessed be He, has retained in His own hands and not entrusted to the hand of any messenger: these are the key of rain, the key of childbirth, and the key of the revival of the dead. . . . The key [*maphteah*] of childbirth, for it is written, **"Now God remembered Rachel; God heeded her and opened her womb"** (Gen. 30:22).

Similarly, *Genesis Rabbah* 45:2 explains, "And Sarai said to Abram, **'Look, the Lord has kept me from bearing'** " (Gen. 16:2) as follows: "Said she, I know the source of my affliction: It is not as people say [of a barren woman], 'she needs a talisman, she needs a charm,' but **'Look, the Lord has kept me from bearing.'** "

Sarai is said to reject the amulets and spells of popular religion,[26] because she knows that it is God who can open the womb whenever God wills it. The aggadic tradition attaches a number of seemingly miraculous elements to this conviction of divine intercession in human conception. Thus, B. Yevamot 64a-b relates that prayer reversed not only the infertility of Abraham and Sarah but prompted God to transform

their actual physical forms to make conception possible, because originally each was of doubtful sex (*tumtumin*). In the same passage, R.
Nahman is said to have stated, in the name of Rabbah b. Abbuha, that
prior to divine response to human entreaties: "Our mother Sarah was
incapable of procreation; for it is said, 'Now Sarai was barren, she had
no child' (Gen. 11:30); [this means] she had not even a womb."

Similar evocations of God's miraculous role in human conception are
evoked in a discussion in *Genesis Rabbah* 72:1 of an excerpt from Hannah's prayer following the birth of Samuel:

> "Men once sated must hire out for bread; / Men once hungry hunger no more.
> / While the barren woman bears seven, / The mother of many is forlorn" (1
> Sam. 2:5). "Men once sated must hire out for bread" applies to Leah, who was
> full with children, yet hired herself [with Reuven's mandrakes (Gen. 30:14)].
> "Men once hungry hunger no more" applies to Rachel, who though hungry for
> children, yet ceased [when she ultimately gave birth]. "While the barren woman
> bears seven" applies to Leah, who was barren, having no womb [and yet] bore
> seven. "The mother of many is forlorn" applies to Rachel, from whom it was
> natural [as the beloved wife] that most of the children should be born, yet she
> anguished. And who caused this? "The Lord deals death and gives life, / Casts
> down into Sheol and raises up" (1 Sam. 2:6).

In this passage, God's primary role in fertility is again emphasized. Men
are like God in their ability to generate new life, but the similarity has
its limits. Men may plant their seed, but only God can open the womb
and God does so according to a divine calculus beyond human understanding. The only way in which humans can play a role in the process
is through prayer.

Eliyyahu Rabbah 18 combines these linked themes of the efficacy of
human prayer and the divine power to enable conception in a passage
devoted to childless biblical couples whose supplications were answered:

> One time as I was travelling from one place to another, an old man accosted
> me and asked: "My master, why is the joy of having children withheld from
> some householders in Israel?" I replied, "Because, my son, the Holy One who
> loves them with an utter love and rejoices in them, purifies them [through suf-
> fering] and brings them to entreat Him urgently for mercy." The old man said,
> "No. The answer is that they have only the satisfaction of lust in their hearts,
> and so God renders the women they wed incapable of bearing children." I re-
> plied, "[Not so], my son. The fact is that we have many householders who drive
> asses for a living [and being long absent from home have only infrequent inter-
> course with their wives]. Men such as these are not likely to have children,
> particularly if they have only one wife. [Hence they urgently entreat God to have
> pity on them and bless them with children. And God answers their prayers] as
> you can see for yourself when you consider our father Abraham [and our mother
> Sarah], who having been childless for seventy-five years, urgently entreated God
> for compassion, whereupon Isaac came, and they rejoiced in him.

Consider Rebecca, who, having been childless for twenty years, urgently entreated God for compassion, whereupon Jacob came, and she and Isaac rejoiced in him. Consider Rachel, who, having been childless for fourteen years before she had either of her children, urgently entreated God for compassion, whereupon both her children came, and she and Jacob rejoiced in them. Consider Hannah, who, having been childless for nineteen years and six months, urgently entreated God for compassion, whereupon her son Samuel came and she rejoiced in him. You have no choice therefore but to accept the reply which I gave you immediately at the beginning of our conversation, namely: Because the Holy One loves householders in Israel with an utter love and rejoices in them, He purifies them [through suffering] in order that they should urgently entreat Him for compassion."[27]

The reiteration in this text of the duration of each woman's childlessness, which lasted in all instances far more than ten years, may certainly be read as a discouragement of the available remedy of divorce in favor of trust in prayer to those in similar situations. Indeed, the primary significance of this text is that in each case of childlessness it cites, the woman—sometimes alone, sometimes with her husband—"entreats God for compassion" and her prayers are answered. These examples of efficacious female prayers must have carried a very powerful message of affirmation for the ordinary Jewish woman, who was generally removed from normative male patterns of worship by custom and lack of education.

Such models of successful supplication, in fact, were extremely important, since rabbinic literature does not perceive women as performing the duty of worship in the same way as men. According to B. Berakhot 20a–20b, women are exempt from participation in prayers which must be recited at specific times. However, that passage teaches that women are not therefore released from the obligation to pray, "because it is an appeal for mercy" which is essential to all. Rather, as Rachel Biale has pointed out, women were believed to fulfil their scriptural duty of prayer by making a personal address to God as they started their day.[28] This distinction between men's prayer, which was undertaken in codified formulas and scheduled at certain times, and women's prayer, which was private and individual in content and time, accords with the general pattern of separation of male and female roles and functions characteristic of rabbinic Judaism. As Biale writes:

Certainly, women at times participated in the set prayers, but this was a matter of personal choice and not a requirement. The private prayer of women did not remain totally individual either. Special prayers for women, or *tehinnot*, were composed for special occasions such as births and weddings. Yet women's prayers remained essentially private, personal, and spontaneous supplication.[29]

According to B. Berakhot 31a, it is a woman, Hannah (1 Sam. 2) whose entreaty to God became a model of supplicative prayer for both women and men.[30]

The Seven Barren Wives

The childless matriarchs were exemplars of the efficacy of prayer and they also became important metaphors for consolation and comfort.[31] Over time, rabbinic enumerations of infertile biblical women whose prayers were answered evolved. Based on an alternate reading of Hannah's invocation to God in 1 Samuel 2:5, "**While the barren woman bears seven**," as "**On seven occasions has the barren woman borne**," these women are said to include Sarah, Rebecca, Leah, Rachel, the wife of Manoah (Samson's mother), and Hannah. The seventh is not an individual who lived in the past but is the personified Israel of some future time, based on Second Isaiah's characterization of Zion as a barren woman: "**Shout, O barren one, / You who bore no child! / Shout aloud for joy, / You who did not travail! / For the children of the wife forlorn / Shall outnumber those of the espoused / —said the Lord**" (Isaiah 54: 1).[32]

A typical example of such an enumeration appears in the homiletical midrash collection *Pesiqta de-Rab Kahana* 20:1. The first section of a sermon based on Isaiah 54:1, "**Shout O barren one**," begins:

"He sets the childless woman (*'akarah*) among her household / As a happy mother of children (*banim*)" (Psalm 113:9). There were seven such barren women: Sarah, Rebecca, Rachel, Leah, Manoah's wife, Hannah, and Zion. Hence the words "He sets the childless woman (*'akarah*) among her household" apply to Sarah [since we read "Now Sarai was barren ('akarah)" (Gen. 11:30), but the words "As a happy mother of children (*banim*) also apply to our mother Sarah: "Sarah suckled children (*banim*)"(Gen. 21:7).

The passage continues with the remaining five biblical barren wives; in each instance biblical proof texts demonstrate both her initial infertile status as an *'akarah* and her ultimate triumph as a mother of children (*banim*).

Pesiqta de-Rab Kahana 20:1 ends with references to the future of Zion:

Finally, the words, "He sets the childless woman among her household" apply to Zion [of whom it is said]: "Shout, O barren one, / You who bore no child!" (Isaiah 54:1); so [too] do the words "As a happy mother of children" [as it says] in, "And you will say to yourself, / 'Who bore me these for me / When I was bereaved and barren, / Exiled and disdained' " (Isaiah 49:21).

In this conclusion and similar homilies, the repeated fulfillment of the prayers of the childless become prophetic consolation texts, pointing to the ultimate restoration and flowering of the nation and Land of Israel.

Special insights into rabbinic views on childlessness can also be derived from the midrashic traditions about each barren biblical couple, as examples from traditions concerning Abraham and Sarah will demonstrate here. One popular theme is the vindication achieved in giving birth after many years of infertility. *Genesis Rabbah* 53:8 proclaims that when Sarah was remembered, numerous barren women were remembered with her. Then, too, many deaf gained their hearing, many blind had their eyes opened, and many who were insane became sane. Moreover, she even increased the light of the sun and the moon. *Genesis Rabbah* 53:9 goes on to describe how all doubters were put to naught, based on: **"And [Sarah] added, Who would have said to Abraham / That Sarah would suckle children! / Yet I have borne a son in his old age"** (Gen. 21:7). This midrash also explains why the biblical verse refers to Sarah suckling "children" since she bore only one son:

Our mother Sarah was extremely modest. Said Abraham to her: "This is not a time for modesty, but uncover your breasts so that all may know that the Holy One, blessed be He, has begun to perform miracles." She uncovered her breasts and the milk gushed forth as from two fountains, and noble ladies [of the nations of the world] came and had their children suckled by her, saying, "We do not merit that our children should be suckled with the milk of that righteous woman." The rabbis said: Whoever came for the sake of heaven became God-fearing. R. Aha said: Even one who did not come for the sake of heaven [but simply to see whether the miracle was true] was given dominion in this world. Yet they did not continue to enjoy it, for when they stood aloof at Sinai and would not accept the Torah, that dominion was taken from them. Thus it is written, **"He undoes the belts of kings, / And fastens loincloths on them"** (Job 12:18).

Nor was the victory purely feminine, for *Genesis Rabbah* 53:10 describes Abraham's feast for Isaac's weaning as follows:

"The child grew up and was weaned, and Abraham held a great feast on the day that Isaac was weaned" (Gen. 21:8). R. Judah said **"A great feast"** (Gen. 21:8) means a feast for great people, for Og and all the great men were there. Said they to Og, "Did you not say that Abraham is like a barren mule and cannot beget child?" "Even now what is [the value of] his gift," replied he; "Is [Isaac] not puny? I can crush him by putting my finger on him." Said the Holy One blessed be He, to him: "What do you mean by disparaging my gift! By your life, you will yet see countless thousands and myriads of his descendants, and your own fate will be to fall into their hands."

A version of this midrash also appears in B. Bava Metzi'a 87a:

"And [Sarah] added, Who would have said to Abraham / That Sarah would suckle children! / Yet I have borne a son in his old age" (Gen. 21:7). How many children then did Sarah suckle? R. Levi said: On the day that Abraham weaned his son Isaac, he made a great banquet, and all the peoples of the world derided him, saying, "Have you seen that old man and woman, who brought a foundling from the street, and now claim him as their son! And what is more, they make a great banquet to establish their claim!" What did our father Abraham do? He went and invited all the great men of the age, and mother Sarah invited their wives. Each brought her child with her, but not the wet-nurse, and a miracle happened to our mother Sarah, her breasts opened like two fountains, and she suckled them all. Yet they still scoffed, saying, "Granted that Sarah could give birth at the age of ninety, could Abraham beget at the age of a hundred?" Immediately the lineaments of Isaac's face changed and became like Abraham's, whereupon they all cried out, "**Abraham begot Isaac**" (Gen. 25:19).

The triumph resonating in these traditions over the achievement of fruitfulness, facilitated by God's miraculous opening of Sarah's womb, reveals again the shame that attached to childlessness for both men and women in rabbinic society. These midrashim also offer the consoling promise that just as Sarah and Abraham endured years of faithful prayer and suffering before they ultimately triumphed, Israel too will advance from present anguish to future exultation in the ultimate unfolding of the divine plan.

Alternate Forms of Generation

It was men who were commanded to procreate and, despite their compassionate treatment of female infertility, the rabbis were primarily concerned with men. In a discussion of the rules of inheritance to be followed when a man dies without any sons in B. Bava Batra 116a, the following statement appears:

R. Johanan said in the name of R. Simeon b. Yohai: The Holy One, blessed be He, is filled with anger against any one who does not leave a son as his heir. For here it is written, "**Further, speak to the Israelite people as follows, 'If a man dies without leaving a son, you shall transfer [veha'avartem] his property to his daughter' **" (Numbers 27:8), and there it is written, "**That day shall be a day of wrath ['ervah]**" (Zephaniah 1:15).

The connection of these two verses is no more than linguistic, since words formed from the same three letter root, 'avr, appear in both, but the sentiment justified by their juxtaposition is extremely disturbing and is debated in the passage that immediately follows:

"**God who has reigned from the first, will hear and humble those who have no successors and fear not God**" (Psalm 55:20).[33] R. Johanan and R. Joshua b. Levi [are in dispute over the meaning of this text]. One says [it refers to] whomever does not leave behind a son. And the other says that [it refers to] whomever does not leave behind a disciple.

In the end, the sages determine that both R. Johanan and R. Joshua b. Levi are in agreement that leaving behind a disciple is the equivalent of leaving behind a son. Similarly, B. Sanhedrin 19b declares: "He who teaches the son of his neighbor the Torah, Scripture ascribes it to him as if he had begotten him."[34] In an appropriate homiletical twist for a society which often valued dedication to scholarship over family obligations, texts such as these resolved issues of male childlessness by constructing students as offspring. Thus, the student fills the place of the natural child, allowing the childless scholar, too, to become a father in Israel.

As Howard Eilberg-Schwartz has pointed out, however, such traditions, which privilege study and the transmission of learning as a form of generation, may also redefine reproduction away from biological fatherhood altogether and project it entirely onto the educational relationship. As students take the place of sons, the need for women disappears altogether. Thus, rabbinic literature preserves the opinion that insemination of Torah knowledge and the production of disciples takes precedence even over the legal obligation to beget biological offspring. In this rabbinic model of cultural generativity, women could become very much dispensable, since they represented "the very antithesis of Torah and Torah study."[35] Eilberg-Schwartz suggests that as the rabbis redefined "barrenness" metaphorically as "a lack of knowledge," they created "a form of reproduction that could dispense with the flesh," writing: "As this substitution took place, the concern with the lineage of male descendants was displaced by a preoccupation with the reproduction and genealogy of knowledge."[36]

Conclusion

Infertility was not an affliction exclusive to women in rabbinic society. Childless men, who were profoundly aware of having failed to fulfill a religious obligation, suffered too. Still, the models of the barren matriarchs, and the accounts of divine responsiveness to their individual prayers must have had singular and empowering resonances for women, whose participation in prayer, at least in public, was neither facilitated by education nor sanctioned by communal norms. The gleefulness with which the vindication of such suffering wives as Sarah is recounted seems proof of a popular female piety that cherished the recollection of biblical women who could communicate so effectively with God.[37] Accounts of the matriarchs' answered prayers and redemption from abasement, as well as their frequent linkage to the happy and fecund future of Zion, must have provided spiritual sustenance to women in a society that limited their access to most avenues of religious affirmation. As chapter 6 will suggest, it may have been together with other women that such infertile wives found support, consolation, and hope.

❦ 6 ❧

"A SEPARATE PEOPLE":
RABBINIC DELINEATIONS OF
THE WORLDS OF WOMEN

The rabbinic sages believed that Jewish society functioned best when its female members remained in the domestic domain under the aegis of male authority. Unaccompanied women who ventured beyond the home risked accusations of immodesty and licentiousness. Rabbinic writings expressed particular uneasiness about women who gathered together in the communal sphere. However, anxieties about female activities were not limited to the public realm. The polygynous and hierarchical nature of rabbinic society meant that female relatives, co-wives, and maidservants occupied a domestic world of women to which men had limited access. Given this consciousness of female propinquity, there was always a rabbinic assumption that women's first loyalties were to each other and that such allegiances might lead them to dupe and deceive men.[1] On the other hand, the biblical record was clear that women, together and as individuals, could be models of exemplary piety and personal transformation. Through an analysis of aggadic traditions focusing on women, this final chapter explores the gender politics implicit in rabbinic renderings of a variety of perceived female behaviors. Central themes involve women's supposed propensity for witchcraft, the fraught relationships of sisters and co-wives, and the ambiguous signification of the foreign woman.

Women among Women: The Polemic against Witches

The rabbis were suspicious of women in groups. If one woman constituted a source of uneasiness, to be avoided in public places and to be strictly fenced off from participation in communal life, then female associations of any kind were especially problematic. Rabbinic legislation and social policy attempted to preclude women from gathering together by exempting them from time-bound ritual obligations, such as synagogue attendance, and from any role in community governance. Judith Romney Wegner has suggested that the conclusion of M. Pesahim 8:7, "Nor may a company be made up of women, slaves, and minors," can be read as prohibiting women from forming fellowship groups (*havurot*), thus ruling out female involvement in Torah study, the most highly esteemed activity of rabbinic culture.[2] Often the *aggadah* associated women who congregated in the public domain with lewd gossip. M. Sotah 6:1, for example, alludes to women who gathered together to spin by moonlight and discuss infidelities that had become public knowledge.

Women in groups were also accused of being witches. While the rabbis took for granted that both men and women had the potential to manipulate the powerful forces operative in the cosmos by reciting efficacious spells, it was assumed that only a few men dabbled in such activities. When individual rabbis did resort to such invocations, their "magic" was generally seen to be for praiseworthy purposes. Women accused of engaging in sorcery, on the other hand, were always suspected of nefarious motives.[3] Moreover, the rabbis connected women's supposed predilection for conjuration with the sexual unreliability and untrustworthiness they also projected onto females in general.

B. Sanhedrin 67a preserves a comment on "You shall not tolerate a sorceress" (Ex. 22:17), to the effect that "most women are involved in witchcraft," while B. 'Eruvin 64b notes in passing that present generations of the daughters of Israel indulge freely in witchcraft. B. Pesahim 111a, in a long discussion of the dangers of pairs of objects or people, warns both of the hazards occasioned by a menstruating woman passing between two men, and of the jeopardy to men passing between two women:

When two women sit at a crossroad, one on one side of the road, and one on the other side of the road, facing each other, they are certainly engaged in witchcraft. What is the remedy [for the male traveller]? If there is another road, let him go through it. If there is no other road and if another man is with him, let them clasp hands and pass through, while if there is no other man, let him say thus: "*Igrat Izlat, Asya, Belusia* [the demons by whose aid you work your witchcraft] have been slain by arrows."

The story in B. Gittin 45a about the two daughters of R. Nahman, discussed in chapter 1, is similar. Here, three converging sources of anxiety—women beyond the boundaries of rabbinic control, assumed female sexual licentiousness, and the dangers of privies—are invoked to claim that these women were witches.[4] Several other rabbinic passages also link sorceresses and human waste, and offer formulas to use against them, as in this passage from B. Pesahim 110a:

Amemar said: The chief of the women who practice sorcery told me: He who meets a female who practices witchcraft should say thus: "Hot dung in perforated baskets for your mouths, O you females who practice sorcery! May your heads become bald! The wind carry off your crumbs, your spices be scattered, the wind carry off the new saffron you are holding, you sorceresses; as long as He showed grace to me and to you, I have not come among [you]; now that I have come among you, your grace and my grace are no longer effective.[5]

Eliezer Berkowits has written that rabbinic anxieties about women and witchcraft should be understood as concern about women exercising powers beyond their appropriate boundaries, generally understood to be confined to the domestic domain.[6] Simcha Fishbane agrees that much of the disquiet expressed in aggadic accounts of female sorcery alludes to groups of women functioning beyond the sphere of the home.[7] Such vehement rabbinic opposition may not only reflect concerns about witchcraft but also fears that Jewish women were involved in pagan practices.[8] Unfortunately, the evidence for women's actual ritual activity is scanty at best. What is apparent in the rabbinic discourse connecting women with sorcery is severe anxiety about the collective potential for disorder that women might create by spending time together beyond the reach of male authority, whether at home or abroad.

These themes converge in M. Avot 2:7, where the following statement is attributed to the first century C.E. sage Hillel:

The more flesh, the more worms, the more possessions, the more anxiety; the more wives, the more witchcraft; and the more bondwomen the more lewdness; the more bondmen the more thieving; the more study of the Law the more life; the more schooling the more wisdom; the more counsel the more understanding; the more righteousness the more peace. If a man has gained a good name he has gained [something] for himself; if he has gained for himself words of the Law he has gained for himself life in the world to come.

In this succinct summary of human possibilities, women who are both free and enslaved are consigned to involvement in sorcery and sexual license, while male slaves are assumed to be dishonest. Only free Jewish men are allowed the potential to achieve meaningful lives, both in this world and the world to come, through their options to choose to function in the communal worlds of worship, study, and leadership. Women, like slaves, had limited alternatives and undesirable choices.

A Counter-Discourse: The Daughters of Zelophehad

The rabbis did not deprecate all female solidarity. A striking counter-example to the assumption that women acting autonomously constitute

danger is found in the very positive portrayals of the daughters of Zelophehad, the biblical sisters of Numbers 27:1–7, who successfully argued that they should inherit from their father, who had died without
male heirs. According to *Sifre Numbers* 133:

> When the daughters of Zelophehad heard that the Land of Israel was being
> apportioned among the males of the tribes but not the females, they consulted
> together as to how to make their claim. They said: The compassion of God is
> not like human compassion. Human rulers favor males over females but the one
> who spoke and brought the world into being is not like that. Rather, God shows
> mercy to every living thing, as scripture says, "**Who gives food to all flesh /
> Whose steadfast love is eternal**" (Ps. 136:24), and "**The sovereign is good to all
> / God's mercy is upon all God's works**" (Ps. 145:9).

In this midrash, the daughter of Zelophehad are represented as canny
and competent women who trusted that divine mercy would transcend
the mutable norms of a human society in which women were subordinate beings. According to the rabbinic sages, these admirable sisters epitomized the females of the wilderness generation who consistently out-
shone their male contemporaries in their faith in God and in their
personal courage. *Numbers Rabbah* 21:10 relates that women of this
era refused to participate in making the golden calf; they also rejected
the disheartening counsel of the spies who warned of the dangers of
invading Canaan. Similarly, the daughters of Zelophehad are said to
have demonstrated their complete confidence in the ultimate fulfillment
of the divine promise when they petitioned Moses to secure their inheritance in the Land of Israel. They constitute a counter-discourse based
in the biblical text that calls into question the general rabbinic distrust
of independent female behavior.

B. Bava Batra 119b praises the daughters of Zelophehad as intelligent
women, since they spoke at an opportune moment. They are also lauded
as scriptural exegetes knowledgeable in Jewish law, since they were
aware of the legal issues involved in their situation; and as sexually
chaste, since they did not marry until their inheritance status was resolved, despite their advanced ages. The rabbis awarded the daughters
of Zelophehad this exalted rank among biblical women because they
prompted Moses to seek divine help in clarifying the laws of succession
of property. The fact that God supported the sisters' claim did not hurt
their standing. According to *Numbers Rabbah* 21:11, by prompting the
expansion of the Torah they earned merit for themselves and their forebears who are listed in Numbers 27:1, including Joseph, the founder of
their tribe. So pious and self-sacrificing were these women that they are
said to have humbled Moses himself.

The actions of the daughters of Zelophehad were approved because they were condoned by the Torah itself. Moreover, their rebellion was limited and they ultimately acceded to male authority when their original point was gained: Their father's inheritance would be preserved only if the daughters agreed to marry men of their own tribe (Num. 36:1–12). Still, these sisters, whose control of male knowledge allowed them to shape their own destinies, at least up to a point, epitomize an untainted instance of female empowerment in rabbinic literature.

Women among Women: Sisters and Co-wives

The connection between polygyny and traffic in the supernatural in M. Avot 2:7, "The more wives, the more witchcraft," is another indication of the dangers the rabbis associated with women in groups. Meir Bar-Ilan has proposed that this statement may allude specifically to a senior wife using spells to prevent her rival from conceiving or appearing attractive to their shared husband.[9] However, these words, which imply that by acceding to his sexual desires and bringing more than one woman into his home, a man risked creating a coven of witches on his own hearth, may also be read as an endorsement of monogamy. Certainly, both biblical and midrashic traditions portray polygynous marriages as contentious and unpleasant for all involved. Even more fraught was the situation, depicted several times in biblical texts and discussed in chapter 5, where one co-wife was fertile and the other was not.

The most extended biblical example of the co-wife motif is found in the matriarchal narratives about Leah and Rachel, the two sisters whom the patriarch Jacob married in Haran (Gen. 29–30.) In this instance the rivalry was heightened because of the sibling relationship between the co-spouses. Moreover, Leah, the unloved and unattractive wife,[10] was fertile, while Rachel, her beautiful and beloved sister, was apparently barren. In fact, it is hard to decide which wife was more miserable—the slighted but fecund Leah, whom her husband was tricked into marrying, or the childless but cherished Rachel.

Rabbinic interpretations of the Leah and Rachel saga tend to reinforce biblical themes and attitudes, particularly in terms of the importance of female fertility.[11] *Genesis Rabbah* 71, for example, preserves several traditions to the effect that it is children who secure a woman's position in her home.[12] Thus, it is striking that aggadic traditions about Rachel and Leah go against the biblical record in stressing the sisters' loyalty to each other, even when competition for one man's affection was central. A frequently repeated tradition relates that Rachel was aware of the likelihood that Laban would deceive Jacob by substituting Leah for herself on the wedding night and warned Jacob of this probability. Thus, Jacob gave Rachel certain tokens so that he would be sure of her identity, even in a dark tent. However, as both B. Megillah 13b and B. Bava Batra 123a relate:

> When night came, she said to herself, Now my sister will be put to shame. So she handed over the tokens to her. So it is written, **"When morning came, there was Leah!"** (Gen. 29:2). Are we to infer from this that up to now she was not Leah? What it means is that on account of the tokens which Rachel gave up to Leah he did not know until then.

This description of Rachel's sisterly consideration for Leah arises out of the textual difficulty of explaining why Jacob did not realize the identity of his new wife until the morning. One must ask whether this midrash depicting Rachel's generosity in preserving her sister from humiliation is a tribute to the possibilities of admirable female behavior and self-sacrifice or a warning to men about the ultimate unreliability of women.

Similar rabbinic traditions praising Rachel for her kindness to her sister reappear in interpretations of **"Now God remembered Rachel"** (Gen. 30:22), the preamble to the birth of Joseph. *Genesis Rabbah* 73: 4 asks, "What did He remember in her favor?" and answers, "Her silence on her sister's behalf. When Leah was being given to him, she knew it, yet was silent." A second tradition in the same place explains that it was because she had brought her rival into her home that God remembered Rachel with a child. This probable reference to the handmaid Bilhah praises Rachel who was willing to risk her own domestic tranquillity in the larger good of providing children for her husband.

Nor did the rabbis doubt the painfulness of Rachel's nobility. Rabbinic perceptions of the depth of Rachel's struggle emerge in the discussion of Rachel's triumphant cry when Bilhah gives birth to a second son, Naphtali: **"A fateful contest I waged with my sister; yes, and I have prevailed"** (Gen. 30:8). *Genesis Rabbah* 71:8 remarks:

> I had perfumed [my couch in preparation of my marriage] but I allowed myself to be persuaded, I exalted my sister above me. R. Johanan interpreted it: "I should have been a bride before my sister. Now had I sent a warning to him, 'Beware, you are being deceived!' would he not have refrained? But I thought, if I am not worthy that the world should be built up through me, let it be built up through my sister."

As these traditions indicate, rabbinic tradition maintains an essentially positive view of Rachel, despite the biblical evidence that she was bitterly jealous of her fecund sister. Even this is turned in Rachel's favor, as *Genesis Rabbah* 71:6 explains that Rachel envied the extent of Leah's good deeds, reasoning, "Were she not righteous, would she have borne children?" *Lamentations Rabbah* Proem 24 also praises Rachel highly.

Leah, on the other hand, does not fare so well. *Genesis Rabbah* 70: 19 presents Leah as complicit and as unrepentant in the deception of Jacob:

In the evening they came to lead her [into the bridal chamber] and extinguished the light. "What is the meaning of this?" he demanded, and they replied: "Do you think we are shameless, like you?" The whole of that night he called her "Rachel," and she answered him. In the morning, however, "**There was Leah**" (Gen. 30:25). He said to her: "What, you are a deceiver and the daughter of a deceiver!" She responded, "Is there a teacher without pupils, and didn't your father call you 'Esau,' and you answered him! So too did you call me [by some-one else's name] and I answered you!"

In this passage, Leah is depicted as a clever woman, well able to hold her own against Jacob's criticism. Accused of trickery to secure her own position in a desirable marriage, she returns fire by citing Jacob's decep-tion of his father to gain the advantage of the birthright. While this anecdote illustrates the larger rabbinic principle that all deeds are repaid in kind, it also reflects a rabbinic appreciation that women had to stra-tegize for their own survival within the narrow confines of the marriage bargain.

The apparent willing effrontery and duplicity that characterized Leah's maneuvers made her a figure of suspicion and opprobrium in aggadic traditions, reinforcing the biblical evidence that she was the dis-dained wife. In its interpretation of "**The Lord saw that Leah was un-loved**" (Gen. 29:31), *Genesis Rabbah* 71:2 relates:

All hated her: sea-travellers abused her, land-travellers abused her, and even the women behind the beams abused her, saying: "This Leah leads a double life: she pretends to be righteous, yet is not so, for if she were righteous, would she have deceived her sister?" R. Judah b. R. Simon and R. Hanan said in the name of R. Samuel b. R. Isaac: When the Patriarch Jacob saw how Leah deceived him by pretending to be her sister, he determined to divorce. But as soon as the Holy One, blessed be He, visited her with children, he exclaimed, "Shall I divorce the mother of these children!" Eventually he gave thanks for her, as it says, "**Then Israel bowed at the head of the bed**" (Gen. 47:31). Who was the head of our father Jacob's bed? Surely Leah.

Here, the rabbinic emphasis on the legal obligation to procreate, dis-cussed in chapters 4 and 5, again comes to the fore. At some level, Leah's character was irrelevant. As long as she bore her husband's children and saved him from sin, Jacob tolerated her as his wife. Ironically, the mid-rash goes on to teach that, perhaps like many reluctant husbands, he ultimately came to appreciate and depend upon her.

Another negative view of Leah was connected to the birth of her daughter Dinah. B. Berakhot 60a preserves the following discussion of a portion of M. Berakhot 9:3: "If a man cried out over what is past, his prayer is vain. Thus, if his wife is pregnant and he says, 'May [God] grant that my wife bear a male child,' this is a vain prayer." In objection to this opinion, the text "**Last, she bore him a daughter, and named her Dinah**" (Gen. 30:21) is cited:

What is meant by "**last**"? Rab said: [This happened] after Leah had passed judgement on herself, saying, "Twelve tribes are destined to issue from Jacob. Six have issued from me and four from the handmaids, making ten. If this child will be a male, my sister Rachel will not be equal to one of the handmaids." Forthwith the child [who was initially male] was turned into a girl, as it says, "**And named her Dinah**" [which means "judgment"].[13]

In other words, Dinah's gender may be construed as a punishment imposed on Leah for her desire to further humble the sister who had acted so generously towards her. Had Leah restrained her envy, her child would have been the eleventh predestined son.

A less punitive interpretation of how Dinah came to be a female is found in *Genesis Rabbah* 72:6, also commenting on "**Last, she bore him a daughter**" (Gen. 30:21):

R. Abba replied: Actually she was created a male, but she was turned into a female through Rachel's prayers when she said, "**May the Lord add another son for me**" (Gen. 30:24). Said R. Hanina b. Pazzi: The matriarchs were prophetesses [who knew that Jacob was destined to have twelve sons], and Rachel was one of the matriarchs. It is not written, "The Lord add other sons to me" but "another son"; she said: "He is yet destined to beget one more; may it be from me!" R. Hanina said: All the matriarchs [Jacob's wives and concubines] assembled and prayed: "We have sufficient males; let her [Rachel] be remembered."

This alternative tradition, which puts Rachel at the center, again speaks to the possibility of female solidarity and compassion. Just as Rachel guarded her sister from humiliation, so Leah, Bilhah, and Zilpah were willing to pray that she be granted a second son. This midrash is also a strong endorsement of the efficacy of female prayers

Still, disquiet about women and their underhanded ways remained. Just as the rabbis were uncomfortable about Leah's apparent willingness to deceive Jacob and betray her sister, so they were distressed by the mandrake episode in which Rachel traded away her husband's attentions in what appeared to be a casual way. *Genesis Rabbah* 72:3 castigated Rachel for treating Jacob's devotion so casually, and explained that it was for this reason that Rachel was not buried with her husband:

R. Simeon taught: Because she [Rachel] slighted that righteous man [Jacob], she was not buried together with him. Thus it says, "**I promise, he shall lie with you tonight, in return for your son's mandrakes**" (Gen. 30:15), with the meaning: With you he will lie in death, but not with me.

For the rabbis, Rachel's arrogant assumption that she could determine Jacob's sexual partners for him provided a ready explanation for her otherwise inexplicable early death and burial on the road to Bethlehem.

According to *Genesis Rabbah* 80:1, Leah, too, revealed her true colors in the transaction over the mandrakes. Aggadic tradition declares that she acted like a harlot when she went to meet Jacob on his return from the fields and baldly declared **"You are to sleep with me, for I have hired you with my son's mandrakes"**(Gen. 30:16).[14] Some statements suggest that Dinah's questionable behavior in going out to visit the daughters of Canaan in Genesis 34, which resulted in her ruin, was predictable from the behavior of her mother. Commenting on the proverb "As the mother, so the daughter," *Genesis Rabbah* 80:1 preserves the following interpretation:

"A cow does not gore unless her calf kicks; a woman is not immoral until her daughter is immoral" [said Kahana]. . . . "If so," said [Resh Lakish] "then our mother Leah was a harlot!" [since we find her daughter Dinah acting immorally]. "Even so," he replied, "because it says, '**Leah went out to meet him**' (Gen. 30:16), which means that she went out to meet him adorned like a harlot; therefore [we find] **"And Dinah, the daughter whom Leah had borne to Jacob, went out"** (Gen 34:1).

The disquiet expressed here about the temerity of both Leah and Dinah is a recurrent theme in rabbinic discourses on women. As previous chapters of this book have shown, any actions by women that might be construed as sexually aggressive or even as immodest are seen as dangerous to a social policy committed to building and maintaining fences against sexual temptation.[15] Unloved by the patriarch Jacob whom she has both deceived and whose sexual attentions she has purchased, Leah is imagined by rabbinic exegetes as brazen and deservedly spurned. The cherished and appealing Rachel, too, is punished for her arrogance in interfering in her husband's sex life, even in the cause of her own fertility.

The deeper meaning of Rachel's and Leah's relationship remains ambiguous to its rabbinic interpreters. As *Genesis Rabbah* 72:1 relates in a meditation on the prayer of Hannah (1 Sam. 2:5–6):

"**Men once sated must hire out for bread**" applies to Leah, who was full of children yet hired herself [in order to beget more]. "**Men once hungry hunger no more**" applies to Rachel, who though hungry for children ceased [giving up her right in favor of Leah]. "**While the barren woman bears seven**" refers to Leah, who [according to midrashic tradition] was barren, having no womb, yet bore seven; "**The mother of many is forlorn**" refers to Rachel, from whom it was natural [given her husband's preference for her] that most of the children should be born, yet she languished. And who caused this? "**The Lord deals death and gives life. Casts down into Sheol and raises up**"(1 Sam. 2:6).

However mysterious the ways of women may be, this midrash affirms that the actions of God are even more so.

Women among Women: Mistress and Foreign Servant

The declaration in M. Avot 2:7, "The more maidservants, the more lewdness," indicates that the relationship between mistress and maidservant, particularly when that maidservant became a sexual partner of the master of the house, was a well known source of domestic stress in both biblical and rabbinic times. The most striking biblical example of such a situation is the story of Sarah and Hagar, where the jealousy of the mistress for her fertile servant is played out against the tensions of Sarah and Abraham's childless marriage that appeared to undermine divine promises of posterity (Gen. 16–21). Here, as elsewhere in biblical narratives, questionable human actions, driven by the most elemental emotions, are presented as fulfilments of a larger predetermined plan.

A significant enigma in the story is why Hagar's pregnancy was so upsetting to Sarai.[16] In a similar situation, the barren Rachel gave her maidservant Bilhah to her husband Jacob, ordering him, "**Consort with her, that she may bear on my knees and that through her I too may have children**" (Gen. 30:6). When Bilhah gave birth, Rachel exulted, "**God has vindicated me; indeed He has heeded my plea and given me a son**" (Gen. 30:7). In that story, Bilhah, who came from the household of Rachel's father, Laban, remained a cipher; she was simply an instrument through whom the desire of her mistress was fulfilled. Why was this not the case with Sarai and Hagar?

One answer may lie in Hagar's ethnic status as an Egyptian. From the perspective of the biblical authors, Israel, at the very moment of its birth as a nation, appeared to be threatened with admixture from an outside source. Sarah is considered to have demonstrated a lack of faith by introducing Hagar into the divine plan for Abram and Sarai and their descendants. Following the long-awaited birth of Isaac, Sarah's natural antipathy to her husband's scornful concubine and the irritation occasioned by the concubine's son take on a larger significance. In protecting her son's inheritance, Sarah is acting to fulfil the divine plan that Isaac, not Ishmael, will carry on the everlasting covenant that God has established with Abraham. The authors of these particular texts are also making some important comments about the importance for Israel of marrying within the group, since the themes of overriding importance for the biblical editors were the covenantal relationship and the unimpeachable genealogy of Israel's mothers and fathers. At a level of deep structure, the story of ancient Israel is one of a lineage and succession constantly in jeopardy and miraculously preserved by the intervention of God.

Rabbinic portrayals of Sarah, the mother of the Jewish people, are extremely positive. B. Bava Metzi'a 87a and B. Yevamot 77a praise her modesty, while in B. Megillah 15a she is said to have been, along with Rahab, Abigail, and Esther, one of the four most beautiful women who ever lived. B. Megillah 14a also enumerates her among the seven female prophets and relates that she was the one whose relationship with God was most direct. According to *Genesis Rabbah* 45:10, "The Holy One, blessed be He, never condescended to hold converse with any woman save with that righteous woman." Perhaps the only blot on Sarah's exemplary life is her relationship with Hagar, her handmaid. Yet even here benevolent interpreters explain the story as much to Sarah's credit as possible, invoking the right of a mistress over her servant and impugning Hagar for her insupportable behavior and foreign origin.

The tradition contends that Hagar was given every benefit in Abraham's household. *Genesis Rabbah* 45:1 relates that Hagar was a daughter of Pharaoh:

When Pharaoh saw what was done on Sarah's behalf in his own house (Gen. 12:17), he took his daughter and gave her to Sarah, saying, "Better let my daughter be a handmaid in this house than a mistress in another house."

Moreover, according to *Genesis Rabbah* 45:3, Sarah gave Hagar to Abraham as another wife, not as a concubine, so that her state was to be one of honor. Sarah is said to have persuaded Hagar to accept her new position with kind words: "Happy are you to be united to so holy a man." When Hagar quickly conceived, the midrash relates that Sarah treated her with solicitude. When ladies came to visit Sarah, she urged them to go and inquire as to Hagar's welfare, as well. *Genesis Rabbah* 45:5, reports that Hagar repaid this kindness with deceit:

Hagar would tell them: My mistress Sarai is not inwardly what she appears to be outwardly: she appears to be a righteous woman, but she is not. For had she been a righteous woman, see how many years have passed without her conceiving, whereas I conceived in one night!

The *aggadah* goes on to say that Sarah chose not to argue the issue with Hagar, but went directly to Abraham with her grievance, lamenting **"The wrong done me is your fault! . . . The Lord decide between you and me"** (Gen. 16:5). Rabbinic tradition deems Sarah's greatest shortcoming not to have been her treatment of Hagar, but her intemperate words to her husband. Several different interpretations of this outburst are preserved in *Genesis Rabbah* 45:5. The simplest is attributed to

Rabbi Judan who explained their meaning in R. Judah's name: "You wrong me with words, since you hear me insulted and yet remain silent." A more complex interpretation is based on "But Abram said, 'O Lord God, what can You give me, seeing that I shall die childless' " (Gen. 15: 2). Sarah's grievance is that Abraham should have said: " 'We shall die childless' [instead of "I shall die childless"], then as He gave you a child so would He have given me."

Abraham tells Sarah in *Genesis Rabbah* 45:6, "I am constrained to do her neither harm nor good," but Sarah feels no such limitation and treats her servant harshly. This unkindness is described in various ways in *Genesis Rabbah* 45:6, perhaps reflecting rabbinic knowledge of how a mistress might oppress her servant: "R. Abba said: She restrained her from cohabitation. R. Berekiah said in R. Abba's name: She slapped her face with a slipper. R. Berekiah said in R. Abba's name: She bade her carry her water buckets and bath towels to the baths." This last, presumably, was work usually done by a slave and was therefore not fitting to Hagar's new status.

In the end, however, the consensus is that Hagar was Sarah's servant and that Sarah dealt with her appropriately. This is the purport of the following comment from *Genesis Rabbah* 40:7, which stresses the unequal nature of the relationship between the two women:

"An angel of the Lord found her . . . and said 'Hagar, slave of Sarai' " (Gen. 16:8). So runs the proverb: "If one man tells you that you have ass's ears, do not believe him; if two tell it to you, order a halter." Thus, Abraham said "Your maid is in your hands" (Gen. 16:6) [and] the angel said "slave of Sarai" (Gen. 16:8). Hence, "And she said, 'I am running away from my mistress Sarai' "(Gen. 16:8).

In this passage, Sarah's less than admirable behavior is justified: A mistress may, after all, do as she wishes with her servant. In this power equation, Hagar is a chattel who was at fault for fleeing her rightful superior.

Rabbinic discomfort with Hagar's Egyptian heritage is also a factor in the negative tenor of these texts. The otherness of the foreign woman evoked significant sexual anxiety in rabbinic discourse.[17] Commenting on "[Ishmael] lived in the wilderness of Paran; and his mother got a wife for him from the land of Egypt" (Gen. 21:21), *Genesis Rabbah* 53:15 relates:

R. Isaac said: Throw a stick into the air, and it will fall back to its place of origin. Thus, because it is written "She had an Egyptian maidservant whose name was Hagar" (Gen. 16:1), therefore it is written, "And his mother got a wife for him from the land of Egypt" (Gen. 21:21).

Ishmael may have been Abraham's acknowledged son, but for the rabbis he was indelibly marked by his mother's origins and was best kept far away from the people of Israel.

This second and final expulsion of Hagar and her son Ishmael is rationalized by the rabbis on the grounds that Ishmael's general behavior was intolerable. This judgment is based on interpretations of Genesis 21:9, "**Sarah saw the son whom Hagar the Egyptian had borne to Abraham playing,**" the verse that immediately precedes Sarah's demand to her husband that Hagar and Ishmael be cast out. According to *Genesis Rabbah* 53:11, Ishmael's "playing" actually referred to various kinds of immorality, including sexual exploitation of women, idolatry, bloodshed, attempts on Isaac's life, and efforts to claim the rights of the firstborn. Such a youth could have no place in Abraham's household.

Perhaps the most disturbing aspect of this story for rabbinic commentators was the foreign Hagar's privilege in receiving two divine visions. B. Me'ilah 17b preserves a tradition that R. Simeon wept and said, "The handmaid of my ancestor's house was found worthy of meeting an angel three times, and I am not even to meet him once." *Genesis Rabbah* 53:14 offers a consolation text for Israel based on the conviction that however much concern God showed Hagar, Israel may be sure of at least equivalent divine solicitude:

"Hear my prayer, O Lord; / give ear to my cry / do not disregard my tears" (Psalm 39:13). You did not keep silent at Hagar's tears; will You keep silent at mine! And should you reply, "Because she was a stranger she was more beloved," then I too am thus, "**For like all my forebears I am an alien, resident with you**"(Ps. 39:13).

The *aggadah* also denigrates Hagar's interaction with the angel of the Lord in *Genesis Rabbah* 45:10, where Hagar is quoted as saying:

I was favored [to see the angel] not only with my mistress [since heavenly beings were frequent visitors to Abraham's household], but even now that I am alone. R. Samuel said: This may be compared to a noble lady whom the king ordered to walk before him. She did so [modestly] leaning on her maid and pressing her face against her. Thus her maid saw [the king] while [the noble lady] did not see him.

For the rabbis, Hagar's visitation, while real, is indicative of her arrogance and lack of shame, as well as of her subordinate status. A pious and modest daughter of Israel knows when to bow humbly before the divine glory. Hagar, an outsider, has again shown herself to be infinitely inferior to her modest and beautiful mistress Sarah, who alone of Abraham's wives was chosen to be the founding mother of Israel.

Similar traditions surround another foreign princess, the Midianite Cozbi, killed with her Israelite lover Zimri by Phinehas, Moses's nephew, in Numbers 25:7–8. Numbers 25:15 identifies Cozbi as the "**Daughter of Zur; he was the tribal head of an ancestral house in Midian,**" and the midrash describes her as a "king's daughter."[18]

B. Sanhedrin 82a denounces Cozbi in a discussion of the consequences for men who have sexual relations with gentile women. Her name is linked to *cazav*, the Hebrew word for "falsehood," and she is castigated in the coarsest terms as a common prostitute. This aggadic passage about Cozbi also reveals the serious problems raised for rabbinic commentators by the marriage of Moses to an outsider, the Midianite Zipporah. In an explanation of Moses' passivity in the face of the events at Shittim (Numbers 25), where Israelite men were seduced into idolatry by Midianite women, and in defense of Phinehas's extreme zealotry, the rabbis explain that Zimri justified his relationship with Cozbi on the grounds that Moses had also taken a foreign consort. Moses was rendered speechless by this challenge and his great-nephew, the fervent Phinehas, had to remind him of the prohibition against cohabitation with foreign women that Moses himself had taught the people when he descended from Mount Sinai. *Numbers Rabbah* 20:24 describes how Moses's failure to act at this moment of crisis demoralized all the Israelites except Phinehas, and concludes that it was in punishment for this public weakness that Moses was buried in an unknown location. The passage concludes, "This serves to teach you that a man must be as fierce as a leopard, swift as an eagle, fleet as a hart, and strong as a lion in the performance of his Maker's will."

Conversion as Domestication: The Fallen Woman Redeemed

According to the aggadic midrash, Hagar was an arrogant foreigner who threatened the divinely ordained succession through Abraham to his son Isaac. Like Cozbi, she also epitomized the dangerous sexual attractions of gentile women. Given the negative rhetoric regarding outsiders that runs through biblical and rabbinic discourse, it is not surprising that these disturbing women were vilified by the rabbis. However, it is also important to attend to those counter-traditions that represent biblical gentiles as models of righteousness beyond the boundaries of Israel and as spiritual seekers who chose to join the Jewish community. Such biblical figures include the Moabite Ruth, who faithfully followed her mother-in-law Naomi back to the land of Israel and ultimately became an ancestor of King David, and the Midianite Jethro, the father-in-law of Moses, who was said in the *aggadah* to have become a proselyte to Judaism.[19] A third example is Rahab, the beneficent harlot who appears in the early chapters of Joshua.

Joshua 2 describes how Rahab, an apparently independent Canaanite woman, provided shelter for the two spies Joshua sent to scout out the land. Defying the king of Jericho, she lied about the hidden men's whereabouts and later helped them to safety over the city walls. Rahab offered several explanations for her generous actions. First, her knowledge of Israel's triumphs preceded the arrival of the spies: **"For we have heard how the Lord dried up the water of the Sea of Reeds for you when you left Egypt; and what you did to Sihon and Og, the two Amorite kings across the Jordan, whom you doomed. When we heard it, we lost heart, and no man had any more spirit left because of you"** (Josh. 2: 10–11). Her second motivation for saving the spies, however, goes beyond hopes for her own safety; Israel's triumphs have awakened her reverence for Israel's God: **"For the Lord your God is the only God in heaven above and on earth below"** (Josh. 2:11).

For these reasons, Rahab rescued the spies, and she was rewarded for her prescience. When Jericho was under siege, Joshua remembered Rahab's goodness to his spies and ordered that both she and her family be escorted to a safe place outside the Israelite camp. Joshua 6:25 confirms the happy ending: **"Only Rahab the harlot and her father's family were spared by Joshua, along with all that belonged to her, and she dwelt among the Israelites—as is still the case. For she had hidden the messengers that Joshua sent to spy out Jericho."**

The biblical story of Rahab is exciting and hortatory and Rahab herself is portrayed as a stalwart woman worthy of praise. The rabbis, however, developed Rahab much further. For them, Rahab became a pre-eminent model of the righteous proselyte, one who went beyond all others in her recognition of God's great powers. Moreover, by imagining her as a repentant fallen woman who found the true God and emerged as a mother in Israel, the rabbis transformed Rahab into an exemplar of the efficacy of Judaism and its traditions in taming the disordering powers of female sexuality.

The degree and success of Jewish proselytism in Second Temple and rabbinic times remains under scholarly discussion.[20] Certainly, the Diaspora of Jews in the Greco-Roman world and increased contacts with sophisticated gentiles provided fertile ground for Jewish conversionary activities. In such a climate, Jewish religious leaders were anxious to find biblical and historical models of proselytes worthy of emulation. Still, the elevation of Rahab to such a role is surprising, since the evidence adduced for her conversion was weak at best, consisting only of her praise of Israel's God in Joshua 2:11 and the later statement in Joshua 6:25 that she continued to dwell in Israel until this day. It may be that Rahab assumed a special importance as a consequence both of her gender and her profession in a rabbinic setting apparently looking for engaging female figures of repentance and conversion. One of the few midrashic *aggadot* set in rabbinic times that deals with a female proselyte has to do with a penitent courtesan who became a Jew and married the student of Torah who had first approached her as a customer. The story ends: "Those very bed-clothes which she had spread for him for an illicit purpose she now spread out for him lawfully."[21] This appealing narrative mirrors the rabbinic adumbrations of Rahab's story. In both instances, risqué details of the heroines' pasts are juxtaposed with the spiritually elevating accounts of the new starts they found within the Jewish community, simultaneously preserving and negating the erotic associations these stories evoked.

Aggadic traditions about Rahab as a proselyte can be divided into several groups. First are those that emphasize her repentance and her sincerity as a convert; a second category details her many distinguished descendants and the honor she received in Israel. It also explains Rahab's reward as a source of consolation for the equally repentant and pious sufferers of Israel. Finally, a third group of traditions revises Rahab's past entirely and transforms her from a harlot to an innkeeper who ultimately married Joshua.

The first rabbinic view of Rahab stresses the efficacy of repentance. That a proselyte and former prostitute could achieve such a name for herself in the annals of Jewish history is proof to all that those who sincerely return to God will achieve salvation, no matter how great their previous sins. To emphasize this point, many sources dwelt on Rahab's past excesses in order to show to even greater advantage her subsequent redemption. *Sifre Zuta* on Numbers 10:28 recounts that four names of disgrace and obscenity pertained to Rahab, and explains that she was called *zonah* (prostitute) because she was unchaste both with the sons of the land as well as with wanderers from outside. B. Zevahim 116a–b related that Rahab came to hear of the parting of the Red Sea and the overwhelming terror that had fallen upon the kings of Canaan because of her intimacy with the great men of her time:

And Rahab the harlot said to Joshua's messengers: **"For we have heard how the Lord dried up the waters of the Sea of Reeds"** (Josh. 2:10) . . . And how did she know this? Because as a master said, There was no prince or ruler who had not possessed Rahab the harlot. It was said: She was ten years old when the Israelites departed from Egypt, and she played the harlot the whole forty years spent by the Israelites in the wilderness. At the age of fifty she became a proselyte. Said she: May I be forgiven as a reward for the cord, window, and flax [that is, for hiding the spies in the flax, and helping them escape with a cord through the window].[22]

This tradition shares in the rabbinic discourse linking women and immorality, particularly in connection with non-Jewish women. But it stresses as well the significant lesson that past wickedness is no bar to present repentance and future salvation. Perhaps the most important message is that women, as well as men, are capable of spiritual transformation and are equally welcomed into the Jewish community. Indeed, Rahab's past excesses are frequently cited as evidence of the breadth of the gates of repentance, as the following homiletic passage from *Pesiqta Rabbati* 40:3 explains:

"He will judge the world and declare it acquitted; But he will minister judgment to the heathen peoples according to the upright" (Ps. 9:9). What is meant by "according to the upright"? R. Alexandri said: He will minister judgment to the heathen people by citing as examples the upright ones among them, the example of Rahab, of Jethro, of Ruth. How will he do so? He will say to each man of the peoples of the earth: "Why did you not bring yourself closer to Me?" And each man of them will answer: "I was wicked, so steeped in wickedness I was ashamed." And God will ask: "Were you more so than Rahab whose house was in the side of the wall so that on the outside she would receive robbers and then whore with them inside? Nevertheless, when she wished to draw near Me, did I not receive her and raise up prophets and righteous men out of her?"

Indeed, Rahab's exemplary descendants, although undelineated in the biblical text, play a major role in her rabbinic metamorphosis as a convert, for despite their humble origin they are said to behave piously while the children of Israel scorn their heritage and practice idolatry. Thus, according to *Pesiqta de-Rav Kahana* 13:4, "A capable servant will dominate an incompetent son/ And share the inheritance with the brothers" (Prov.17:2), is said to refer to the superiority of the descendants of Rahab:

R. Abba bar Kahana applied to Israel the verse: "You are not as the harlot who made her deeds comely" (Ezek. 16:31),[23] and then said, Let the descendant of a shameless woman who made her deeds comely present himself and reprimand the son of a comely woman who made her deeds shameless. You find that all of those words of Scripture which are used in tribute to Rahab contain a reproach of Israel. Thus, Rahab is quoted as saying, "Now, since I have shown loyalty to you, swear to me by the Lord that you in turn will show loyalty to my family" (Josh. 2:12); and of Israel it is said, "Surely they swear falsely" (Jer. 5:2). Rahab is quoted as saying, ". . . spare the lives of my father and mother" (Josh. 2:13; but to Israel it is said, "Fathers and mothers have been humiliated within you"(Ezek. 22:7).

Here, then, the proselyte's righteous behavior puts to shame the sinners of Israel: the marginalized harlot has shown herself more worthy than the children of the house. And here, too, is proof that repentance can cleanse even the most tarnished of pasts.

Rahab's high standing among all proselytes stems from her whole-hearted confession of God's sovereignty, for this is how the rabbis understand her praise of Israel's diety in Joshua 2:11, as in this passage found in *Mekhilta* 'Amalek 3 and *Deuteronomy Rabbah* 2:26–27:

> The rabbis say Jethro attributed reality to idols, as it is said, **"Now I know that the Lord is greater than all gods"** (Ex. 18:11). Naaman partly acknowledged them, as it is said, **"Now I know that there is no God in the whole world except in Israel"** (2 Kings 5:15). [But] Rahab placed God in heaven and upon earth, as it is said, **"For the Lord your God is the only God in heaven above and on earth below"** (Josh. 2:11).

In the minds of the rabbis, Rahab's reward was that she numbered priests and prophets of Israel among her descendants. In a long passage on the benefits granted sincere proselytes, *Numbers Rabbah* 8:9 considers her example:

> In the same manner we find in connection with Rahab the harlot, that because she brought spies into her house and rescued them, the Holy One, blessed be He, accounted it unto her as though she had performed the act for Him, and bestowed her reward. In confirmation of this it says, **"The woman, however, had taken the two men and hidden Him"** (Josh.2:4).[24] What reward did she receive? Some of her daughters were married into the priesthood and bore sons who stood and performed service upon the altar and entered the Sanctuary, where, uttering the Ineffable Name of God, they would bless Israel. These sons were: Baruch, the son of Neriah, Seraiah, the son of Mahseiah, Jeremiah, the son of Hilkiah, and Hanamel, the son of Shallum.[25]

Other listings of Rahab's descendants are even longer. *Ruth Rabbah* 2:1 counts, "Ten priests who were also prophets descended from Rahab the harlot: Jeremiah, Hilkiah, Seraiah, Mahseiah, Hanamel, Shallum, Baruch, Neriah, Ezekiel, and Buzzi; while some add that Huldah the prophet was also a descendant of Rahab the harlot." The midrash continues:

> R. Judah says: Huldah the prophet was also among the descendants of Rahab the harlot, as it is said, **"So Hilkiah the Priest . . . went to Huldah the prophet, the wife of Shallum the son of Tikvah"** (2 Kings 22:14), and it says [elsewhere, in connection with Rahab], **"You tie this length (*tikvat*) of crimson cord"** (Josh. 2:18).

This tenuous evidence is typical of all the proof texts linking Rahab to her supposed descendants since there are no biblical indications of whom they might actually have been. That the Rabbis would use it indicates their strong desire to establish her position as an accepted convert and mother of worthy descendants.

Rahab's professed relationship to the female prophet Huldah led to the development of a further rabbinic tradition which redounded to her credit, her supposed marriage to Joshua. The following account in B. Megillah 14b explains the family tree:

R. Nahman said: Huldah was a descendant of Joshua. It is written here [in connection with Huldah] "**The son of Harhas** (*harhas*)" (2 Kgs 22:15), and it is written in another place [in connection with Joshua] "**In Timnath-Heres** (*heres*)" (Judg. 2:9). Ena Saba cited the following in objection to R. Nahman: "Eight prophets who were also priests were descended from Rahab the harlot, namely Neriah, Baruch, Seraiah, Mahseiah, Jeremiah, Hilkiah, Hanamel, and Shallum." R. Judah said: "Huldah the prophetess was also one of the descendants of Rahab the harlot" . . . He replied: "Ena Saba . . . the truth can be found by combining my statement and yours. We must suppose that she became a proselyte and Joshua married her."[26]

A final group of comments on the conversion of Rahab are consolation texts addressed to the suffering community of Israel. J. Berakhot 4: 4 and *Ecclesiastes Rabbah* 5:6 recount that when Hezekiah, King of Judah, became ill and turned his face to the wall, as recounted in 2 Kings 20:2, the wall he faced was the wall of Rahab:

He spoke before Him: Lord of the Universe, she saved two lives for You and You saved many lives for her, [for as] R. Simeon ben Yohai taught: Even if there were two hundred men in her family and they were connected with two hundred families, they were all saved through her merit; for it is not written here, "her family," but "**All her** *families* **they brought out**" (Joshua 6:23).[27] How much more [said Hezekiah] [should You save me] seeing that my ancestors gathered unto You all proselytes.

Similar discussions of Rahab, like those focused on other converts, end with refrains assuring Israel that the divine grace shown to the proselyte will not be withheld from the worthy of Israel. Thus, *Sifre Numbers* 78 says of Rahab that even though she came of a people about whom it was written, "**And you shall not let a soul remain alive**" (Deut. 20: 16), "yet because she brought herself near, the All-Present drew her close, [and] how much more so is this true of Israel, when they do the will of the All-Present!"[28]

All these remarks about Rahab reveal a favorable rabbinic attitude towards female converts and testify to a willingness to welcome any sincere proselyte. As the putative wife of Joshua and the forebear of priests and prophets, she became a shining model of all that a righteous individual might achieve, regardless of her past. And by the example of her gender, as well, she is eloquent testimony that the God of Israel was accessible to all who seek divine shelter. At the same time, however, Rahab's conversion may be seen as a form of domestication. This formerly notorious prostitute, who epitomized all the dangers of the gentile temptress, was rendered benign when she adopted the non-threatening guise of a compliant Jewish wife and mother.[29]

Since Rahab is said to have become so intimately connected with prominent figures in Israel, as wife and as ancestor, it is not surprising to find another concurrent strain of rabbinic tradition that maintains that Rahab was not a harlot at all, but was instead involved in inn-keeping, or some other respectable trade.[30] To launder her past in this way, however, seriously undercut the main tradition of the warm reception Judaism offered the repentant harlot. The powerful prototype of redemption Rabah represented was immeasurably weakened because it was the transformation of the fallen woman into a mother in Israel that confirmed the rabbinic message that neither gender, foreign origins, nor a dubious past were a barrier to those who sincerely wished to join the Jewish people.

Conclusion

Some of the male-constructed paradigms of women discussed in this chapter reveal a profound rabbinic distrust of females, particularly in groups, who appeared to evade the reach of male authority. The resulting association of women with witchcraft is reinforced by parallel discourses framing women as sexually unreliable and potentially dangerous to men. Conversely, aggadic delineations of biblical heroines reveal that God's marvelous purposes can be manifest in the details of women's lives. In these midrashic narratives, conflicts among women are seen to advance Israel's destiny in unexpected ways, while moments of shared sympathy provide inspiring models of feminine conduct. The glowing portrayals of Sarah, Rachel, and the daughters of Zelophehad depict women who fulfilled male expectations almost to the utmost degree. In sharp contrast is the antipathy aimed at Leah and Dinah, and the gentiles, Hagar and Cozbi, all of whom were understood to have breached the boundaries of appropriate female behavior through deception, immodesty, and presumption.

Most strikingly, in the loving depiction of Rahab's journey from sinful prostitute to pious proselyte and Joshua's devoted wife, midrashic tradition demonstrated how otherness could be vitiated, foreign origins superceded, threatening sexuality defused, and disturbing female independence undercut. In the details of Rahab's rehabilitation through conversion, rabbinic chagrin over women's confusing and conflicting propensities was revealed and resolved.

AFTERWORD

When the daughters of Zelophehad heard that the land of Israel was being apportioned among the males of the tribes but not the females, they consulted together as to how to make their claim. They said: The compassion of God is not like human compassion. Human rulers favor males over females but the One who spoke and brought the world into being is not like that. Rather, God shows mercy to every living thing, as Scripture says, "Who gives food to all flesh / Whose steadfast love is eternal" (Ps. 136: 24) and "The Sovereign is good to all / God's mercy is upon all God's works" (Ps. 145: 9).

(*Sifre Numbers* 133)

The sages, who formed, compiled, and edited rabbinic literature over several centuries and across a large geographic area, were all men. Although the estimable body of writing the rabbis produced expresses diverse points of view on virtually every conceivable topic, it preserves very few female voices. Contemporary students of this tradition must begin with the knowledge that rabbinic literature is inherently oriented towards men, conveying a one-sided picture of Jewish life, religious ritual, and spirituality in late antiquity. Moreover, the apparent multivocality of rabbinic literature rests on a number of inalterable principles and beliefs. Among them is the conviction of woman's secondary status as a created being who is other than man in her abilities and talents and of lower status in human society.

Female alterity begins with the corporeal. Women are defined by their bodies and by bodily functions. As objects of temptation and sources of pollution, they are experienced by men as both sexually attractive and physically repellant. Moreover, as passive vessels who do not generate new life, females are anomalous bystanders to the convenantal relationship between God and Israel. Yet women are acknowledged to be essential to men at the same time as they portend potential problems. In the rabbis' ideal vision of the world, this dilemma is resolved by confining females to domestic enabling roles, facilitating the endeavors of their husbands and sons.

Patriarchy was not unique or original to rabbinic social policy. It was typical of all the societies among whom the Jews of the rabbinic period lived. What is remarkable in rabbinic Judaism is the acknowledgement of the consequences of patriarchy for women. As the midrash cited above articulates, the sages had no illusions about the many drawbacks of women's secondary status. In this book I have discussed aggadic enumerations of the ways in which women's lot was undesirable from a male standpoint and I have delineated how the rabbis justified these inequities as inherent in female creation. I have also shown that to subordinate women is not to condemn them to perdition. The rabbis knew that God's mercy extends to every living thing. Numerous examples cited in these pages demonstrate that rabbinic teachings affirm women's basic humanity and their access to the divine through prayer and suffering.

Rabbinic representations of women's lives are mediated through a conservative and androcentric religious sensibility. Generally unmoored to specific times or places, aggadic texts tell us very little about actual individuals or female undertakings. Women who display modesty and selflessly support the scholarly endeavors of their husbands and sons receive high praise. However, rabbinic literature also preserves many oblique and disapproving references to women's activities and concerns, both within and beyond the domestic realm. Midrashic narratives about sisters who collude together; daughters who follow their mother's examples, whether good or bad; and disputes between women and their maidservants, reflect anxieties about what the rabbis imagined went on in women's lives when men were absent. Polemics against supposed female involvement in witchcraft, imprecations about the brazenness of women who venture unveiled into the marketplace, and warnings to men against converse with all females express profound uneasiness about women in the public domain. Such reprehension may indicate discomfort with actual social settings in which active and influential women were involved in religious rituals, successful businesses, and friendship circles with other women. That the rabbis can imagine the daughters of Zelophehad consulting together for a positive purpose affirms not only their acquaintance with wise and capable females but also their muted admission of the deleterious consequences for women of their restrictive social policy.

Rabbinic Judaism's formation of the feminine affirmed female alterity. All women were "a separate people" whose secondary mode of creation and deficient moral judgment accounted for their significant disadvantages in comparison to men. This did not mean, however, that all females were the same. The rabbinic world was characterized by dichotomies and separations, and so, too, was their perceived world of women. As this book has demonstrated, midrashic women include Jews and gentiles, free women and maidservants, married women and unmarried minors, faithful wives and suspected adulteresses, widows and levirate widows, divorcées and 'agunot. Similar distinctions divide modest homebodies from immodest gadabouts, and the pious wives of rabbis and rabbinic students from the wives of people derelict in their observance of ritual obligations.[1] The fertile wife fulfilled social expectations while infertility was a source of distress for both women and men. Due to her biological functions, a woman could move from a state of ritual cleanness to a condition in which she could convey ritual impurity to her husband. Locating the moment of this metamorphosis is a major concern of rabbinic legislation concerning the *niddah*.

The foreign woman was a particular focus of rabbinic sexual and social anxieties. As many biblical examples warned, the seductive beauty of the ethnic other could lead Jewish men away from faithful worship of God and observance of divine commandments. Offspring from such exogamous unions were lost to the Jewish community and, as in the case of the biblical Ishmael, could even threaten the intended line of inheritance. Among midrashic solutions to this threat was to incorporate such women into the Jewish community and welcome them under the "wings of the Shekhinah," a rabbinic euphemism for conversion. The midrashic domestication of Rahab the harlot into a devout proselyte, wife of Joshua, and mother of priests and prophets in Israel, discussed in chapter 6 of this volume, is a central example of this phenomenon. The biblical Rahab epitomized personal autonomy, communal stature, sexual encounters with a variety of partners, and independent religious thinking. The rabbis neutralized her threatening propensities by subjecting her to all the disabilities seen as appropriate and essential for Jewish women.

Rabbinic literature is a product of the needs and assumptions of small circles of learned sages living through particular historical circumstances over a span of five or six centuries. The patriarchal stance towards women that characterizes its legal pronouncements and non-legal narratives was neither unique to this Jewish community nor more oppressive or restrictive than the mores of contemporaneous cultures. However, the consequences of the general construction of women expressed in these texts have been long lasting and often pernicious in stifling female intellectual, spiritual, and social possibilities. The manifold changes in women's status in Judaism and in the larger world at the beginning of the twenty-first century offer strong grounds for hope that all such limitations on female aspirations will soon disappear.

At the conclusion of one of his talmudic readings, Emmanuel Levinas wrote that the most glorious title for God, cited in Psalm 68: 6, is "Father of orphans and champion of widows." He suggests that dedication to this God is epitomized by the act of study:

Consecration to God: his epiphany, beyond all theology and any visible image, however complete, is repeated in the daily Sinai of [human beings] sitting before an astonishing Book, ever again in progress because of its very completeness.[2]

I have emended Levinas's words to read "human beings" rather than the original "men," just as I read the first segment of Genesis 1: 27 as, "And God created human beings in God's image." The "astonishing Book" of revelation that Levinas describes as "ever again in progress" represents a "daily Sinai" because it demands continuous rereading and constant reinterpretation. Women and men of this present moment, as much as our rabbinic sages, are also a part of this ongoing process of study and discovery.

NOTES

INTRODUCTION (PP. I–I2)

1. Simone de Beauvoir, *The Second Sex*. Translated and edited by H. M. Parshley (New York: Vintage Books, 1989), p. 37.

2. Shaye J. D. Cohen, "Why Aren't Jewish Women Circumcised?" in *Gender and the Body in the Ancient Mediterranean*, ed. Maria Wyke (Oxford: Blackwell Publishers, 1998), pp. 136–154, p. 136.

3. For a thorough English language bibliographic guide to rabbinic literature and its contexts, see Eliezer Diamond, "The World of the Talmud," in *The Schocken Guide to Jewish Books*, ed. Barry W. Holtz (New York: Schocken Books, 1992), pp. 47–69. Robert Goldenberg, "Talmud," and Barry W. Holtz, "Midrash," in *Back to the Sources: Reading the Classic Jewish Texts*, ed. Barry W. Holtz (New York: Summit Books, 1984), pp. 128–175, and pp. 176–211 respectively, provide clear introductions to the literary documents and approaches of talmudic and midrashic texts. For recent historical overviews of portions of the rabbinic period, see Shaye J. D. Cohen, "Judaism to the Mishnah, 135–220 C.E.," and Isaiah Gafni, "The World of the Talmud: From the Mishnah to the Arab Conquest," both in *Christianity and Rabbinic Judaism: A Parallel History of Their Origins and Early Development*, ed. Hershel Shanks (Washington, D.C.: Biblical Archaeology Society, 1992), pp. 195–224, and pp. 225–266 respectively. For literary approaches to midrashic literature, see the essays in *Midrash and Literature*, ed. Geoffrey H. Hartman and Sanford Budick (New Haven, CT: Yale University Press, 1986); also James L. Kugel, *In Potiphar's House: The Interpretive Life of Biblical Texts* (New York: HarperCollins, 1990); and Jeffrey L. Rubenstein, *Talmudic Stories: Narrative Art, Composition, and Culture* (Baltimore: The Johns Hopkins University Press, 1999).

4. Jacob Neusner, *Method and Meaning in Ancient Judaism*, (Missoula, MT: Scholars Press, 1979), p. 83.

5. Daniel Boyarin, *Carnal Israel: Reading Sex in Talmudic Culture* (Berkeley: University of California Press, 1993), p. 27.

6. On the unreliability of rabbinic attributions, see Jacob Neusner, *In Search of Talmudic Biography. The Problem of the Attributed Saying* (Chico, Calif.: Scholars Press, 1984). In three recent studies, Tal Ilan, *Jewish Women in Greco-Roman Palestine: An Inquiry into Image and Status*. Texts and Studies in An-

cient Judaism 44 ((Tübingen: J.C.B. Mohr, 1995); idem, *Yours and Mine are Hers: Retrieving Women's History from Rabbinic Literature* (Leiden: E. J. Brill, 1997), and idem, *Integrating Women into Second Temple History*. Texts and Studies in Ancient Judaism 76 (Tübingen: J.C.B. Mohr, 1999), has demonstrated ways in which information about specific women and women's activities in the social, economic, political, intellectual, and religious history of the Second Temple and rabbinic periods may be retrieved from rabbinic documents.

7. While this book does not take a comparative approach, it is important to state that rabbinic constructions of women were significantly influenced by the cultural mores of the various times and places in which rabbinic literature was formed. I agree with Charlotte Elisheva Fonrobert, *Menstrual Impurity: Rabbinic and Christian Reconstructions of Biblical Gender* (Stanford, Calif.: Standford University Press, 2000), p. 161, that it is vital to emphasize that all women in late antiquity lived under patriarchal conditions, and that any knowledge we have of women's lives during that period is "reflected mostly through an androcentric lens in Jewish and Christian as well as Greco-Roman literature." Other recent comparative studies include Ross S. Kraemer, "Women's Judaism(s) at the Beginning of Christianity," in *Women and Christian Origins*, ed. Ross S. Kraemer and Mary Rose D'Angelo (New York: Oxford University Press, 1999), pp. 50–79; idem, *Her Share of the Blessings: Women's Religions Among Pagans, Jews, and Christians in the Greco-Roman World* (New York: Oxford University Press, 1992); and Michael L. Satlow, *Tasting the Dish: Rabbinic Rhetorics of Sexuality* (Atlanta: Scholars Press, 1995); idem, *Jewish Marriage in Antiquity* (Princeton: Princeton University Press, 2001).

8. Among scholars who have shown how late antique Jewish views of issues connected with women varied from location to location, reflecting the dominant culture of a given environment, or who have emphasized particular geographic areas in their work are Daniel Boyarin, *Carnal Israel: Reading Sex in Talmudic Culture* (Berkeley: University of California Press, 1993); Isaiah Gafni, "The Institution of Marriage in Rabbinic Times," *The Jewish Family: Metaphor and Memory*, ed. David Kraemer (New York: Oxford University Press, 1989), pp. 13–30; Miriam Peskowitz, *Spinning Fantasies: Rabbis, Gender, and History* (Berkeley: University of California Press, 1997); and Michael L. Satlow, *Tasting the Dish: Rabbinic Rhetorics of Sexuality* (Atlanta: Scholars Press, 1995).

9. Recent books, in addition to those cited in notes 6 and 7 above, include Meir Bar-Ilan, *Some Jewish Women in Antiquity* (Atlanta, Scholars Press, 1998); David Biale, *Eros and Jews: From Biblical Israel to Contemporary America* (New York: Basic Books, 1992); Rachel Biale, *Women and Jewish Law: An Exploration of Women's Issues in Halakhic Sources* (New York: Schocken, 1984); Daniel Boyarin, *Unheroic Conduct: The Rise of Heterosexuality and the Invention of the Jewish Man* (Berkeley: University of California Press, 1997); Charlotte Elisheva Fonrobert, *Menstrual Purity: Rabbinic and Christian Reconstructions of Biblical Gender* (Stanford: Stanford University Press, 2000); Judith Hauptman, "Feminist Perspectives on Jewish Studies: Rabbinics," in *Feminist Perspectives on Jewish Studies*, ed. Shelly Tenenbaum and Lynn Davidman (New Haven: Yale University Press, 1994), pp. 40–61; idem, *Rereading the Rabbis: A Woman's Voice* (Boulder: Westview Press, 1998); Jacob Neusner, *Androgynous Judaism: Masculine and Feminine in the Dual Torah* (Macon, Ga.: Mercer University Press, 1993); idem, *How the Rabbis Liberated Women* (Atlanta Scholars

Press: 1998); and Judith Romney Wegner, *Chattel or Person? The Status of Women in the Mishnah* (New York: Oxford University Press, 1988).

10. See, for example, Rachel Adler, *Engendering Judaism: An Inclusive Theology and Ethics* (Philadelphia: Jewish Publication Society, 1998); Judith Plaskow, *Standing Again at Sinai: Judaism from a Feminist Perspective* (San Francisco: Harper, 1990); and see Ellen Umansky "Jewish Feminist Theology," in Eugene B. Borowitz, *Choices in Modern Jewish Thought: A Partisan Guide.* 2nd ed. (West Orange, N.J.: Behrman House, 1995), pp. 313–340.

11. Judith Hauptman, *Rereading the Rabbis*, p. 9.

CHAPTER 1 (PP. 13–43)

1. Some of the content of this chapter appeared in different form in the following essay, Judith R. Baskin, "Woman as Other in Rabbinic Literature," in *Judaism in Late Antiquity.* Part 3, Volume 2:*Where We Stand: Issues and Debates in Ancient Judaism*, ed. Jacob Neusner and Alan J. Avery-Peck (Leiden: E. J. Brill, 1999), pp. 177–196. On the crucial point that rabbinic literature does not necessarily reflect any particular social or historical reality as much as an imagined, idealized social order, see Jacob Neusner,*Method and Meaning in Ancient Judaism*, Brown Judaic Studies 10 (Missoula, Mont.: Scholars Press, 1979), p. 83, n. 3; Ross Shepard Kraemer, *Her Share of the Blessings* pp. 93–94, 99, 102; and idem, "Jewish Women and Christian Origins: Some Caveats," in *Women and Christian Origins*, ed. Ross Shepard Kraemer and Mary Rose D'Angelo (New York: Oxford University Press, 1999), pp. 35–49, 35–38; and Tal Ilan, *Mine and Yours are Hers: Retrieving Women's History from Rabbinic Literature* (Leiden: E. J. Brill, 1997).

2. This statement in B. Shabbat 62a is found in a technical discussion of M. Shabbat 6:3 which specifies the jewelry a woman is permitted to wear on the Sabbath, differentiating between acceptable ornaments and objects which could be construed as burdens, which are not allowed. The talmudic discussion of this *mishnah* begins with the ruling of the sage 'Ulla that whatever applies to a woman in this particular instance does not apply to a man, and vice versa. R. Joseph concludes from this that " 'Ulla holds that women are a separate people," or as the phrase is sometimes translated, "women are a nation unto themselves." Emphasizing the inherent unreliability of the female, as opposed to the steadiness of the male, the talmudic discussion ultimately progresses from whether women may or may not wear such items as perfume flasks on the Sabbath to *aggadot* connecting perfumed women to a variety of vulgar and immoral behaviors. Finally, the *sugya* graphically details the unpleasant physical afflictions such immodest women will receive as punishment. For further discussion of this and other passages indicating significant rabbinic discomfort with the female body and overt female sexuality, see pp. 34–35 below. In his discussion of the situation of women as reflected in the medieval documents of the Cairo Genizah, Shlomo Dov Goitein, *A Mediterranean Society. Vol 3: The Family* (Berkeley: University of California Press, 1978), pp. 354–355, cites B. Shabbat 62a as a rabbinic expression of "man's inability or unwillingness to understand his womenfolk or to let them participate in his own pursuits." Tal Ilan, *Integrating Women into Second Temple History.* Texts and Studies in Ancient Judaism 76

(Tübingen: J.C.B. Mohr, 1999), p. 1, observes that in this statement 'Ulla "was not giving a positive, factual assessment of what women were, but typically, and candidly, stating what they were not." See Mayer Gruber, "The Status of Women in Ancient Judaism," in *Judaism in Late Antiquity*. Part 3, Volume 2: *Where We Stand: Issues and Debates in Ancient Judaism*, ed. Jacob Neusner and Alan J. Avery-Peck (Leiden: E. J. Brill, 1999), pp. 151–176, for the ways in which the rabbis systematically exempted women from social and religious rights they had held in earlier periods of Jewish history.

3. Most of the laws pertaining to genital emissions are found in Leviticus 12–18; they apply to both men and women. Many apply to the *niddah*, or menstruating woman, who is considered ritually impure for seven days from the beginning of the menstrual flow. Her impurity can be transferred to persons, utensils, and clothes. A woman is also deemed unclean for a period of seven days after giving birth to a male child, and fourteen after a girl. For 33 additional days after delivering a boy and 66 after a girl, she is forbidden to enter the Temple or to touch hallowed things. The discussion in M. Niddah 3: 5–7 focuses on whether and when a woman who suffers a miscarriage is treated as one who has given birth, in terms of ritual impurity. For further discussion of the *niddah* in rabbinic Judaism, see pp. 22–29 below, and notes 30–41.

4. According to Leviticus 12:6–12, following the completion of her period of purification, a new mother must bring both a burnt offering and a sin offering to the Tent of Meeting. The nature of each sacrifice depends on her economic means. In B. Niddah 31b, a student asks why a woman would be required to bring a sacrifice after childbirth. R. Simeon b. Yohai suggested it was because of oaths she may have sworn during the pains of labor to have no further intercourse with her husband. In the part of the passage not quoted here, R. Joseph is said to reject this teaching on the grounds that such an oath, made under the duress of pain, would be easily absolved by a sage once she had regretted it and did not require a sacrifice, at all. Moreover, he points out that the sacrifice required for cancelling an oath is not the same as the sacrifice required for a woman who has given birth, so that oaths have nothing to do with offerings required in Leviticus.

5. On the rabbinic extension of separation between husband and wife during *niddut*, see pp. 25–27 below.

6. Parallels to this segment of B. Niddah 31b appear in a number of sources including *Genesis Rabbah* 17:8 and *Avot de-Rabbi Nathan* B, ch. 9; they are discussed in detail in chapter 3 of this volume. On the explanation for the desirability of the male superior position in sexual intercourse, see Judith Romney Wegner, "The Image and Status of Women in Classical Rabbinic Judaism," in *Jewish Women in Historical Perspective*, ed. Judith R. Baskin. 2nd ed. (Detroit: Wayne State University Press, 1998), p. 78. See chapters 3 and 4 below on its implications for the justification of female debilities and the sexual politics of marriage.

7. As Judith Plaskow has written in *Standing Again at Sinai: Judaism from a Feminist Perspective* (New York: Harper and Row, 1990), p. 63, "Women are objects of the law but neither its creators nor agents. *Halakhot* concerning the religious sphere assume a world in which women are 'enablers.' Women create the preconditions for men and male children to worship and study Torah, but women cannot do these things themselves without becoming less effective in their relational role."

8. See, for example, Philip Birnbaum, trans.,*Ha-Siddur Ha-Shalem: Daily Prayer Book* (New York, 1949), pp. 15–17. Judith Hauptman, in *Rereading the Rabbis: A Woman's Voice* (Boulder:Westview Press, 1998), argues, on p. 237, that the purport of these blessings is that "the real reason a man should thank God for not being a woman is not his higher status but his greater level of ritual obligation. . . . A Jewish man's superiority flows from his being commanded by his Creator." See chapter 3 for further discussion of the similarities and differences between women and slaves in rabbinic thought. In the contemporary traditional liturgy, the order of slave and woman are reversed, so that gratitude for not having been created a woman is the third of the blessings recited.

9. Scholarly studies detailing how rabbinic legislation improved women's legal status beyond the mandates of biblical law in a number of areas include Judith Hauptman, *Rereading the Rabbis,* and Jacob Neusner, *How the Rabbis Liberated Women* (Atlanta:Scholars Press, 1998). For a convincing demonstration of how the rabbis at the same time deliberately limited women's opportunities in a number of areas connected with public domain activities including study, ritual participation, worship, as well as the personal status issue of the right to initiate divorce, see Gruber, "The Status of Women." On rabbinic justifications of constraints on women, see chapter 3 below.

10. Very little is known about the details of women's lives during the different times and places in which rabbinic Judaism was being composed. For some insights on Jewish women's economic, public, and religious activities in the Roman Empire based on both rabbinic and non-rabbinic sources, including archeological remains, papyri, and inscriptions, see Bernadette Brooten, *Women Leaders in the Ancient Synagogue* (Chico, Calif.: Scholars Press, 1982); Miriam Peskowitz,*Spinning Fantasies: Rabbis, Gender, and History* (Berkeley: University of California Press, 1997); Ross S. Kraemer, "Women's Judaism(s) at the Beginning of Christianity," in Ross S. Kraemer and Mary Rose D'Angelo, eds., *Women and Christian Origins* (New York: Oxford University Press, 1999), pp. 50–79; idem, "Jewish Women in the Diaspora World of Late Antiquity," in Judith R. Baskin, ed., *Jewish Women in Historical Perspective.* 2nd ed. (Detroit: Wayne State University Press, 1998), pp. 46–72; Hannah Safrai, "Women and the Ancient Synagogue," in Susan Grossman and Rivka Haut, eds., *Daughters of the King: Women and the Synagogue* (Philadelphia: Jewish Publication Society, 1992), pp. 39–50; and Tal Ilan, *Jewish Women in Greco-Roman Palestine: An Inquiry into Image and Status.* Texts and Studies in Ancient Judaism 44 (Tübingen, J.C.B. Mohr: 1995); idem, *Yours and Mine are Hers: Retrieving Women's History from Rabbinic Literature* (Leiden: E. J. Brill, 1997), and idem,*Integrating Women into Second Temple History.* Texts and Studies in Ancient Judaism 76 (J.C.B. Mohr: Tübingen, 1999); and pp. 41–42 below. Studies of women's lives in late antiquity in the major center of Jewish life in Sassanian Iran/Iraq are sorely lacking; see, however, Rebecca Lesses, "Exe(o)rcising Power: Women as Sorceresses, Exorcists, and Demonesses in Babylonian Jewish Society of Late Antiquity," *Journal of the American Academy of Religion* 69, 2 (2001): 343–375.

11. For a fuller discussion of wives as enablers of their husbands' study, see, chapter 4 below. A similar statement appears in B. Sotah 21a in the context of whether a woman can earn the merit that attaches to Torah study by enabling others to study: "Rabina said: It is certainly merit of [the study of] Torah [that causes the water swallowed by a woman accused of adultery to suspend its

effect]; and when you argue that she is in the category of one who is not com-manded and fulfils, [it can be answered] granted that women are not so com-manded, still when they have their sons taught Scripture and Mishnah and wait for their husbands until they return from the schools, should they not share [the merit] with them?" On women and Torah study, see chapter 3.

12. On women as light minded, see the extensive discussion of *Genesis Rab-bah* 18:2 in chapter 3. Michael Satlow, *Tasting the Dish: Rabbinic Rhetorics of Sexuality* (Atlanta: Scholars Press, 1995), p. 158, points out that "light minded" is a euphemism for women's fundamental sexual unreliability. For praise of wives, see Judith Hauptman, "Images of Women in the Talmud," in Rosemary Radford Ruether, ed., *Religion and Sexism: Images of Women in Jewish and Christian Traditions* (New York: Simon and Schuster, 1974); pp. 184–212; and chapter 4 below.

13. See Hauptman, *Rereading the Rabbis: A Woman's Voice*; and Neusner, *How the Rabbis Liberated Women*.

14. On this and similar topics, see also Rachel Biale, *Women and Jewish Law: An Exploration of Women's Issues in Halakhic Sources* (New York: Schocken Books, 1984), and see chapter 4 below.

15. On wife and mother as "house," see chapter 4, p. 88 below.

16. For a detailed discussion of rabbinic understandings of what it meant to be created in the divine image, see chapters 2 and 3. On the numerous dilemmas inherent in ancient and rabbinic Judaism's perception of God as masculine and the corollary, that human masculinity was expressed through procreation, see Howard Eilberg-Schwartz, *God's Phallus and Other Problems for Men and Monotheism* (Boston: Beacon Press, 1994); and Jacob Neusner, *Androgynous Judaism: Masculine and Feminine in the Dual Torah* (Macon: Mercer University Press, 1993).

17. Howard Eilberg-Schwartz, *The Savage in Judaism: An Anthropology of Israelite Religion and Ancient Judaism* (Bloomington: University of Indiana Press, 1990), pp. 171. See also Lawrence A. Hoffman, *Covenant of Blood: Cir-cumcision and Gender in Rabbinic Judaism* (Chicago: University of Chicago Press, 1996).

18. Shaye J. D. Cohen "Why Aren't Jewish Women Circumcised?" in *Gender and the Body in the Ancient Mediterranean*, ed. Maria Wykes (Oxford: Black-well, 1998), pp. 136–154; p. 148.

19. Cohen, "Why Aren't Jewish Women Circumcised?" p. 149.

20. Cohen, "Why Aren't Jewish Women Circumcised?" p. 150.

21. Howard Eilberg-Schwartz, *The Savage in Judaism: An Anthropology of Israelite Religion and Ancient Judaism* (Bloomington: Indiana University Press, 1990), pp. 175–176.

22. B. Shevuot 18b; see Satlow, *Tasting the Dish*, p. 303; and chapter 4 below on further discussion of ways to guarantee male offspring.

23. Recent works on this topic in Greco-Roman medicine include Joan Cad-den, *The Meaning of Sex Differences in the Middle Ages: Medicine, Natural Philosophy, and Culture* (Cambridge: Cambridge University Press, 1993); and Lesley Ann Dean-Jones, *Women's Bodies in Classical Greek Science* (Oxford: Clarendon Press, 1994); both are discussed in Helen King, "Reading the Female Body," in *Gender and the Body*, ed. Wykes, pp. 199–203.

24. Jan Blayney, "Theories of Conception in the Ancient Roman World," in

The Family in Ancient Rome: New Perspectives, ed. Beryl Rawson (London: Routledge, 1986), pp. 230–239; p. 234.

25. Jan Blayney, "Conception in the Ancient Roman World," p. 234.

26. In its biblical context in Leviticus 12:2, the Hebrew verb form *tazri'a*, "brings forth seed," is meant as a synonym for the succeeding verb form *v'yaldah*, "bears." Since the rabbis accepted the principle that there is no repetition in the biblical text, they understood *tazri'a* as referring to the female emission of semen which they believed occurred when a woman experienced an orgasm during sexual intercourse. The more standard translation of this verse is "When a woman in childbirth bears a male."

27. On the development of rabbinic regulations regarding marital separation and on popular resentment of this legislation, see pp. 25–27 below.

28. Sherry Ortner, "Is Female to Male as Nature is to Culture?" in *Women, Culture and Society*, ed. Michelle Zimbalist Rosaldo and Louise Lamphere (Stanford, Calif.: Stanford University Press, 1971), pp. 67–87, pp. 73–74, p. 87.

29. Michelle Zimbalist Rosaldo, "Women, Culture, and Society: A Theoretical Overview," in *Women, Culture and Society*, ed. Rosaldo and Lamphere, pp. 17–42, pp. 31–32.

30. Jean Soler, "The Dietary Prohibitions of the Hebrews," *The New York Review of Books* 26 (14 June, 1976), pp. 28–31, p. 29. This article also appears in *Food: A Culinary History from Antiquity to the Present*, under the direction of Jean-Louis Flandrin and Massimo Montanari; English edition by Albert Sonnenfeld (New York: Columbia University Press, 1999), pp. 46–54.

31. Soler, "Dietary Prohibitions," p. 30. For further discussion of the importance of rabbinic Judaism's categorization of reality in relation to women, see Judith R. Baskin, "The Separation of Women in Rabbinic Judaism," in *Women, Religion and Social Change*, ed. Yvonne Yazbek Haddad and Ellison Banks Findly (Albany: State University of New York Press, 1985), pp. 3–18; pp. 12–13; and see the anthropologist Mary Douglas, *Purity and Danger: An Analysis of the Concepts of Pollution and Taboo* (New York: Praeger, 1966), pp. 53–57, who points out that holiness is exemplified by completeness and demands that individuals conform to the class to which they belong. She writes, p. 57, that holiness achieves physical expression by rules of avoidance.

32. *Niddah* means "one who is excluded or expelled"; Shaye J. D. Cohen, "Menstruants and the Sacred in Judaism and Christianity," in *Women's History and Ancient History*, ed. Sarah B. Pomeroy (Chapel Hill: University of North Carolina Press, 1991), pp. 273–299, p. 292 n.4, writes that in the Hebrew Bible *niddah* often means "pollution" (as at Lev. 12 and 15), but that Ezekiel 18:6, 22:10, and Lamentations 1:8 anticipate the rabbinic use of the word as referring to a menstruating woman.

33. As in biblical Judaism, the rabbis saw ritual purity as a religious ideal; ritual uncleanness, on the other hand, necessitated a separation from the Divine. According to the *Encyclopedia Judaica*, "Purity," the three main causes of ritual impurity in biblical Judaism are leprosy, issue from human sexual organs, and the dead bodies of certain creatures, particularly human corpses. For a discussion of six sets of biblical passages dealing with ritual impurity in connection with the *niddah*, see Cohen, "Menstruants and the Sacred in Judaism and Christianity," pp. 274–276.

34. Eilberg-Schwartz, *Savage in Judaism,* pp. 184–185. On the connection of women with death, see below, chapter 3.

35. Cohen, "Menstruants and the Sacred," pp. 275–276; he notes, p. 275, that "intercourse with a menstruant is the only shared element between the 'ritual' or physical impurities of Leviticus 11–15 and the 'dangerous' or sinful impurities of Leviticus 18." See also Tikva Frymer-Kensky, "Pollution, Purification, and Purgation in Biblical Israel," in *The Word of the Lord Shall Go Forth: Essays in Honor of David Noel Freedman,* ed. Carol Meyers (Winona Lake, Ind.: Eisenbraun's, 1983), pp. 399–414.

36. David Biale, *Eros and the Jews: From Biblical Israel to Contemporary America* (New York: Basic Books, 1992), p. 42. On the rabbinic emphasis on procreation, see chapter 5 in this volume.

37. Hauptman, *Rereading the Rabbis,* pp. 148–150. For detailed accounts of biblical, rabbinic, and post-rabbinic legislation concerning the *niddah,* see Rachel Biale, *Women and Jewish Law,* pp. 147–174; Shaye J. D. Cohen, "Menstruants and the Sacred'; and idem, "Purity and Piety: The Separation of Menstruants from the Sancta," in *Daughters of the King: Women and the Synagogue,* ed. Susan Grossman and Rivka Haut (Philadelphia: Jewish Publication Society, 1992), pp. 103–116; Yedidyah Dinari, "The Customs of Menstrual Impurity: Their Origin and Devolpment," *Tarbiz* 49 (1979–80):302–324 [Hebrew]; Charlotte Elisheva Fonrobert, *Menstrual Purity: Rabbinic and Christian Reconstructions of Biblical Gender* (Stanford:Stanford University Press, 2000); Tirzah Meacham, "An Abbreviated History of the Development of the Jewish Menstrual Laws," in *Women and Water: Menstruation in Jewish Life and Law,* ed. Rahel S. Wasserfall (Hanover, N.H.: Brandeis University Press, 1999), pp. 23–39; and Judith Romney Wegner, *Chattel or Person? The Status of Women in the Mishnah* (New York: Oxford University Press, 1988).

38. Tirzah Meacham, "An Abbreviated History," in *Women and Water,* ed. Wasserfall, pp. 29–32, and her appendices A and B, pp. 255–261. See also Hauptman, *Rereading the Rabbis,* pp. 156–160. While precisely dating and locating the origins of the prescription of the seven white days is all but impossible, it is the case that their observance, together with immersion in a *mikveh* (ritual bath) following their completion, became the norm for Jewish women everywhere in the centuries after the completion of the Babylonian Talmud. Immersion following *niddah* is never expressly mandated in rabbinic halakhah, but its practice is assumed. On this topic, see Hauptman, pp. 166–168. On issues connected with the rabbinic assumption of authority in distinguishing among different kinds of female blood flows, see Charlotte Fonrobert, "Yalta's Ruse: Resistance against Rabbinic Menstrual Authority in Talmudic Literature," in *Women and Water,* ed. Wasserfall, pp. 60–81, and idem, *Menstrual Purity,* pp. 118–125.

39. Hauptman, *Rereading the Rabbis,* p. 160, suggests the possibility of Zoroastrian influences in this increased stringency. Meacham, "An Abbreviated History," in *Women and Water,* ed. Wasserfall, p. 32, notes parallel negative attitudes towards the menstruating woman in Roman writers like Pliny. Biale, *Women and Jewish Law,* writes, p. 167, that it became common in medieval Europe for Jewish women to absent themselves from synagogue and other public places during their period of *niddut,* even though the rabbinic laws of *niddah* proper do not exclude a woman from such activities. In "Menstruants and the Sacred," Cohen points to a sixth or seventh century text, *Baraita de Niddah,*

probably written in the Land of Israel, as responsible for a major and negative shift in popular attitudes towards the dangerous influence of the menstruant who, according to this tract, must be distanced, not only from her husband, but is also forbidden to enter a synagogue, to come into contact with sacred books, to pray, or to recite God's name. On this phenomenon in medieval context, see also Judith R. Baskin, "Women and Ritual Immersion in Medieval Ashkenaz: The Sexual Politics of Piety," in *Judaism in Practice: From the Middle Ages through the Early Modern Period*, ed. Lawrence Fine, (Princeton: Princeton University Press, 2001), pp. 131–142; and Sharon Koren, "Mystical Rationales for the Laws of Niddah," in *Women and Water*, ed. Wasserfall, pp. 101–121.

40. Cohen, "Purity and Piety," p. 113, and second citation, p. 108.

41. On the danger of death for women who do not obey the rules of menstrual separation, see chapter 3. On women as a source of danger to men, see also Mordechai A. Friedman, "Tamar, a Symbol of Life: The 'Killer Wife' Superstition in the Bible and Jewish Tradition," *Association for Jewish Studies Review* 15:1 (Spring, 1990): 23–61; and pp. 27–29 below.

42. Fonrobert, *Menstrual Purity*, p. 21, pp. 38–39, p. 40.

43. Mayer Gruber, "The Status of Women in Ancient Judaism," pp. 166–167; Daniel Boyarin, *Carnal Israel*, pp. 180–81. Gruber, "The Status of Women in Ancient Judaism," does note, pp. 167–68, that Jewish men have been content to let women believe that the reason for their exclusion from study of Torah was because of their susceptibility to menstrual impurity.

44. The pitfalls to men of contact with attractive women who are not their wives is already a significant theme in biblical literature, as, for example, in the stories of Joseph and Potiphar's wife (Gen. 39) and David and Bathsheba (2 Sam. 12), and the warnings tendered in Proverbs 6–7. This theme is also very well documented in rabbinic writing; see Satlow, *Tasting the Dish*, pp. 155–167. Biale, in *Eros and Jews*, writes, p. 57, of "the fundamental rabbinic ethic that accepted the sexuality of women as a biological fact but required that men 'conquer their desire' (*yetzer*). As women are condemned to be prisoners of their own biology, incapable of willed sexual restraint, there is no point in teaching them the law." However, see the story of the prostitute in B. Menahot 44a, who was so impressed by the self-restraint of a scholar that she gave up her profession and converted to Judaism. On this midrash, see chapter 6 below.

45. Jacob Neusner, *Method and Meaning in Ancient Judaism*, p. 97. Hauptman, *Rereading the Rabbis*, p. 30, offers what she refers to as a dissenting view to the effect that the rabbis preferred to impose as many barriers as possible between men and women out of recognition "that their own sexual nature makes social interchange with women impossible." However, I suggest that the view of women as sexually unreliable need not conflict with the conviction of the strength of male desire; rather the two combine to create an atmosphere of danger around women requiring effective controls and social separation to prevent moral chaos.

46. Satlow, *Tasting the Dish*, pp. 158–159.

47. For further discussion of B. Nedarim 20a–20b, see chapter 4 of this volume; for a similar remark, see B. Shabbat 64b, "Whoever looks upon a woman's little finger is as though he gazed upon the pudenda."

48. Hauptman, *Rereading the Rabbis*, pp. 54.

49. The Wisdom of Ben Sira is a Jewish work of the second century B.C.E. now found in the Apocrypha. The text in Ben Sira does not mention witchcraft,

and in fact this *sugya* interweaves citations from Ben Sira with rabbinic editorial comments. On the rabbinic connection between perceived female sexual licentiousness and witchcraft, see comments below, and Satlow, *Tasting the Dish*, p. 146. On the connections established between women and witchcraft in rabbinic Judaism, see Meir Bar-Ilan, "Witches in the Bible and in the Talmud," and Simcha Fishbane, "Most Women Engage in Sorcery," both in *Approaches to Ancient Judaism. New Series*, ed. Herbert W. Basser and Simcha Fishbane, Vol. 5 (Atlanta: Scholars Press, 1993), pp. 7–32 and 143–166; and chapter 6 below. For images of women in the Wisdom of Ben Sira, see Claudia V. Camp, "Understanding a Patriarchy: Women in Second Century Judaism Through the Eyes of Ben Sira," in *"Women Like This": New Perspectives on Jewish Women in the Greco-Roman World*, ed. Amy-Jill Levine (Atlanta: Scholars Press, 1991), pp. 1–39, esp. pp. 34–37; Warren C. Trenchard, *Ben Sira's View of Women* (Chico, Calif.: Scholars Press, 1982); and especially Tal Ilan, " 'Wickedness Comes from Women' (Ben Sira 42:13): Ben Sira's Misogyny and its Reception by the Babylonian Talmud," in idem, *Integrating Women into Second Temple History*, pp. 155–174.

50. For further discussion of rabbinic fears of unfaithful wives, see chapter 4 below. On the dangers of women gathering together, see chapter 6.

51. The entire *sugya* at B. Shabbat 62b is extremely disturbing. It first links women who wear perfume flasks with those who engage in sexually immoral behavior: "This refers to people who eat and drink together, join their couches, exchange their wives, and make their couches foul with semen that is not theirs," before moving on to the discourse on seductive women, uncouth men, and their shared culpability in the fall of Jerusalem.

52. B. Nazir 59a forbids such methods of hair removal to men on the basis of **"A woman must not put on man's apparel, nor shall a man wear woman's clothing; for whoever does these things is abhorrent to the Lord your God"** (Deut. 22:5).

53. According to Bernadette Brooten, *Women Leaders in the Ancient Synagogue*, pp. 103–138, analysis of archaeological, literary, and epigraphical evidence relating to women and the synagogue reveals that there is currently no evidence from antiquity that women were routinely separated from men in Jewish worship, nor that women sat in upstairs galleries or adjacent rooms. Similarly, Hannah Safrai, "Women and the Ancient Synagogue," in *Daughters of the King*, ed. Grossman and Haut, pp. 39–49, cites the work of Samuel Safrai who also agreed there was no archeological or literary evidence in the ancient period to indicate that there was a separate place for women in the synagogue. Emily Taitz, "Women's Voices, Women's Prayers: The European Synagogue of the Middle Ages," in *Daughters of the King*, ed. Grossman and Haut, pp. 59–71, notes, p. 62, that separation of the sexes does not appear to become a hard-and-fast ruling until the late twelfth or early thirteenth centuries. See also, Norma Baumel Joseph, "*Mehitzah*: Halakhic Decisions and Political Consequences," in *Daughters of the King*, ed. Grossman and Haut, pp. 117–134, for the history of this custom.

54. Tikva Frymer-Kensky, *In the Wake of the Goddesses: Women, Culture and the Biblical Transformation of Pagan Myth* (New York: The Free Press, 1992), p. 203.

55. Frymer-Kensky, *In the Wake of the Goddesses*, p. 211, p. 202, and passim, pp. 203–212.

56. Boyarin, *Carnal Israel*, p. 94. Boyarin, writes, pp. 77–78, "Hatred and fear of women, as such and as a central theme of culture, develop in Hellenistic Judaism out of a disposition toward procreation that can be traced to certain Greek cultural sources fundamentally different from the biblical one." See also p. 100, where Boyarin contrasts Greek stories about Pandora with the biblical vision of Eve as two very different configurations of androcentrism. He argues that in the Greek version, which was transmitted to late antiquity and the Middle Ages, "woman is a mark of evil and a source of danger for man and indeed essentially evil in her very nature," as opposed to biblical and rabbinic Judaisms where women's social and sexual functions, while subordinate to men's, are "valued highly and represented not as an evil that has befallen 'man' but as a mark of God's beneficence to man."

57. Boyarin, *Carnal Israel*, p. 106.

58. Boyarin, *Carnal Israel*, p. 94. For studies of the negative ways in which women are constructed in some medieval Jewish literatures, see Judith Dishon, "Images of Women in Medieval Hebrew Literature," in *Women of the Word*, ed. Judith R. Baskin, pp. 35–49; and Judith R. Baskin, "From Separation to Displacement: Perceptions of the Feminine in Sefer Hasidim," *Association for Jewish Studies Review* 19:1 (Spring, 1994):1–10. For the *Alphabet of Ben Sira*, a composition dated to the Muslim world in the Geonic period which preserves a significant amount of misogynistic *aggadah*, see the translation by Norman Bronznick in *Rabbinic Fantasies: Imaginative Narratives from Classical Hebrew Literature*, ed. David Stern and Mark Jay Mirsky (Philadelphia: Jewish Publication Society, 1990), pp. 167–202.

59. Boyarin, *Carnal Israel*, p. 96. For an analysis of various medieval Jewish views about sexuality, see David Biale, *Eros and the Jews*, pp. 60–120.

60. Boyarin, *Carnal Israel*, p. 245.

61. In a later work, *Unheroic Conduct: The Rise of Heterosexuality and the Invention of the Jewish Man* (Berkeley: University of California Press, 1997), p. 25, n. 76, Boyarin writes that contrary to his expressed view in *Carnal Israel* that the anti-misogynist voice is dominant in rabbinic writings, he has now concluded that it is impossible to identify dominant and subordinate ideologies. He believes that I have made the "contrary (but identical) mistake" in finding a misogynist strain dominant. In fact, I have never claimed that this is the case; I argue here, as I have elsewhere, that in constructing women as essentially other than men, rabbinic literature does leave plentiful room for the expression of negative views about those women who depart from the secondary enabling roles rabbinic Judaism deems appropriate for them, while preserving positive representations of compliant women, as well.

62. See, for example, Mordechai A. Friedman, "Tamar, a Symbol of Life: The 'Killer Wife' Superstition in the Bible and Jewish Tradition," *Association for Jewish Studies Review* 15:1 (Spring, 1990): 23–61; quote on p. 24: See also chapter 3 below.

63. Mayer Gruber, "The Status of Women in Ancient Judaism," pp. 151–176, p. 172.

64. Jacob Neusner, *Androgynous Judaism: Masculine and Feminine in the Dual Torah* (Macon: Mercer University Press, 1993), writes, p. vii, "God wants holy Israel now to embody traits defined as feminine, woman to the nations' ravishing man, so that, in the world that is coming, Israel may find itself transformed into man—but man still with woman's virtues."

65. Gruber, "The Status of Women," p. 173.
66. Boyarin, *Unheroic Conduct*, pp. 156–157.
67. Boyarin, *Unheroic Conduct*, pp. 144–145.
68. Boyarin, *Unheroic Conduct*, p. 179. On the question of women studying Torah, see Boyarin, *Carnal Israel*, pp. 169–179, who contends that there was a significant difference between the Babylonian and Palestinian Talmuds on this issue. Although neither community endorsed such study, he argues that Palestinian rabbis at least discussed Ben Azzai's minority opinion in M. Sotah 3:4, that a man is obligated to teach his daughter Torah, while the Babylonian sages found the very notion of female involvement in Torah study so threatening they thoroughly eliminated any reference to the very possibility from their deliberations. Rather the Babylonian sages, in what was to become the dominant tradition for medieval and early modern Judaism, focus on the vicarious merit women achieve through furthering the Torah study of the males of their family. For further discussion of issues connected with women's involvement in Torah study, see chapter 3 of this volume.
69. Boyarin, *Unheroic Conduct*, both citations p. 153.
70. I thank Susan Sered for this insight about the collusion of women in maintaining social structures and institutions that are oppressive to them and their participation in the persecution of women who appear to rebel against the system.
71. Friedman, "Tamar: A Symbol of Life," p. 39; on Homa and her situation, see Friedman's remarks, pp. 36–39.
72. See Mayer I. Gruber, "The Status of Women," on systematic rabbinic efforts to remove women's rights in both the public and private domains; and see idem, "Women in the Cult According to the Priestly Code," in idem, *The Motherhood of God and Other Studies* (Atlanta:Scholars Press:, 1992), pp. 49–68; and see chapter 3 of this volume.
73. Ross Shephard Kraemer, *Her Share of the Blessings: Women's Religions Among Pagans, Jews, and Christians in the Greco-Roman World* (New York: Oxford University Press, 1992), pp. 93–94, 99, 102; idem, "Jewish Women in the Diaspora World of Late Antiquity," in *Jewish Women in Historical Perspective*, ed. Judith R. Baskin, 2nd ed. (Detroit: Wayne State University Press, 1998), pp. 46–72; and idem, "Women's Judaism(s) at the Beginning of Christianity," in *Women and Christian Origins*, ed. Ross Shepard Kraemer and Mary Rose D'Angelo (New York: Oxford University Press, 1999), pp. 50–79.
74. On Babata and the archive of papyrus documents connected with her personal and business affairs, as well as those of several other women, see *The Documents from the Bar Kokhba Period in the Cave of Letters: Greek Papyri*, ed. Naphtali Lewis, Judean Desert Studies No. 2 (Jerusalem: Israel Exploration Society, 1989), pp. 229–250; Tal Ilan, *Integrating Women into Second Temple History*, pp. 215–262; and Ross S. Kraemer, "Women's Judaism(s) at the Beginning of Christianity," in *Women and Christian Origins*, ed. Ross S. Kraemer and Mary Rose D'Angelo (New York: Oxford University Press, 1999), pp. 53–59, 61–62. On Berenice, a member of the Herodian royal family who had a love affair with the Roman general Titus, see Kraemer, "Women's Judaism(s)," in *Women and Christian Origins*, ed. Kraemer and D'Angelo, pp. 54–56.
75. Bernadette Brooten, *Women Leaders in the Ancient Synagogue* (Chico, Calif.: Scholars Press, 1982).
76. Kraemer, *Her Share of the Blessings*, p. 123.

77. Brooten, *Women Leaders*, p. 150.

78. Kraemer, *Her Share of the Blessings*, p. 100.

79. On women as bolsters to their husbands, see B. 'Eruvin 100b, and chapters 3 and 4 below. For women's economic activities, see Shulamit Valler, "Business Women in the Mishnaic and Talmudic Period," *Women in Judaism: A Multidisciplinary Journal* 12, 2 (2001); www.utoronto.ca/wjudaism/journal/vol2n2.

CHAPTER 2 (PP. 44–64)

1. An earlier version of parts of the first section of this chapter appeared as "Rabbinic Judaism and the Creation of Woman," *Shofar* 13: 4 (Fall, 1995): 68–73. Reprinted in *Judaism Since Gender*, ed. Miriam Peskowitz and Laura Levitt (New York: Routledge, 1997), pp. 125–130. While the Hebrew *'adam* in Genesis 1:26 is most often translated as "man," it seems to me that "humanity" or "human beings" is more accurate in this context of a simultaneous creation of woman and man.

2. For a review of modern source critical study of the Hebrew Bible, see Richard Elliott Friedman, *Who Wrote the Bible?* (San Francisco: Harper, 1987); on these particular passages, see pp. 50–51, 234–236.

3. See, for example, Friedman, *Who Wrote the Bible?* p. 236, who writes, "The Eden story is from J, which never suggests that humans are created in God's image. The creation account is from P, which never includes powerful plants or talking snakes. And the redactor included both stories whole, so we cannot tell whether he was even aware of this exquisite coalescence of the two or not." There are a number of feminist readings of these passages, including Tikva Frymer-Kensky, *In the Wake of the Goddesses: Women, Culture, and the Biblical Transformation of Pagan Myth* (New York: Basic Books, 1992), pp. 108–110, 140–143; Carol Meyers, *Discovering Eve: Ancient Israelite Women in Context* (New York: Oxford University Press, 1988), pp. 72–94; Phyllis Bird, "Male and Female He Created Them: Gen 1:27b in the Context of the Priestly Account of Creation," *Harvard Theological Review* 74:2 (1981):129–159; and Ilana Pardes, *Countertraditions in the Bible: A Feminist Approach* (Cambridge: Harvard University Press, 1992), pp. 13–38.

4. The usual translation of Psalm 139:5 is: "You hedge me before and behind / You lay your hand upon me."

5. For further discussion of this aggadic midrash of the androgyne and its significance in rabbinic Judaism, see pp. 60–64 below; and see Daniel Boyarin, *Carnal Israel: Reading Sex in Talmudic Culture* (Berkeley: University of California Press, 1993), pp. 42–46; and Wayne Meeks, "The Image of the Androgyne: Some Uses of a Symbol in Early Christianity," *History of Religions* 13 (1974): 165–208. While the rabbis never directly address the possibility of a separate female who was created at the same time as Adam, there are oblique references to such a being in rabbinic literature. On the "first Eve" and her conflation with folklore about Lilith, see pp. 56–60 below.

6. In Genesis 2:19, **"And the Lord God formed out of the earth all the wild beasts and all the birds of the sky . . . ,"** by contrast, *vayyitzer* ("formed") is spelled with one *yod*; therefore, the double *yod* in this verse is seen to demands exegetical comment. For a philosophical reading of this text that also affirms

the social necessity of male/female hierarchy, see Emmanuel Levinas, "And God Created Woman," collected in *Nine Talmudic Readings*, trans. Annette Aronowicz (Bloomington: University of Indiana Press, 1990, pp. 161–177.

7. This passage is also cited by Gary Anderson, "The Garden of Eden and Sexuality in Early Judaism," in *People of the Body: Jews and Judaism from an Embodied Perspective*, ed. Howard Eilberg-Schwartz (Albany: State University of New York Press, 1992), pp. 47–68, in a discussion of the connection between marriage and sexual pleasure. He suggests, p. 59, that the language of the blessing in which Eve is described as "an eternal building (*binyan*)" is a wordplay on **"And the Lord God built (*banah*) the rib . . . into a woman"** (Gen. 2:22), writing, "This midrash understands the verb to connote not simply the divine act of creation but also the nature of that creation." Anderson goes on to say that "Eve is to become more than a partner to Adam; she is to be a propagator, a provider of children." I would disagree with this active characterization. Eve does not propagate. Rather, in a well known biblical metaphor, discussed in chapter 1 and chapter 4 of this book, she is a house (*bayit*), a passive vessel, in which the unborn child is deposited, develops, and is nurtured; see also, p. 88 below.

8. On this midrash, see chapter 1, pp. 15–16 above. This midrash also appears in *Avot de Rabbi Nathan* B 9; and in altered form in *Genesis Rabbah* 17:8, discussed in chapter 3: "R. Joshua was asked: 'Why does a man come forth [at birth] with his face downward, while a woman comes forth with her face turned upwards?' '[He answered], 'The man looks toward the place of his creation [the earth], while the woman looks towards the place of her creation [the rib].' "

9. Reuven Kimelman, "The Seduction of Eve and the Exegetical Politics of Gender," *Biblical Interpretation* 4:1 (1996): 1–39; pp. 17–18.

10. On the centrality of the male superior position in sexual intercourse to rabbinic constructions of male dominance over women, see my discussion of the medieval formulation of the myth of Lilith as the "first Eve," pp. 56–60 below. On readings of Genesis 1:28, as indicated here, see *B. Yevamot 65b* and *Genesis Rabbah* 8:12. On implications for women and the obligation to procreate, see chapter 5.

11. The phrase *"yad l'yad,"* at the beginning of Proverbs 11:21 translates literally as "hand to hand." The *Jewish Publication Society Tanakh* indicates that the meaning of the Hebrew is uncertain, and translates the phrase as "assuredly."

12. On the exegetical history of this verse, see Jeremy Cohen, *"Be Fertile and Increase, Fill the Earth and Master It": The Ancient and Medieval Career of a Biblical Text* (Ithaca: Cornell University Press, 1989).

13. On the exemption of women from the legal obligation to procreate, see below chapter 5.

14. On Dinah, see, for example, *Genesis Rabbah* 80:1–12, particularly the comments on **"Now Dinah . . . went out to visit the daughters of the land"** (Gen 34:1), which attributes all the terrible events connected with this episode to Dinah's immodesty in going out on her own, and see, chapter 4, p. 109 below. On controlling the movements of one's wife, see chapter 4.

15. The Hebrew letters in each word, *mem, aleph, dalet*, are the same, although differently arranged.

16. For this interpretation *ne'esah* ("is made") is read instead of *na'aseh* (**"Let us make"** [Gen. 1:26]).

17. A similar passage appears in *Genesis Rabbah* 45:5 in which women are said to be greedy, eavesdroppers, slothful, envious, scratchers, talkative, prone to steal, and gadabouts, with many of the same proof texts. Another extended midrash, *Genesis Rabbah* 17:8, discussed in detail in chapter 3, begins with the assumption that women's inherent weaknesses are a result of the secondary nature of their creation and progresses to blaming women for bringing disorder and death into the world. Ephraim E. Urbach, in *The Sages: The World and Wisdom of the Rabbis of the Talmud* (Cambridge: Harvard University Press, 1987), writes, p. 421, that the primary consequence of human disobedience in the Garden of Eden was that death came into being; he argues: "The story of Adam's sin does not purport in the Bible to explain men's sins and weaknesses." While Urbach cites Ben Sira 25:28, **"From a woman did sin originate, and because of her we all die,"** and *Genesis Rabbah* 17:8 on female culpability for mortality, he uses these texts only to support his argument that Judaism has no concept of original sin or predestination, not to investigate the ways in which rabbinic literature constructs women as the cause of human mortality. On the folklore tradition that some women are sources of death, see Mordechai A. Friedman, "Tamar, a Symbol of Life: The 'Killer Wife' Superstition in the Bible and Jewish Tradition," *Association of Jewish Studies Review* 15 (1990): 23–62.

18. Tirzah Meacham, "Woman More Intelligent than Man: Creation Gone Awry," in *Approaches to Ancient Judaism. New Series 5: Historical, Literary, and Religious Studies*, ed. Herbert W. Basser and Simcha Fishbane (Atlanta: Scholars Press, 1993), pp. 59–60.

19. On Deborah and Huldah, see B. Megillah 14b and chapter 1, p. 32. Judith Hauptman, "Images of Women in the Talmud," in *Religion and Sexism: Images of Women in Jewish and Christian Traditions*, ed. Rosemary Radford Ruether (New York: Simon and Schuster, 1974), p. 204, cites the example of Rabbi Samuel's daughters who "not only quoted Jewish law, but actually utilized it in a shrewd way in order to obtain permission to marry a *kohen* [priest] after having been returned from captivity" (B. Ketubbot 23a). While the daughters did marry, they died untimely deaths (J. Ketubbot 2:6). Judith Hauptman, *Rereading the Rabbis: A Woman's Voice*, (Boulder: Westview Press, 1998) states, p. 9, that almost every negative aggadic statement about women can be offset by another that says just the opposite, but I find that negative remarks and attitudes expressed towards women far outnumber positive statements.

20. See Judith R. Baskin, "The Separation of Women in Rabbinic Judaism," in *Women, Religion and Social Change*, ed. Y. Y. Haddad and E. B. Findly (Albany: State University of New York Press, 1985), pp. 6–7; and Hauptman, "Images of Women," pp. 201–204. For several stories of how a rabbi was bested by a woman and by children, represented as strikingly unusual events, see B. 'Eruvin 53b. For another account of the refutation of a heretic by a woman, in this case Rabban Gamliel's daughter, see B. Sanhedrin 39a.

21. On named women in rabbinic literature, see Tal Ilan, *Mine and Yours are Hers: Retrieving Women's History from Rabbinic Literature* (Leiden: E. J. Brill, 1997), pp. 278–318, who points out, p. 279, that, issues of historicity aside, "In the entire rabbinic corpus only fifty-two women are mentioned by name (as opposed to about a thousand men)." For rabbinic delineations of two named women, Beruriah and Yalta, see chapter 3.

22. On rabbinic views of marriage, see chapter 4 below. B. Berakhot 61a is quite similar: "It teaches that [God] built Eve after the fashion of a storehouse.

Just as a storehouse is narrow at the top and broad at the bottom so as to hold produce, so a woman is narrower above and broader below so as to hold the embryo." In this *sugya*, God is also said to have braided Eve's hair before bringing her to Adam (the passage makes an etymological connection between a regional term for braiding hair, "*binyata*" ("building"), and the phrase in Genesis 2:22 describing the formation of Eve, **"And the Lord God built (*vayyiven*)".** On the connection of loosened hair with immodesty, uncontrolled sexuality, and demonic qualities, see pp. 58–60 below, and chapter 3, pp. 68, 74, 77.

23. Judith Romney Wegner, "The Image and Status of Women in Classical Rabbinic Judaism," in *Jewish Women in Historical Perspective*, ed. Judith R. Baskin, 2nd ed. (Detroit: Wayne State University Press, 1998), p. 84. The blessing Wegner cites can be found in Philip Birnbaum, trans., *Daily Prayer Book [Ha-Siddur Ha-Shalem]* (New York: Hebrew Publishing Company, 1949). Wegner writes, p. 98 n. 35, "Perhaps it is no accident that the male worshiper continues immediately with three blessings praising God for not having made him a gentile, a slave, or a woman." On this blessing, see chapter 1 above, pp. 16–17.

24. *Midrash Ha-Gadol* to Genesis, 1:74, cited in Meacham, "Woman More Intelligent than Man," p. 60.

25. Meacham, "Woman More Intelligent than Man," p. 60.

26. Meacham writes, "Fortunately, real women were not so easily subjugated, which is why creation went awry." (p. 61)

27. See chapter 4, p. 111 below.

28. The text raises an immediate objection to this statement since the letter *samekh* first appears in the verse: **"The name of the second river is Gihon, the one that winds (*sovev*) through the whole land of Cush"** (Gen. 2:11). The response is: "The text refers there to rivers." This second use of *samekh* is the first that refers to a human being.

29. Daniel Boyarin, *Carnal Israel*, pp. 88–90.

30. This cryptic comment preserves a triple pun on *pa'am*, "instance" or "time," *pa'amon*, "bell," and the verb *pa'am*, "to trouble" or "disquiet." The full passage from Exodus 28:31–35 discusses the pure blue **"robe of the ephod"** to be worn by the high priest. The reference to a "golden bell" is found in verses 33–35: **"On its hem make pomegranates of blue purple, and crimson yarns, all around the hem, with bells of gold between them all around: a golden bell and a pomegranate, a golden bell and a pomegranate, all around the hem of the robe. Aaron shall wear it while officiating, so that the sound of it is heard when he comes into the sanctuary before the Lord and when he goes out—that he may not die."**

31. On a similar aggadic explanation, attributed to R. Meir, for the separation of husband and wife when she is a *niddah*, see chapter 1, p. 22. A number of traditions referring to a certain "Matrona" appear in rabbinic literature. Many scholars have understand *matrona* as a general term for a Roman lady interested in Jewish traditions. Tal Ilan has suggested that Matrona is the proper name of an actual Jewish woman who engaged in some level of Jewish scholarly discourse. On the corpus of aggadic material concerning Matrona and their meanings, see Tal Ilan, "Matrona and Rabbi Jose: An Alternative Interpretation," *Journal for the Study of Judaism* 25 (1994): 18–51, and idem, *Mine and Yours are Hers*, pp. 240–262, 297–310.

32. *Genesis Rabbah* 22:2 recounts that Eve gave birth at one time to Cain and a twin sister, and to Abel and two twin sisters. This legend is apparently meant to answer the question of whom the children of Adam and Eve, in the absence of information about further human creations, could have married.

33. There are references to Lilith in B. 'Eruvin 100b, "[A woman must] grow long hair like Lilith"; B. Niddah 24b, "Rab Judah citing Samuel ruled: If an abortion had the likeness of Lilith its mother is unclean by reason of the birth, for it is a child, but it has wings"; B. Shabbat 151b, "R. Hanina said: One may not sleep in a house alone, and whoever sleeps in a house alone is seized by Lilith," a probable reference to the belief that Lilith is responsible for nocturnal emissions; and B. Bava Batra 73b, which relates an anecdote about the prodigious speed of the demon "Hormin, the son of Lilith." *Numbers Rabbah* 16:25 preserves a reference to Lilith killing her own children. For a discussion of the place of "liliths" as evil female spirits invoked on incantation bowls in Sassanian Babylonia, see Rebecca Lesses, "Exe(o)rcising Power: Women as Sorceresses, Exorcists, and Demonesses in Babylonian Jewish Society of Late Antiquity," *Journal of the American Academy of Religion* 69, 2 (2001): 343–375. Lesses, argues, p. 354, that these bowls, some of which use rabbinic divorce formulas to exorcise demons, can be considered as originating in the same cultural milieu as the Babylonian Talmud, although they were far from an exclusively Jewish phenomenon. She writes, p. 356, that "one prominent characteristic of the liliths is that they attack people in the sexual and reproductive realm of life."

34. On aggadic references to the demonic descendants of Adam and Lilith, see Gershom Scholem, *Origins of the Kabbalah*, ed. R. J. Zwi Werblowsky (Princeton: Princeton University Press,1987), p. 296, n.191; and Joseph Dan, "Samael, Lilith, and the Concept of Evil," *Association for Jewish Studies Review* 5 (1980):17–40, p. 20.

35. An annotated English translation of the *Alphabet of Ben Sira* by Norman Bronznick appears in *Rabbinic Fantasies: Imaginative Narratives from Classical Hebrew Literature*, ed. David Stern and Mark Jay Mirsky (Philadelphia: Jewish Publication Society, 1990), pp. 167–202. For a critical edition of this text, see Eli Yassif, *Sippurei Ben Sira* (Jerusalem: Magnes Press, 1984).

36. *The Alphabet of Ben Sira*, "Question 5," in *Rabbinic Fantasies*, ed. Stern and Mirsky, pp. 183–184. On the Lilith legend in the Middle Ages, and on amulets and other defenses against her, see Joshua Trachtenberg, *Jewish Magic and Superstition* (New York: Jewish Publication Society, 1970), pp. 36–37, 101, 169.

37. *Encyclopedia Judaica* 11:246–47. On the demonic roles played by Lilith in medieval Jewish mysticism, see Scholem, *Origins of the Kabbalah*, pp. 295–97; and Dan, "Samael, Lilith, and the Concept of Evil."

38. Dan, "Samael, Lilith, and the Concept of Evil," pp. 22.

39. The Septuagint is the oldest Greek translation of the Hebrew Bible, probably translated in Alexandria, Egypt, during the first half of the third century B.C.E. *Encyclopedia Judaica* 2:236, "Adam," notes a similar midrashic tradition (*Mekhilta*, Pisha 14) to the effect that translators of the Septuagint changed **"Let us make man in our image, after our likeness"** (Gen. 1:26) to **"I will make man in my likeness and image,"** presumably in order to remove any suggestion of polytheism. In fact, no such version of this verse appears in any existing Septuagint texts. On this issue, see Boyarin, *Carnal Israel*, p. 36, n.9.

40. Jeremy Cohen, *"Be Fertile and Increase,"* p. 87. For parallels to this midrash and further discussion of some of its implications, see Cohen, pp. 83–98.

41. One of the best known examples of a similar narrative occurs in Plato's *Symposium* 189d, 190d. On this parallel and others, see Urbach, *The Sages*, p. 228; and Boyarin, *Carnal Israel*, p. 43. For the various uses of this legend in early Christianity, see Meeks, "The Image of the Androgyne."

42. Philo of Alexandria, *De opificio mundi* 134. On Philo's negative views of women in general and his reading of the Genesis creation narratives in particular, see Judith Romney Wegner, "Philo's Portrayal of Women—Hebraic or Hellenic?" in *"Women Like This": New Perspectives on Jewish Women in the Greco-Roman World*, ed. Amy Jill Levine (Atlanta: Scholars Press, 1991), pp. 41–66; pp. 45–51.

43. Boyarin, *Carnal Israel*, p. 43; also see pp. 17–18.

44. *Carnal Israel*, p. 43; see also, Cohen, *"Be Fertile and Increase"*, pp. 90–98, on polemical aspects of rabbinic discourses on human sexuality and procreation.

45. *Carnal Israel*, pp. 45–46.

46. Gary Anderson, "The Garden of Eden," pp. 59–63; quote on p. 63.

47. It is worth reiterating that rabbinic texts tell us very little about the actualities of women's lives in any particular time or place.

CHAPTER 3 (PP. 65–87)

1. See *Avot de Rabbi Nathan B* 9; B. Niddah 31b; ; chapter 1, pp. 15–16; and chapter 2, pp. 49–51 for the connections between creation and the male superior position in sexual intercourse.

2. See chapter 2, pp. 53–55. Many of these same queries and responses appear in B. Niddah 31b, although that passage concludes on a more positive note regarding women: "Why is a woman's voice sweet and a man's voice is not sweet? He [derives his voice] from the place from which he was created [the earth] and she [derives hers] from the place from which she was created [a bone can be made to produce certain musical notes]. Thus it is said, 'Let me hear your voice;/ For your voice is sweet/ And your face is comely' (Song of Songs 2:14)." Sweetness of voice is also problematic, however, since it is a sexual incitement (B. Berakhot 24a); see chapter 1, pp. 15–16, 35–36.

3. Isaiah M. Gafni, "The Institution of Marriage in Rabbinic Times," in *The Jewish Family: Metaphor and Memory*, ed. David M. Kraemer (New York, 1989), pp. 21–25; see chapter 4, note 63, for documentary evidence of a polygynous marriage in the Land of Israel in the second century C.E.

4. Leila Leah Bronner, "From Veil to Wig: Jewish Women's Hair Covering," *Judaism* 42:4 (Fall, 1993): 465–477, p. 468. Veiling may have been considered even more essential for women in public in Babylonia than in the Land of Israel. On veiling of women in the ancient world, see Molly Myerowitz Levine, "The Gendered Grammar of Ancient Mediterranean Hair," in *Off with Her Head! The Denial of Women's Identity in Myth, Religion, and Culture*, eds. Howard Eilberg-Schwartz and Wendy Doniger (Berkeley: University of California Press, 1995), pp. 76–130. She assumes it was the norm for Jewish women to cover or bind their hair from biblical times on, noting, p. 104, that a stage in the ritual

undergone by the *sotah*, the wife suspected of adultery, involved the public entangling of her hair, an indication of her sexually suspect status. She writes, pp. 104–105, "Indeed, the immense body of rabbinic legislation regarding the covering of married women's hair all derives from the disheveled hair of the hapless *sotah*."

5. On this passage, see Mordechai A. Freidman, "Tamar, a Symbol of Life: The 'Killer Wife' Superstition in the Bible and Jewish Tradition," *Association for Jewish Studies Review* 15:1 (Spring, 1990): 23–61, pp. 36–39.

6. The linkage of women with death constitutes a distinctive strand in the rabbinic discourse about women and the dangers they represent. Similar notions are found as well in Jewish Hellenistic literature, including Wisdom of Ben Sira 25:24: "The beginning of sin is from woman and because of her we all die." Friedman, "Tamar: A Symbol of Life" has traced recurring superstitions associating particular women with "life-endangering demonic forces" through biblical, rabbinic, and medieval sources. While such views, he argues, were never mainstream and were generally rejected by authoritative voices, the fact that they keep reappearing in various rabbinic associations of women and death indicates the deep resonance they found within rabbinic culture.

7. Meir Bar Ilan, "The Keening Women," in idem, *Some Jewish Women in Antiquity* (Atlanta: Scholars Press, 1998), pp. 52–77; p. 72.

8. Bar Ilan, "The Keening Women, pp. 60–61.

9. Bar Ilan, "The Keening Woman," pp. 73–74; quote above, pp. 75–76.

10. Galit Hasan-Rokem, *Web of Life: Folklore and Midrash in Rabbinic Literature* (Stanford: Stanford University Press, 2000), trans. Batya Stein, both quotes on p. 111.

11. Bar Ilan, "The Keening Woman," p. 72, n. 52, suggests that women's separate keening at funerals may also bear implications for women's praying separately from men. The antiquity of such customs can be seen in the description of mourning in Zechariah 12:12–14: "**The land shall wail, each family by itself: the family of the House of David by themselves, and their womenfolk by themselves; the family of the House of Nathan by themselves, and their womenfolk by themselves.**"

12. Carol Meyers, *Discovering Eve: Ancient Israelite Women in Context* (New York: Oxford University Press,1988), p. 161. M. Ta'anit 4:8 preserves an intriguing reference to a twice yearly event when unmarried girls would don borrowed white garments and dance in the vineyards in front of unmarried men seeking wives.

13. Ross Shepard Kraemer, *Her Share of the Blessings: Women's Religions Among Pagans, Jews, and Christians in the Greco-Roman World* (New York: Oxford University Press, 1992), p. 97. Kraemer notes, p. 97, that women may not have been responsible for purchasing food since that would have required them to venture into public markets. On concern about women in the public domain of the marketplace, see, chapter 4, pp. 112–114 below. While wealthy women may have had slaves who did much of the actual food purchasing and preparation, wives were still considered responsible for supervision and observance of the dietary laws.

14. In the midrash collection *Tanhuma*, Noah 1, these three precepts are described as both punishments and as atonement for women's guilt: "And since Scripture says, '**Whoever spills the blood of Adam so within man shall his blood be spilled**' (Gen. 9:6), her blood is spilled as punishment in surety, and she

observes the blood of menstrual purity that it may atone for the spilling of Adam's blood in perpetuity." The text in the Buber edition of *Tanhuma,* Noah I, stresses atonement rather than punishment: "Since Adam was the head of His creation of the world and Eve deceived him, bringing upon him that which was said 'For you are dust and to dust you shall return,' so the Holy One said: May there be given to her the commandment of menstrual purity that there may be atonement for that blood which she spilled in perpetuity."

15. The rest of the passage in *Avot de-Rabbi Nathan* B, ch. 9, concludes: "Why was the commandment of dough offering given to woman and not to man? For Adam was the pure dough offering of the Holy One blessed be He and she defiled it. Therefore she was given the commandment of dough offerings in order to atone for the dough offering she had defied. Why was the commandment of candle-lighting given to woman and not to man? Adam was the candle of the Holy One blessed be He who lit the way for all who would be born and she extinguished it. Therefore she was given the commandment of candle-lighting in order to atone for the candle she extinguished."

16. Other explanations for women's premature deaths in this passage include washing diapers on the Sabbath. In addition, this text also appears to imply that premature deaths of wives (and children) may not always be due to their own fault, but might occur as punishment for their husband's sins.

17. Kraemer, *Her Share of the Blessings,* p. 100.

18. Kraemer, *Her Share of the Blessings,* p. 107.

19. Kraemer, *Her Share of the Blessings*, p. 99. For the medieval period, see Shaye J. D. Cohen, "Purity, Piety, and Polemic: Medieval Rabbinic Denunciations of 'Incorrect' Purification Practices, in Rahel R. Wasserfall, ed., *Women and Water: Menstruation in Jewish Life and Law* (Hanover, N.H.: Brandeis University Press, 1999), pp. 82–100; and Judith R. Baskin, "Women and Ritual Immersion in Medieval Ashkenaz: The Sexual Politics of Piety," in *Judaism in Practice: From the Middle Ages through the Early Modern Period*, ed. Lawrence Fine (Princeton: Princeton University Press, 2001), pp. 131–142.

20. Daniel Boyarin, *Carnal Israel: Reading Sex in Talmudic Culture* (Berkeley: University of California Press, 1993), p. 94.

21. Boyarin, *Carnal Israel,* p. 94.

22. Most of these curses are also found in *Avot de-Rabbi Nathan* A, ch. 1, which also relates that three decrees were decreed against Adam on the day of his disobedience and three were also decreed against Eve. Discussion of the decrees against Eve are based on: "And to the woman He said, 'I will make most severe/ Your pangs in childbearing;/ In pain shall you bear children./ Yet your urge shall be for your husband,/ And he shall rule over you" (Gen. 3:16). The text reads: " 'Most severe' teaches that when a woman is menstruating, at the beginning of her period she is in pain. 'I will make' teaches that the first time a woman cohabits it is painful for her. 'Your pangs' teaches that the first three months after a woman has conceived, her face turns ugly and pallid." For ten decrees against Eve listed in *Avot de-Rabbi Natan B* 42, see p. 78 below.

23. This verse (Job 35:11) is usually translated, "Who gives us more knowledge than the beasts of the earth,/ Makes us wiser than the birds of the sky."

24. On polygyny, see note. 3 above.

25. See, chapter 1, pp. 41–42 above. On women's business activities, particularly in connection with owning and administering property, see Shulamit

Valler, "Business Women in the Mishnaic and Talmudic Period," *Women in Judaism: A Multidisciplinary Journal* 2:2 (2001).

26. See, chapter 2, p. 55 above.

27. Other examples include M. Berakhot 3:3: "Women and slaves and minors are exempt from reciting the *Sh'ma* and from wearing phylacteries," and M. Sukkah 2:7: "Women, slaves and minors are exempt from [the law of] the Sukkah."

28. See chapter 1, p. 16.

29. On *lilith* as a night spirit in ancient Near Eastern folklore who seduces men and harms children, see chapter 2, pp. 56–60 above. Rebecca Lesses, "Exe(o)rcising Power: Women as Sorceresses, Exorcists, and Demonesses in Babylonian Jewish Society of Late Antiquity," *Journal of the American Academy of Religion* 69,2 (2001): 343–375, writes, p. 358, that "the demonic image of the *lilith*'s long, flowing, and disheveled hair [on incantation bowls from Sassanian Babylonia] may shed some light on the significance of women's uncovered hair in rabbinic literature." She suggests that this statement in B. 'Eruvin 100b "connects women's demonic and bestial nature to their sexual subordination to men."

30. Meir Bar Ilan, "Prayers by Women," in idem, *Some Jewish Women in Antiquity*, writes, pp. 112–113, that "The exclusion of women from praying in a social context, that is, not in a synagogue; and the spontaneous quality of their prayers, highlight the anti-establishment, or individualistic aspect of their prayers"; and goes on to say that "Since feminine prayers were considered unimportant, they were excluded from the canonization of normative—that is, masculine—prayer." He discusses, p. 93 n.38, several *halakhot* which, according to B. Berakhot 31 a–b and other sources, are said to be derived from Hannah's prayer. On Hannah's prayer, see Dvora Weisberg, "Men Imagining Women Imagining God: Gender Issues in Classic Midrash," in *Agendas for the Study of Midrash in the Twenty-First Century*, ed. Marc Lee Raphael (Williamsburg, Va.: Department of Religion, William and Mary College, 1999), pp. 63–83; and chapter 5 below. On the permissibility of prayer in the vernacular, a necessity for women since few learned Hebrew, see B. Sotah 32a–33a, and Ruth Langer, *To Worship God Properly: Tensions between Liturgical Custom and Halakhah in Judaism* (Cincinnati: Hebrew Union College Press, 1998), pp. 22–23.

31. Saul Berman, "The Status of Women in Halakhic Judaism," in *The Jewish Woman*, ed. Elizabeth Koltun (New York: Schocken, 1976), pp. 114–128, p. 123. And see Rachel Biale, *Women and Jewish Law* (New York: Schocken, 1984), pp. 10–17.

32. Judith Hauptman, in "Women and Prayer: An Attempt to Dispel Some Fallacies," *Judaism* 42:1 (winter 1993), pp. 94–103 and "Some Thoughts on the Nature of Halakhic Adjudication: Women and *Minyan*," *Judaism* 42:4 (fall, 1993), pp. 396–413, offers a close re-examination of the issues involved in rabbinic sources concerned with women and prayer. She concludes that women, like men, have always been obligated to pray several times a day according to a fixed liturgy. See idem, *Rereading the Rabbis: A Woman's Voice* (Boulder: Westview Press, 1998), pp. 229–231.

33. Judith Romney Wegner, *Chattel or Person? The Status of Women in the Mishnah* (New York: Oxford University Press, 1988), pp. 147–148.

34. On the general exclusion of women from study in rabbinic Judaism, see Boyarin, *Carnal Israel,* pp. 167–196; idem, "Reading Androcentrism against the

Grain:Women, Sex and Torah Study," *Poetics Today* 12:1 (spring, 1991): 29–53.

35. Boyarin, *Carnal Israel*, p. 177. See also Mayer Gruber, "The Status of Women in Ancient Judaism," in *Judaism in Late Antiquity*. Pt. 3, vol. 2: *Where We Stand: Issues and Debates in Ancient Judaism*, ed. Jacob Neusner and Alan J. Avery-Peck (Leiden: E. J. Brill, 1999), pp. 151–176, who demonstrates the variety of ways in which the rabbis of the Talmud deliberately disempowered women in the communal domains of prayer and study.

36. Examples of Beruriah's astuteness appear in B. Pesahim 62b, B. Berakhot 10a, and B. 'Eruvin 53b–54a. In her detailed analysis of "The Historical Beruriah," Tal Ilan, *Integrating Women into Second Temple History* (Tübingen: Mohr Siebeck, 1999), pp. 176–179, discusses the legal ruling attributed to Beruriah in Tosefta Kelim Bava Metzi'a 1:6 and finds no reason to doubt the authenticity of the tradition. However, she finds it no accident that this ruling appears in the Mishnah at Kelim 11:4 with no reference to Beruriah (pp. 179–180). A second ruling in Tosefta Kelim Bava Metzi'a 4:17, attributed to a woman, the daughter of R. Hananya ben Teradion, has also been linked with Beruriah. On the uncertainty of this identification, see Ilan, *Integrating Women*, pp. 176–178.

37. For a recent review of scholarship demonstrating the lack of historicity in references to Beruriah in the Babylonian Talmud, see Tal Ilan, "The Historical Beruriah, Rachel, and Imma Shalom," *Association for Jewish Studies Review* 22:1 (1997): 1–17, particularly pp. 1–8; and David Goodblatt, "The Beruriah Traditions," *Journal of Jewish Studies* 26 (1975):68–85, who demonstrates through comparisons of Babylonian Talmud texts with Palestinian traditions that in several of the Babylonian Talmud citations, Beruriah's name had simply been inserted into pre-existing literary compositions.

38. Ilan, *Integrating Women*, p. 194.

39. Boyarin, *Carnal Israel*, p. 183.

40. Rachel Adler, "The Virgin in the Brothel and other Anomalies: Character and Context in the Legend of Beruriah," *Tikkun* 3, no. 6 (1988):28–32, 102–105, p. 32.

41. Boyarin, *Carnal Israel*, p. 178; Ilan, *Integrating Women*, pp. 189–194, believes this unpleasant tale originates with Rashi.

42. Ilan, *Integrating Women*, p. 180.

43. Boyarin, *Carnal Israel*, p. 196

44. Judith Hauptman, "Feminist Perspectives on Jewish Studies: Rabbinics," in *Feminist Perspectives on Jewish Studies*, ed. Shelly Tenenbaum and Lynn Davidman (New Haven: Yale University Press, 1994), pp. 54–57.

45. Boyarin, *Carnal Israel*, pp. 169–170.

46. See chapter 1, pp. 41–42.

47. On the marketplace as an anxiety-filled location for rabbinic culture, see Cynthia Baker, "Bodies, Boundaries, and Domestic Politics in a Late Ancient Marketplace," *Journal of Medieval and Early Modern Studies* 26:3 (Fall 1996): 391–418, and chapter 4, pp. 112–114.

48. On Yalta, see Tal Ilan, *Integrating Women into Second Temple History*, pp. 171–174; and Rachel Adler, "Feminist Folktales of Justice: Robert Cover as a Resource for the Renewal of Halakhah," *Conservative Judaism* 45/3 (1988): 40–56.

49. On this episode, see Charlotte Elisheva Fonrobert, "Yalta's Ruse: Resis-

tance against Rabbinic Menstrual Authority in Talmudic Literature," in *Women and Water: Menstruation in Jewish Life and Law*, ed. Rahel R. Wasserfall (Hanover, N.H.: Brandeis University Press, 1999). pp. 60–81; and idem, *Menstrual Purity: Rabbinic and Christian Reconstructions of Biblical Gender* (Stanford: Stanford University Press, 2000), pp. 118–126.

50. There are indications elsewhere in the Talmud that this was often done as a courtesy to the women of the household. See for example B. Bava Metzi'a 87a, where various suggestions are put forward as to why the angels who visited Abraham in Genesis 18 asked after Sarah: "R. Jose the son of R. Hanina said: In order to send her the wine-cup of benediction." The issue is whether women are obligated to partake of the cup or whether it is simply sent to them as a courtesy. 'Ulla makes quite clear that women are not obligated and shouldn't be encouraged to think they are. Another example of a ritual in which women were said to have been included as a courtesy even though their participation had no validity can be found in B. Hagigah 16b and also in *Sifra Leviticus* at Leviticus 1:5 in connection with animal sacrifice in Second Temple times. 'Ulla is not even prepared to go this far and it is this lack of civility that enrages Yalta.

51. See Tal Ilan, "Ben Sira in the Babylonia Talmud," in *Integrating Women*, pp. 171–174, on possible connections of Yalta's answer, "Gossip comes from peddlers and vermin from rags," to Ben Sira 42:13, "**For from garments comes the moth, and from a woman comes woman's wickedness**," and Ben Sira 11:29, "**Many are the wounds inflicted by peddlars.**"

52. Rachel Adler, "Feminist Folktales of Justice," pp. 50–51.

53. Adler, "Feminist Folktales of Justice," p. 52.

54. A similar message of disdain for a woman's pretensions, regardless of her social prestige, also seems to be embedded in the brief reference to Yalta in a complicated passage in B. Qiddushin 70a–70b.

CHAPTER 4 (PP. 88–118)

1. An earlier version of some of the material in this chapter appeared in Judith R. Baskin, "Silent Partners: Women as Wives in Rabbinic Literature," in *Active Voices: Women in Jewish Culture*, ed. Maurie Sacks (Urbana and Chicago: University of Illinois Press, 1995), pp. 19–37. On human marriage as symbolic of the relationship between God and the Jewish people, see Arthur Green, "Bride, Spouse, Daughter: Images of the Feminine in Classical Jewish Sources," in *On Being a Jewish Feminist: A Reader*, ed. Susannah Heschel (New York: Schocken, 1983), pp. 248–260; Moshe Idel, "Sexual Metaphors and Praxis in the Kabbalah," in *The Jewish Family: Metaphor and Memory*, ed. David Kraemer (Oxford: Oxford University Press, 1989), pp. 197–224; Jacob Neusner, "Judaism," in *Women and Families*, ed. Jacob Neusner (Cleveland: The Pilgrim Press, 1999), pp. 50–82, pp. 53–68; and below, pp. 99–100. Michael L. Satlow's important book on this topic, *Jewish Marriage in Antiquity*, (Princeton: Princeton University Press, 2001), appeared as this volume was being completed.

2. Cynthia Baker, "Bodies, Boundaries, and Domestic Politics in a Late Ancient Marketplace," *Journal of Medieval and Early Modern Studies* 26,3 (fall 1976): 391–418, goes even further in her discussion of the dangers rabbinic Judaism projects onto women who wander beyond the domestic setting, sug-

gesting, p. 408, that the rabbinic concern surrounding women who venture into the public domain "is as much rabbinic anxiety about the creation and preservation of cultural identity and cultural boundaries as it is male anxiety about female sexuality and the limits of control."

3. Judith Romney Wegner, *Chattel or Person? The Status of Women in the Mishnah* (New York, 1988), p. 44; and see Isaiah Gafni, "The Institution of Marriage in Rabbinic Times," in *The Jewish Family: Metaphor and Memory*, ed. David Kraemer pp. 13–30. For an analysis of marriage as acquisition in most pre-modern societies, see Gayle Rubin, "The Traffic in Women: Notes on the 'Political Economy' of Sex," in *Toward an Anthropology of Women*, ed. Rayna R. Reiter (New York: Monthly Review Press, 1975), pp. 157–210.

4. Judith Hauptman, *Rereading the Rabbis: A Woman's Voice* (Boulder: Westview, 1998), p. 60.

5. On consent to marriage, see Hauptman, *Rereading the Rabbis*, pp. 69–74. Hauptman argues, pp. 73–74, that such innovations represent a progression over time from women being married off by their fathers, to women having the right of consent, to women negotiating their own marriages. It seems more likely to me that different situations are represented here. The young girl almost certainly entered into a marriage contracted for her by her parents or guardians. It seems unlikely that in most cases such a bride would be in a position to give informed consent to the choices her elders had made for her. On the other hand, a financially independent adult woman, whether widowed, divorced, or previously unmarried, could certainly make her own choices and negotiate her own marriage.

6. Hauptman, *Rereading the Rabbis*, p. 68.

7. Wegner, *Chattel or Person*, p. 71; these obligations are discussed, ibid., pp. 71–75; Gafni, "Institution of Marriage," pp. 15–17, notes that there was always room for individual flexibility in negotiating these provisions. The wife's right to conjugal attentions, discussed further below, is based on Exodus 21:10: **"If he marries another, he must not withhold from this one her food, her clothing, or her conjugal rights."**

8. See "Husbands and Wives," *EJ* 8:1120–1128, for the full particulars of spousal rights and duties, both as laid out in rabbinic literature and as interpreted and modified in the rabbinic tradition of the medieval and early modern periods. A written *ketubbah* for all marriages became the norm by medieval times.

9. Hauptman, *Rereading the Rabbis*, p. 61. As Hauptman notes, p. 67, the transformation of what had been a bride-price paid to the bride's family at the time of marriage to the delayed payment at the end of a marriage, demonstrates how "the *ketubbah* consolidates some basic rights for women, even though it leaves patriarchy in place."

10. See Gafni, "Institution of Marriage," p. 16, who cites T. Ketubbot 4:7 and J. Ketubbot 5:2, 29b, for a case in which "Yehoshua, son of R. Aqiva married a woman and stipulated with her that she would feed and support and teach him Torah." "Teaching him Torah" implies that she would financially support his Torah studies.

11. On women in infertile marriages who petition the court to compel their husbands to grant them a divorce, see, chapter 5, pp. 127–128 below.

12. On divorce and its consequences, see Wegner, *Chattel or Person*, pp. 80–84; Rachel Biale, *Women and Jewish Law*, pp. 70–101, especially pp. 84–89; and "Divorce," *EJ* 6:122–135. On the aggadic tendency to condemn divorce,

see pp. 114–117 below. Further legal improvements (*takkanot*) in women's marital status were instituted by medieval Jews living in Christian lands. On these *takkanot*, attributed to R. Gershom b. Judah (960–1028), that provide that women cannot be divorced against their wills, and that a man may be married to only one woman at a time, see Biale, *Women and Jewish Law*, pp. 49–52; and Ze'ev W. Falk, *Jewish Matrimonial Law in the Middle Ages* (Oxford: Oxford University Press, 1966). On Jewish marriage in the Muslim sphere, see Mordechai Akiva Friedman, *Jewish Marriage in Palestine: A Cairo Genizah Study*. 2 vols. (Tel Aviv and New York: Tel Aviv University and The Jewish Theological Seminary of America, 1980), and idem, "Marriage as an Institution: Jewry under Islam" in *The Jewish Family*, ed. Kraemer, pp. 31–45; and idem, *Jewish Polygyny in the Middle Ages* [Hebrew] (Jerusalem: Bialik Institute, 1986).

13. Mayer I. Gruber, "The Status of Women in Ancient Judaism," in *Judaism in Late Antiquity* 3:2: *Where We Stand: Issues and Debates in Ancient Judaism*, ed. Jacob Neusner and Alan J. Avery-Peck (Leiden: E. J. Brill, 1999), pp. 151–176, pp. 162–163. Friedman, *Jewish Marriage in Palestine*, writes of medieval documents found in the Cairo Genizah, vol. 1, p. 19: "Most conspicuous in the Palestinian tradition is the provision which entitled both parties to initiate divorce proceedings," typical of the mutuality characteristic of these documents which describe marriage as a "partnership." He notes that "This contrasts sharply with the Babylonian *ketuba* which essentially may be characterized as a testimony of unilateral obligations undertaken by the husband to the wife." The evidence for female initiated divorce in late antique Judaism includes references in the *Antiquities* of Josephus at XV, vii, 10 and XVIII, vol. 4; in the New Testament (Mark 10:11–12 : "Who divorces his wife and marries another commits adultery against her; and if she divorces her husband and marries another, she commits adultery"); and Aramaic papyrus documents from the Judaean Desert dating from 134 or 135 C.E. There is a growing body of scholarly literature on this subject. In addition to the bibliography cited in Gruber, see Bernadette Brooten, "Könnten Frauen in Alten Judentum die Scheidung betrieben? Überlegung zu Mk 10, 11–12 und I Kor 7, 10–11," *Evangelische Theologie* 42 (1982): 65–80; Tal Ilan, "A Divorce Bill? Notes on Papyrus *XHev/Se* 13," in idem, *Integrating Women into Second Temple History*. Texts and Studies in Ancient Judaism 76 (Tübingen: Mohr Siebeck, 1999), pp. 253–262; idem, "Notes and Observations on a Newly Published Divorce Bill from the Judaean Desert," *Harvard Theological Review* 89/2 (1996): 195–212; and Ross Shepard Kraemer, "Women's Judaism(s) at the Beginning of Christianity," in *Women and Christian Origins*, ed. Ross Shepard Kraemer and Mary Rose D'Angelo (New York: Oxford University Press, 1999), pp. 50–79, pp. 57–59.

14. Gruber, "The Status of Women," writes, p. 163 n. 45, "The eisegesis of Deut. 24 reflected in *Sifre Deuteronomy* and canonized in the Mishnah and in Orthodox and Conservative Judaism today is, therefore, historically speaking, an aberration, for which Jewish women have paid dearly for over two millennia."

15. Wegner, *Chattel or Person*, p. 176.

16. Female behavior construed as immodest in M. Ketubbot 7:6 includes going out with uncovered head, spinning in the marketplace, or speaking with other men. For discussion of these offences as transgressions against the boundaries between public and private domains, see Baker, "Bodies, Boundaries and Domestic Politics," and my discussion on pp. 112–114 below.

17. Wegner, *Chattel or Person*, pp. 84–85.

18. David Biale, *Eros and the Jews*, p. 50. Similarly, the husband had complete freedom to introduce whatever sexual practices he preferred within marriage, even if his wife objected. Any efforts on her part to direct marital sexuality were condemned as immodest. On this topic, see pp. 107–109 below.

19. M. Ketubbot 5:6 specifies: "The duty of marriage enjoined in the Law is: every day for those that are unoccupied; twice a week for laborers; once a week for ass-drivers; once every thirty days for camel-drivers; and once every six months for sailors."

20. Michael Satlow, *Tasting the Dish: Rabbinic Rhetorics of Sexuality*, Brown Judaic Studies 303 (Atlanta: Scholars Press, 1995), pp. 266–268, p. 318.

21. Satlow, *Tasting the Dish*, p. 319. Both Michael Satlow, throughout his book, and David Biale, *Eros and the Jews*, pp. 49–59, offer a great deal of evidence on differences in attitudes towards sexuality between the rabbinic communities in the Land of Israel and in Babylon. Generally, they argue that attitudes in the Land of Israel tended to be more ascetic while the Babylonian rabbis appeared to have a more complex understanding of human sexuality both inside and outside of marriage. Both Satlow and Biale point out that attitudes and practices in the larger environments in which Jews lived had significant influence on rabbinic formulations of sexuality.

22. Satlow, *Tasting the Dish*, p. 160, p. 286. Satlow maintains, however, pp. 158–160, that while the rabbis believed that male sexual desires were stronger than those of women they were also convinced that men could restrain themselves while women, once in a state of sexual desire, lacked any self-control; see chapter 1 below.

23. Wegner, *Chattel or Person*, p. 79. It is important to note in this discussion that the rabbis did not believe that a man should compel his wife to have sex. The *moredet* was not understood as a woman who refused sexual relations with her husband because she found him physically repugnant (divorce was a recognized recourse in such cases), but a woman who refused sex as an act of rebellion and assertion of power against her husband to the point that he was forced to the humiliating expedient of appealing to a rabbinic court. In the case of an unhappy marriage, a wife may have resorted to this expedient as a way of forcing a divorce, even at the cost of her *ketubbah*.

24. On aggadic traditions about men who left home for long periods of time to study with the rabbis, see pp. 101–105 below.

25. "Household" (*bayit*, literally "house") is understood here, and in the proof texts that follow, to refer to a wife, and therefore the verse is understood as "You shall . . . rejoice" *only* when there is a wife to rejoice with you.

26. See, for example, *Leviticus Rabbah* 8:1.

27. The larger passage at B. Sotah 2a, in which this statement appears, is discussed more fully on p. 112 below.

28. Daniel Boyarin, Carnal Israel, p. 136. On this theme, also see Biale, *Eros and the Jews*, pp. 46–48, 58–59; Satlow, *Tasting the Dish*, pp. 269 ff, p. 314; and pp. 102–103 in this volume.

29. This passage, which also appears in B. Sanhedrin 76b, is immediately followed in B. Yevamot 62b by parallel statements that a man who has no wife is not a proper man and a man who has no land is not a proper man.

30. Satlow, *Tasting the Dish*, pp. 158–159.

31. Prior to this statement, M. Sotah 3:4 presents the debate, in the context

of the woman accused of adultery, over whether a father should teach his daughter Torah, discussed in chapter 3, pp. 81–83. R. Joshua's statement about women's preference for sexual attention rather than material comfort immediately follows R. Eliezer's remark that teaching a woman Torah is teaching her lasciviousness.

32. Jacob Neusner, "Judaism," in *Women and Families,* ed. Neusner, pp. 59–60.

33. On the implications for Jewish mysticism of constructing marriage as a spiritual metaphor, see Moshe Idel, "Sexual Metaphors and Praxis in the Kabbalah," in *The Jewish Family: Metaphor and Memory,* ed. David Kraemer (New York: Oxford University Press, 1989), pp. 197–224; and Judith R. Baskin, "From Separation to Displacement: The Problem of Women in *Sefer Hasidim,*" *Association for Jewish Studies Review* 19:1 (1994):1–18.

34. Tal Ilan, *Mine and Yours are Hers: Retrieving Women's History from Rabbinic Literature* (Leiden: Brill, 1997), pp. 274–277. Ilan points out that in six narratives in four different rabbinic documents, Rabbi Aqiva's wife is named only once, as Rachel, in what is likely the latest text (*Avot de-Rabbi Nathan* A). Ilan doubts this name is historical. Instead, she believes it was derived from an earlier version of the tale (B. Ketubbot 63a) where the saying "as ewe (*rahela*) follows ewe, so a daughter's acts are like those of her mother" is cited to describe Rabbi Aqiva's wife and her daughter, who is also said to have disdained riches to marry a poor man of great talent. Parallels between the story of Rabbi Aqiva and his wife and the biblical romance of Jacob and Rachel may also have played a role in yielding the appellation "Rachel." Ilan believes that the real name of Rabbi Aqiva's wife, as with most women mentioned in rabbinic texts, remains unknown. See Boyarin, *Carnal Israel,* pp. 150–152, on the metaphor of shepherd and ewe that he sees as key to the Aqiva/Rachel narratives.

35. Steven D. Fraade, "Ascetical Aspects of Ancient Judaism," in *Jewish Spirituality: From the Bible Through the Middle Ages,* ed. Arthur Green (New York: Crossroads Press, 1986), pp. 253–288, p. 275. On attitudes towards celibacy and asceticism in rabbinic Judaism, see also Eliezer Diamond, "Hunger Artists and Householders: The Tension between Asceticism and Family Responsibility among Jewish Pietists in Late Antiquity," *Union Seminary Quarterly Review* 48 (1996): pp. 28–47; and Boyarin, *Carnal Israel,* p. 47, pp. 134–36, 139–141, 163–66.

36. Eilberg-Schwartz, *The Savage in Judaism,* pp. 230–231, p. 233. He notes, p. 231, in reference to T. 'Eduyyot 3:4, "The Tosefta . . . suggests that the title of 'sage' is itself predicated on one's disciples being remembered. . . . It is as if the title 'rabbi' is authorized by the production of a genealogy. Just as a man who has not produced children cannot be a 'father,' so a man who does not have memorable disciples cannot be a 'rabbi.' " For fuller discussion of the implications of the obligation of male procreation, see chapter 5, p. 138.

37. David Biale, *Eros and the Jews,* pp. 58–59

38. Boyarin, *Carnal Israel,* pp. 165–166. He notes, p. 136, that the conflict between the demands of marriage and the imperative to total devotion to study remained unresolved in rabbinic culture. See also Biale, *Eros and the Jews,* p. 55; and Satlow, *Tasting the Dish,* p. 278, who finds a general "redactorial drift" elsewhere in the Babylonian Talmud, as well, towards lessening female conjugal rights when they interfered with male prerogatives.

39. Euripedes, "Alcestis," transl. Richard Lattimore, in *The Complete*

Greek Tragedies, ed. David Grene and Richard Lattimore (Chicago: The University of Chicago Press, 1959), vol. 3, pp. 1–53. I am certainly not claiming direct influence here, but this or similar stories of self-sacrificing wives and miraculous resurrections may well have circulated throughout the Greco-Roman world. Daniel Boyarin, *Carnal Israel*, pp. 157–158, provides a detailed comparison of the story of R. Hananiah b. Hakinai in B. Ketubot 62b with an apparently earlier version of this tale in the Palestinian text *Genesis Rabbah* 95 on Genesis 46:30 and points out that the *Genesis Rabbah* version, in which R. Hananiah b. Hakinai's wife is not restored to life, is wholly critical of R. Hananiah's negligence in leaving his wife and family for so long, indicative of Palestinian disapproval of this practice, unlike the Babylonian version with its miraculous resolution.

40. Boyarin, *Carnal Israel*, p. 158.

41. On this proverb, see n. 34 above.

42. Boyarin, *Carnal Israel*, p. 156, n. 37, is no doubt correct in assuming that the variant in the text, "You have remembered your *dove*," achieved by changing the initial letter in "*your whore*," was added by a later editor who found the original text too disturbing to leave unaltered.

43. Satlow, *Tasting the Dish*, p. 278.

44. Satlow, *Tasting the Dish*, p. 13.

45. Satlow, *Tasting the Dish*, writes, p. 331, of the overwhelming influence of sexual mores in the larger environment in determining rabbinic views in both the land of Israel and in Babylon. Although Palestinian rabbinic rulings on sexuality occasionally differ from their Greek and Roman equivalents, he believes that in general they are based upon a common language, shared thought-categories, and assumptions. Satlow suggests that the Babylonian rabbis, who were similarly affected by the very different culture in which they were living, were apparently working with quite different assumptions about sexuality and sometimes did not fully grasp the import of the teachings transmitted to them from Palestine.

46. See below, Chapter One, pp. 22–29 below, for the development of rabbinic legislation concerning the *niddah* and its implications for marital sexuality.

47. David Biale, *Eros and the Jews*, p. 42.

48. *Tanhuma* B., *Naso*, f.16a, par. 13.

49. Imma Shalom was the wife of the first-century sage, R. Eliezer, and is also said to have been the sister of the Patriarch Rabban Gamliel. As David Biale, *Eros and the Jews*, p. 249, n. 110, points out, the talmudic editor understands the term "to converse" in this passage to mean actual conversation, when "Imma Shalom is actually using it in the euphemistic rabbinic sense of sexual intercourse (*le-sapper im isha*)." On the doubtful historicity of many of the traditions associated with Imma Shalom, see Tal Ilan, "The Quest for the Historical Beruriah, Rachel, and Imma Shalom," *Association for Jewish Studies Review* 22:1 (1997): pp. 1–17.

50. B. Yevamot 61b, "Even though a man has children, he must not remain without a wife," may be read as an endorsement of sexual expression as a purpose of marriage. For another ascetic view of marital sexuality, see B. Gittin 70a, which objects to any position in sexual intercourse other than male superior.

51. Boyarin, *Carnal Israel*, pp. 115–116.

52. Marital rape is also condemned in B. 'Eruvin 100b. On this topic, see Satlow, *Tasting the Dish*, pp. 286–288.

53. See B. 'Eruvin 100b for a similar version of this passage, followed immediately by a discussion of the ten curses of Eve which include the fact that a wife cannot solicit her husband for sex directly: " 'And he shall rule over you' (Gen. 3:16) teaches that while the wife solicits with her heart the husband does so with his mouth." See, chapter 3, p. 75 above.

54. For R. Hananiah b. Hakinai's unnamed wife, see pp. 103–104 above. She, like R. Akiva's wife, is a paradigm of passive self-sacrifice.

55. Versions of this anecdote are found in *Leviticus Rabbah,* 34:14, where it is brought to justify the interpretation that "Hide not thyself from thine own flesh" (Isa. 57:7) "refers to a man's divorcée"; and in J. Ketubot 11:3, f. 34b, line 61, where the story ends as follows: "Nevertheless, sounds were heard in the night, and they heard her say, 'The pain I suffered in my body [when my husband beats me] was better than the pain I now suffer within me.' "

56. On the folklore tradition that some women are sources of death to men, see Mordechai Akiva Friedman, "Tamar, A Symbol of Life: The 'Killer Wife' Superstition in the Bible and Jewish Tradition," *Association for Jewish Studies Review* 15 (1990), pp. 23–62; chapter 1, p. 27, and chapter 3 pp. 68–70.

57. A parallel passage, T. Ketubot 7:6–7, adds that such a woman also goes out with unseemly clothes, acts without shame in front of her male and female slaves and her neighbors, and washes and bathes in the public bath with anyone. On the "vocal woman," see B. Ketubbot 72b where the accepted definition is "one who makes her voice heard on marital matters."

58. Cynthia Baker, "Bodies, Boundaries, and Domestic Politics in a Late Ancient Marketplace," *Journal of Medieval and Early Modern Studies* 26:3 (fall 1996), p. 403.

59. Baker, "Bodies, Boundaries, and Domestic Politics," p. 407.

60. Baker, "Bodies, Boundaries, and Domestic Politics," p. 408.

61. Numbers 25 describes the behavior of the Israelites encamped at Shittim during the wilderness wanderings who "profaned themselves by whoring with the Moabite women, who invited the people to the sacrifices for their god. The people partook of them and worshiped that god" (Num. 25:1–2). This behavior provokes divine wrath, and only when the ringleaders are killed, does a plague which had raged among the people abate.

62. The meaning of the Hebrew here is uncertain, yielding either "A hateful one put away," or, as the JPS *Tanakh* translates it, "For I detest divorce, said the Lord, the God of Israel" (Mal. 2:16); this uncertainty forms the crux of the debate in the B. Gittin 90 a–b passage.

63. Gafni, "Institution of Marriage," pp. 21–23. However, polygyny was far from unknown in the Land of Israel. Ross Shepard Kraemer, "Women's Judaism(s) at the Beginning of Christianity," in *Women and Christian Origins*, ed. Kraemer and D'Angelo, pp. 57–59, discusses documents found in a cave in the Judean Desert, including two marriage contracts written in Aramaic, belonging to Babata, a Jewish woman of the second century C.E. The second of Babata's two marriages, around the year 125 C.E. was a polygynous marriage with a certain Judah. On polygyny, see also n. 12 above.

CHAPTER 5 (PP. 119–140)

1. Some of the contents of this chapter appeared in a different form in my essay, "Rabbinic Reflections on the Barren Wife," *Harvard Theological Review*

82 (1989): 1–14. On the subject of procreation in rabbinic law and exegesis, see also Judith Hauptman, *Rereading the Rabbis: A Woman's Voice* (Boulder: West-view Press, 1998), pp. 130–146; Jeremy Cohen, *"Be Fertile and Increase, Fill the Earth and Master It," The Ancient and Medieval Career of a Biblical Verse* (Ithaca: Cornell University Press, 1989); David M. Feldman, *Marital Relations, Birth Control and Abortion in Jewish Law* (New York: Schocken, 1968, 1975), pp. 46–59; Rachel Biale, *Women and Jewish Law* (New York: Schocken, 1984), pp. 98–203; Louis Epstein, *Marriage Laws in the Bible and Talmud* (Cambridge: Harvard University Press, 1942); and *Sex Laws and Customs in Judaism* (New York: KTAV, 1967); and the discussion below. David Daube, in *The Duty of Procreation* (Edinburgh: The University of Edinburgh Press, 1977), presents a comparison of societal attitudes towards procreation in the Hebrew Bible, rabbinic Judaism, classical antiquity and early Christianity.

   2. For rabbinic constructions of female roles, see chapters 1 and 4 above; and also Jacob Neusner, "Thematic or Systemic Description: The Case of Mishnah's Division of Women," in *Method and Meaning in Ancient Judaism*, Brown Judaic Studies 10 (Missoula, Mont.: Scholars Press, 1979), pp. 79–100, p. 100. That control of woman's sexuality is the issue here is made clear by Judith Romney Wegner, "Dependency, Autonomy and Sexuality: Woman as Chattel and Person in the System of the Mishnah," *New Perspective on Ancient Judaism* 1, ed. Jacob Neusner, Peder Borgen, Ernest S. Frerichs and Richard Horsley (Lanham, Md., New York, London: University Press of America, 1987), pp. 89–102. Wegner points out, p. 91, that if a legal relationship is present "in which some man owns the exclusive right to use or dispose of a woman's biological function," "the system classifies the woman as legally dependent on the man in question; if not the system grants her legal autonomy." Here, and in more detail in idem, *Chattel or Person? The Status of Women in the Mishnah* (New York: Oxford University Press, 1988), Wegner argues that the Mishnah perceives of woman as chattel rather than person only when the context is control of her sexual and reproductive function.

   3. Feldman, *Marital Relations,* pp. 46–47, notes that traditionally Genesis 9: 1, and especially 9:7, the divine charges to Noah and his sons to "Be fruitful and multiply," were taken as the first commandment concerning procreation, while the directive in Genesis 1:28, was said, based on B. Ketubbot 5a, to be for "blessing only." B. Yevamot 63b remarks that the command in Genesis 9:7 occurs where it is because it directly follows the prohibition of murder, "in order to liken one who abstains from having children to one who sheds blood."

   4. See Hauptman, *Rereading the Rabbis,* pp. 132–136, where she argues that the Tosefta to Yevamot 8:4 also appears to hold that women are obligated to have offspring. Clearly, as the discussion below of B. Yevamot 65b indicates, there was a strong minority tradition that read Genesis 1:28 literally and insisted that the commandment to be fertile and increase applied to both men and women.

   5. See chapter 2, pp. 51–52 and chapter 4, pp. 108–109, for discussion of midrashic traditions about Dinah and the risks for women in entering the public domain.

   6. See chapter 1, pp. 20–22, on the roles of man, woman, and God in forming the embryo.

   7. See chapter 2, first Eve, pp. 56–60.

   8. B. Nedarim 64b.

9. Biale, *Women and Jewish Law*, p. 202.

10. On rabbinic views concerning contraception, see Biale, *Women and Jewish Law*, pp. 203–218; and Feldman, *Marital Relations*, pp. 109–250.

11. Feldman, *Marital Relations*, p. 54, n. 49.

12. The same interpretation of Numbers 5:28 also appears in B. Sotah 26a, In that text, R. Ishmael points out to R. Aqiva the consequences of a literal understanding of the verse: "In that case, all barren women will seclude themselves and be visited, and since this one did not seclude herself she will be the loser [by not conceiving]." The ranking of desirable traits in offspring, with the addition in B. Sotah 26a that "if she formerly bore girls, she will now give birth to boys," is an interesting insight into rabbinic prejudices.

13. Feldman, *Marital Relations*, p. 54.

14. See, chapter 2, pp. 50–51 above.

15. See chapter 3, pp. 83–87 above.

16. See Hauptman, *Rereading the Rabbis*, pp. 132–136, on the ways in which T. Yevamot 8:4–6 differs from M. Yevamot 6:6. Hauptman believes, p. 135, that the Tosefta maintains an "egalitarian requirement" that women, too, are legally obligated to procreate, a minority point of view which is rejected by the Mishnah and the Babylonian Talmud.

17. For more on Sarai and Hagar, see chapter 6.

18. Similar traditions are preserved in T. Yevamot 8:5–6, *Genesis Rabbah* 45:3, and J. Yevamot 6:6, 7c. *Genesis Rabbah* 45:3 suggests that the years of Sarai's childlessness outside the land of Canaan/Israel did not count in the ten-year tally because her childlessness in that case could have been punishment of Abram and Sarai for the sin of living outside the land.

19. On the issue of Jewish polygamy in rabbinic times, see chapter 4, pp. 116–117 and n. 63; Epstein, *Marriage Laws*, pp. 3–25; and Ze'ev W. Falk, *Jewish Matrimonial Law in the Middle Ages* (London: Oxford University Press, 1966), pp. 1–10.

20. Medieval rabbinic sources, cited by Epstein, *Marriage Laws*, pp. 25–33, and Falk, *Jewish Matrimonial Law*, pp. 13–34, verify that in a childless situation, a man usually preferred taking a second spouse to divorce. Mordechai A. Friedman, *Jewish Polygyny in the Middle Ages. New Documents from the Cairo Genizah* (Jerusalem: The Bialik Institute, Tel Aviv University, 1986), presents a number of medieval documents, pp. 153– 204, describing polygynous marriages because of the infertility of the first wife. Similarly, Falk indicates, p. 13, that the case of the childlessness of the first wife was one of the major reasons for polygyny in medieval Jewish society, and, pp. 14–15, that polygyny in this instance continued to be permitted among Ashkenazic Jewry, even for several centuries after the eleventh century ban attributed to R. Gershom b. Judah. On p. 29, Falk indicates that the barren wife would apparently be given a choice over whether she wished a divorce or would permit a co-wife. Although the divorced wife would have the option to remarry, it seems likely that in most cases she would prefer to stay within an already established marriage and household. As Epstein notes, pp. 32–33, in connection with the Sephardic Jewish sphere, "Even with the pre-nuptial agreement for monogamy, in case the wife was childless, it was wisdom on her part not to raise objection of the husband's designs to marry another, because the law would not sustain her protests. The law took the attitude that an agreement that interferes with the husband's duty of procreation is contrary to public policy and therefore not valid . . ." I thank

Professor Mordechai Friedman for our conversation on this point. Similar situations are also possible in present day Israel. S. Zalman Abramov, *Perpetual Dilemma. Jewish Religion in the Jewish State* (Rutherford, N.J.: Fairleigh Dickinson University Press, 1976), writes, p. 187, that according to modern Israeli law, a husband may be given permission to remarry without the dissolution of his previous marriage, since a Jewish religious marriage may be polygamous, according to the Penal Law Amendment (Bigamy) Law of 1959, section 5, which states that such a marriage is valid, "If a new marriage was contracted after permission to marry had been granted by a final judgement of the rabbinical court, and the judgement had been approved by the two Chief Rabbis of Israel." I thank Professor Judith Romney Wegner for this reference.

21. The refusal of a husband in an infertile marriage to divorce his wife for any number of reasons must have been a frequent situation and, in fact, is approved by much of the aggadic material cited below in this chapter. The medieval sage Maimonides inveighs against what must have been a commonplace circumstance, insisting that a childless husband must make every effort to fulfill his halakhic obligation: "If he refuses to divorce her, he should be compelled to do so, by being scourged with a rod until he divorces her . . . or else [he must] marry another wife capable of giving birth" (*Mishneh Torah*, Book of Women: Marriage, 15:7, trans. Isaac Klein, *The Code of Maimonides, Book Four* (New Haven: Yale University Press, 1972), p. 95. This interpretation reappears in the *Shulkan Aruch*, Eben HaEzer 154:10. Moses Isserles, however, ruling for Ashkenazic Jewry, comments on this text that "Nowadays one does not force the issue of the requirement to procreate."

22. On negative rabbinic attitudes to divorce, see chapter 4, pp. 114–117.

23. See, for example, *Genesis Rabbah* 71:6, where the verse is interpreted in context.

24. See B. Yevamot 64a for speculation on why the patriarchs appeared to be infertile.

25. For more discussion of Leah and her sister Rachel, see chapter 6.

26. Although the correct translation of this passage is questionable, it seems likely that it contains a reference to one of the most popular safeguards against infertility, the amulet. References to material in Jewish folklore concerning remedies for barrenness, including amulets, may be found in Theodor Gaster, *The Holy and the Profane* (New York: William Sloane Associates, 1955), pp. 1–8; Raphael Patai, "Jewish Folk-cures for Barrenness," *Folklore* 54 (1943):117–124; and idem, "Jewish Folk-cures for Barrenness," *Folklore* 56(1945):208–218; and Joshua Trachtenberg, *Jewish Magic and Superstition. A Study in Folk Religion* (New York: Atheneum, 1939; reprint 1970), see appropriate entries in index.

27. *Eliyyahu Rabbah* 18 (p. 99).

28. Biale, *Women and Jewish Prayer*, p. 20.

29. Biale, p. 20. Chava Weissler, "The Traditional Piety of Ashkenazic Women," in *Jewish Spirituality. From the Sixteenth Century to the Present*, ed. Arthur Green (New York: Crossroad, 1987), pp. 245–275, has discussed the development of *tkhines* (supplication) literature in the early modern period and provides bibliographical information on such earlier studies as exist. A methodological framework for this material is suggested in her "The Religion of Traditional Ashkenazic Women: Some Methodological Issues," *Association for Jewish Studies Review* 12 (1987): 73–94. See also idem, *Voices of the Matri-*

archs: Listening to the Prayers of Early Modern Women (Boston: Beacon Press, 1998).

30. See the passage in B. Berakhot 31a beginning, "R. Hamnuna said: How many of the most important laws [relating to prayer] can be learned from these verses relating to Hannah." On Hannah's prayer, see chapter 3, pp. 79–80 and p. 185, n. 30. See also, Dvora Weisberg, "Men Imagining Women Imagining God: Gender Issues in Classic Midrash," in *Agendas for the Study of Midrash in the Twenty-First Century*, ed. Marc Lee Raphael (Williamsburg, Va.: Department of Religion, William and Mary College, 1999), pp. 63–83.

31. Mary Callaway, *Sing, O Barren One: A Study in Comparative Midrash*, Society for Biblical Literature Dissertation Series 91 (Atlanta: Scholars Press, 1986), discusses the important roles that accounts of the barren matriarchs have played in popular piety in a number of periods of Jewish and Christian history.

32. On this theme, see Callaway, pp. 59–65.

33. Psalm 55:20 is usually translated, "God who has reigned from the first, who will have no successor, hears and humbles those who have no fear of God."

34. See also B. Sanhedrin 99b where the same statement is attributed to Resh Lakish. B. Sanhedrin 19b also teaches that "he who brings up an orphan in his home, Scripture ascribes it to him as though he had begotten him."

35. Howard Eilberg-Schwartz, *The Savage in Judaism: An Anthropology of Israelite Religion and Ancient Judaism* (Bloomington: Indiana University Press, 1990), pp. 230–231, p. 233.

36. Eilberg-Schwartz, *The Savage in Judaism*, p. 232, p. 234.

37. Weissler, "Traditional Piety," has studied many supplicatory prayers for Jewish women in the early modern period. Discussing an eighteenth-century text called the *Shloyshe she'orim*, attributed to a female author (p. 253) she notes (pp. 265–266) the importance of the theme of women's helping to bring about Israel's redemption, and she comments as well (pp. 266–267) on the significant roles played by the matriarchs, who are generally missing from the standard liturgy, in this group of women's prayers, and in *tkhines* (supplication) literature in general. She writes, p. 267, that "this assertion of the power of mothers may have been particularly important to women living in the uncertain conditions of Jewish Eastern Europe, who were in fact powerless to protect their families from many of the dangers that beset them." No doubt, positive homiletical references to the matriarchs and appeals to their merits and efficacy fulfilled a similar function for Jewish women of earlier periods.

CHAPTER 6 (PP. 141–160)

1. Some of the contents of this chapter appeared in different form in Judith R. Baskin, "The Rabbinic Transformations of Rahab the Harlot," *Notre Dame English Journal. A Journal of Religion in Literature* 11 (1979): 141–157. For an example of the rabbinic conviction of women's unreliability, see Charlotte Elisheva Fonrobert, *Menstrual Purity: Rabbinic and Christian Reconstructions of Biblical Gender* (Stanford: Stanford University Press, 2000), p. 147, who describes the rabbis' uneasiness about depending on "reliable" women to examine other women's bodies when testimony of an intimate nature was required by rabbinic courts, because such examinations could create "a space for women

that [was] not under rabbinic control." As she notes, "The issue clearly does not concern [the women's] abilities to recognize the signs of physical maturity. Rather, the suspicion appeared to be that women might give a 'gender-biased' testimony on behalf of a girl [intending] to protect her."

2. Judith Romney Wegner, "The Image and Status of Women in Classical Rabbinic Judaism," in *Jewish Women in Historical Perspective.* 2nd ed., ed. Judith R. Baskin (Detroit: Wayne State University Press, 1998), pp. 73–100, p. 80.

3. Simcha Fishbane, "Most Women Engage in Sorcery," *in Historical, Literary, and Religious Studies,* ed. Herbert W. Basser and Simcha Fishbane, Approaches to Ancient Judaism, ed. Jacob Neusner, n.s., 5 (Atlanta: Scholars Press, 1993), pp. 143–166, 152–153. See also Rebecca Lesses, "Ex(o)rcising Power: Women as Sorceresses, Exorcists, and Demonesses in Babylonian Jewish Society of Late Antiquity," *Journal of the American Academy of Religion* 69:2 (2001): 343–375. She writes, p. 364, "The definition of sorcery as belonging essentially to women's nature is part of the overall rabbinic project that defines gender. Women's subordinate role in the rabbinic religious community makes them suspect."

4. Michael Satlow, *Tasting the Dish: Rabbinic Rhetorics of Sexuality* (Atlanta: Scholars Press, 1995), p. 146, cites a number of texts to support his contention that the connection among women, sexual license, and witchcraft is both implicit and explicit in rabbinic literature.

5. See chapter 1, pp. 33–34. The rabbis saw the privy as a dangerous nexus between this world and the world of demons. See J. Hagigah 2:2, 77d for a story about how R. Simeon ben Shetah hanged eighty witches in Ashkelon who lived in a single cave and "harmed the world." Meir Bar-Ilan, "Witches in the Bible and in the Talmud," in *Historical, Literary, and Religious Studies,* ed. Herbert W. Basser and Simcha Fishbane, Approaches to Ancient Judaism, ed. Jacob Neusner, n.s., 5 (Atlanta: Scholars Press, 1993) pp. 7–32, p. 11, suggests that this story may represent an attack on Jewish women's perceived attraction to idolatry.

6. Eliezer Berkowits, *Jewish Women in Time and Torah* (Hoboken: KTAV Publishing, 1990), pp. 24–25, cited in Fishbane, "Most Women Engage in Sorcery," p. 153.

7. Simcha Fishbane, "Most Women Engage in Sorcery," p. 154.

8. On papyrus evidence of Jewish women's involvement in magic, see Ross Shepard Kraemer, *Her Share of the Blessings: Women's Religions Among Pagans, Jews, and Christians in the Greco-Roman World* (New York: Oxford University Press, 1992), pp. 108–109. She notes, p. 109, that the rabbinic texts against Jewish women's practice of magic "offer us a polemical judgment of what was likely to have been widespread popular religion, and worth far more exploration as evidence of women's piety." On Jewish women's exposure to pagan customs, see Kraemer, ibid, pp. 100–101. Also see Bar-Ilan, "Witches in the Bible and Talmud," p. 28, n.14. For detailed documentation on Jewish women's use of amulets and incantation bowls in Sassanian Babylonia, see Lesses, "Ex(o)rcising Power," pp. 354–362. Lesses also discusses the positive rabbinic depiction of Abaye's foster mother who is portrayed as possessing knowledge of incantations and female rituals (see, e.g., B. Shabbat 66b). Concerning rabbinic citations of this unnamed woman's medical knowledge, see Fonrobert, *Menstrual Purity,* pp. 151–158.

9. Bar-Ilan, "Witches in the Bible and Talmud," p. 11.

10. The general conviction of biblical readers that Rachel surpassed Leah in beauty is based on: **"Now Laban had two daughters; the name of the older one was Leah, and the name of the younger was Rachel. Leah had weak eyes; Rachel was shapely and beautiful"** (Gen. 29:16–17).

11. See chapter 5 for rabbinic views on the dilemma of infertility.

12. See *Genesis Rabbah* 71:1 and 71:2; and chapter 5, pp. 130–131.

13. *Genesis Rabbah* 72:6 also cites this verse as proof that God can change the sex of an embryo in the womb, together with a proof text from Jeremiah 18:6: ". . . O House of Israel, can I not deal with you like this potter?—says the Lord. Just like clay in the hands of the potter, so are you in my hands."

14. *Genesis Rabbah* 72:5 offers more positive interpretations of Leah's role in the mandrakes episode, centering on her wish to add to Jacob's progeny and the particular contributions to Israel of the tribes of Issachar and Zebulun who were born as a result of the sisters' bargain. See also B. Nedarim 20b, and chapter 4 above, pp. 108–109.

15. The rabbinic projection of sexual unreliability onto women is discussed in more detail in chapters 1 and 4.

16. This scenario was common throughout the ancient Near East. P. Kyle McCarter, Jr., "The Patriarchal Age: Abraham, Isaac and Jacob," in *Ancient Israel: A Short History from Abraham to the Roman Destruction of the Temple*, ed. Hershel Shanks (Washington, D.C.: Biblical Archaeology Society, and Englewood Cliffs, N.J.: Prentice-Hall, 1988), pp. 1–30, writes, that "the responsibility of a barren wife to provide a slave woman to her husband for the purpose of bearing children is cited in Old Babylonian, Old Assyrian and Nuzi texts (all from the [second millennium B.C.] Middle Bronze Age), but also in a twelfth-century Egyptian document and a marriage contract from Nimrud, dated 648 B.C." See also, Jo Ann Hackett, "Rehabilitating Hagar: Fragments of an Epic Pattern," in *Gender and Difference in Ancient Israel*, ed. Peggy L. Day (Minneapolis: Fortress Press, 1989), pp. 12–27.

17. Michael Satlow, *Tasting the Dish*, pp. 146 ff., points out that rabbinic texts consistently connect adultery and licentiousness with gentiles. He discusses rabbinic attitudes and rabbinic legislation regarding sexual relations between Jews and gentiles on pp. 84–95. Fonrobert, *Menstrual Purity*, p. 270, n. 22, suggests that practices and traditions centered on ritual purity and impurity determine women's "ethnic" difference in rabbinic literature. She believes the rabbis constructed categories of "otherness" among women by distinguishing the bodies of Jewish women and their discharges from those of non-Jewish women. As Fonrobert remarks, this topic deserves further research.

18. Some traditions portray the highly born Cozbi as the innocent victim of her father's hatred for Israel. According to *Numbers Rabbah* 21:3, Zur was so anxious to ensnare the Israelites that he coerced his own daughter into harlotry.

19. For more information on Ruth and Jethro as converts, see Bernard Bamberger, *Proselytism in the Talmudic Period* (New York: KTAV Publishing House, 1968), pp. 182–191, 194–199. On Jethro, see also Judith R. Baskin, *Pharaoh's Counsellors: Job, Jethro, and Balaam in Rabbinic and Patristic Tradition* (Chico, Calif.: Scholars Press, 1983), pp. 47–61.

20. On Jewish proselytism in rabbinic times, see Bamberger, *Proselytism in the Talmudic Period*; William Braude, *Jewish Proselyting in the First Five Centuries of the Common Era* (Providence: Brown University, 1940); Shaye J. D.

Cohen, "Conversion to Judaism in Historical Perspective: From Biblical Israel to Post-Biblical Judaism," *Conservative Judaism* 36, 4 (summer, 1983):31–45; idem, *The Beginnings of Jewishness: Boundaries, Varieties, Uncertainties* (Berkeley: University of California Press, 1999); and Gary G. Porton, *The Stranger Within Your Gates: Converts and Conversion in Rabbinic Literature* (Chicago: University of Chicago Press, 1994), who examines rabbinic evidence concerning the place of the convert within the Jewish community.

21. This *aggadah*, which originates in a discussion of the importance of wearing *tzitzit* (ritual fringes), relates how the young scholar was about to approach a beautiful prostitute on an elevated bed of gold when "all of a sudden the four fringes [of his garment] struck him across the face" and he slipped and fell to the ground. The prostitute was so impressed by this that she resolved to become a Jew. The story appears in B. Menahot 44a and *Sifre Numbers* 115. Of converts mentioned in rabbinic literature, Bamberger, in *Proselytism*, pp. 221–266, lists far more men than women. Given this dearth of female exemplars, the great attention paid to the biblical figures of Ruth and Rahab is understandable.

22. This tradition links Joshua 5:1, "And it came to pass, when all the kings of the Amorites, that were beyond the Jordan westward, and all the kings of the Canaanites, that were beyond the sea, heard how that the Lord had dried up the waters of the Jordan from before the children of Israel, until they were passed over, that their hearts melted, neither was there any spirit in them anymore, because of the children of Israel"; and Joshua 2:10, "For we have heard how the Lord dried up the water of the Red Sea before you, when you came out of Egypt; and what you did unto the two kings of the Amorites, that were beyond the Jordan, unto Sihon and Og, whom you utterly destroyed," and assumes that Rahab had gained special knowledge of the power of Israel's God because of her intimate relations with the kings of Canaan. *Mekhilta*, 'Amalek 3 preserves a similar tradition.

23. In the Jewish Publication Society *Tanakh*, this verse is translated, "Yet you were not like a prostitute, for you spurned fees; [you were like] the adulterous wife who welcomes strangers instead of her husband."

24. Joshua 2:4 reads *titzpeno*, "she hid him," rather than the expected "she hid them." The rabbis seized on this textual incongruity as the basis for a homiletical proof of Rahab's conversion and piety.

25. See also *Sifre Numbers* 78 for a similar enumeration of Rahab's descendants. In line with the generally positive rabbinic attitude towards proselytes, descendants of converts are often said to have become priests. Thus, *Exodus Rabbah* 19:4 comments on, "Let not the stranger lodge outside" (Job 31:32), as follows: "The Holy One does not disqualify a creature, but receives all. The gates are open at every hour, and anyone who wants to enter may enter . . . Said R. Berekhiah: To whom does this verse apply? [It means] that the proselytes are destined to be priests serving in the Temple and they are destined to eat of the showbread in that their daughters will marry into the priesthood."

26. *Ecclesiasates Rabbah* 8:10 also preserves this tradition, although in a form crediting Joshua with Rahab's conversion.

27. The text of Joshua 6:23 gives the plural *mishpehoteha*, "families," rather than the expected singular, "family."

28. This passage also appears in *Sifre Zuta* on Numbers 10:28.

29. Rabbinic transformations of Rahab into a respectable Jewish mother may

also be part of a response to her important role as a precursor of the gentile Church in early Christian traditions. Rahab is mentioned three times in the New Testament, in Matthew 1:4–5, Hebrews 11:31, and James 2:25. In Matthew, she is listed among the ancestors of Jesus as the wife of Salmon and the mother of Boaz. In Hebrews, Rahab is cited as an example of the efficacy of faith, for "By faith Rahab the harlot did not perish with those who were disobedient, because she had given friendly welcome to the spies." In James, however, Rahab is an example of the necessary combination of works with faith: "You see that a man is justified by works and not by faith alone. And in the same way was not also Rahab the harlot justified by works when she received the messengers and sent them out another way. For as the body apart from the spirit is dead, so faith apart from works is dead" (James 2:24–26). The repentant New Testament prostitute, Mary Magdalene, is also a clear parallel to Rahab. For further discussion of Rahab in early Christian writings and art, see Baskin, "Rabbinic Transformations of Rahab the Harlot;" Jean Daniélou, "Rahab as a Type of the Church," in *"Sacramentum Futuri": From Shadows to Reality* (London: Burns and Oates, 1960), pp. 244–260; and Hermann L. Strack and Paul Billerbeck, *Kommentar zum Neuen Testament aus Talmud und Midrash* (Munich: Beck, 1922–26), vol. 1, pp. 20–23.

30. On Rahab as innkeeper, see *Sifre Numbers* 78. Innkeeping was also a problematic occupation for women that was often associated with prostitution (see B. Yevamot 122a). Rahab is closely linked with linen making in *Ruth Rabbah* 2:1, which provides a full identification of those Israelites said to be descended from Rahab. One midrashic thread argues that "And the families of the house of them that wrought fine linen" (I Chron. 4:21) refers to "Rahab the harlot who concealed the spies in flax (Josh. 2:6)." Segments of these *aggadot* are also found in *Sifre Numbers* 78 and *Sifre Zuta* on Numbers 10:28. For more discussion of Rahab's supposed descendants and occupations, see Baskin, "Rabbinic Transformations of Rahab the Harlot."

AFTERWORD (PP. 161–164)

1. See M. Gittin 5: 9 for a discussion of the extent to which the wives of the rabbinic elite should associate with the wives of unlearned men.

2. Emmanuel Levinas, "The Nations and the Presence of Israel: From the Tractate Pesahim, 118b," in idem, *In the Time of the Nations*, trans. Michael B. Smith (Bloomington: University of Indiana Press, 1994), pp. 92–108, p. 108.

BIBLIOGRAPHY

SELECTED PRIMARY SOURCES AND TRANSLATIONS

Avot de-Rabbi Nathan. Edited by Solomon Schechter. Vienna, 1887. Reprint, New York: Philip Feldheim, 1967.
Babylonian Talmud. Vilna: Romm, 1880–1886.
The Babylonian Talmud. Translated into English with notes, glossary and indexes under the editorship of Isidore Epstein. 18 vols. London: Soncino Press, 1936–1952.
Daily Prayer Book [*Ha-Siddur Ha-Shalem*]. Translated by Philip Birnbaum. New York: Hebrew Publishing Company, 1949.
The Fathers According to Rabbi Nathan. Translated by Judah Goldin. Yale Judaica Series 10. New Haven: Yale University Press, 1955.
The Fathers According to Rabbi Nathan: A Translation and Commentary. Translated by Anthony J. Saldarini. Leiden: E. J. Brill, 1975.
Jerusalem Talmud. Venice 1523. Reprint, Leipzig, 1925.
Josephus Flavius. *Jewish Antiquities.* Loeb Classical Library. Translated by H. St. J. Thakeray, R. Marcus, and L. H. Feldman. London: Heinemann, 1925–1965.
Mekhilta de Rabbi Ishmael. Edited by Jacob Lauterbach. 3 vols. Philadelphia: Jewish Publication Society, 1933–1935.
Midrash Bereshit Rabba. Edited by J. Theodor and H. Albeck. 2nd ed. 3 vols. Jerusalem: Wahrmann, 1965.
Midrash Rabbah. Translated by Harry Freedman, Maurice Simon, and Isidore Epstein. 9 vols. London: Soncino Press, 1938.
Midrash Tanhuma. New York: Horev, 1926.
Midrash Tanhuma. Edited by Solomon Buber. Vilna: Romm, 1885.
The Mishnah. Edited by H. Albeck. 6 vols. Tel Aviv and Jerusalem: Dvir, The Bialik Institute, 1988.
The Mishnah: Translated from the Hebrew with Introduction and Brief Explanatory Notes. Translated by Herbert Danby. Oxford: Oxford University Press, 1933.
Pesiqta de-Rav Kahana. Edited by Bernard Mandelbaum. 2 vols. New York: Jewish Theological Seminary, 1962.
Pesikta de-Rab Kahana: R. Kahana's Complication of Discourses for Sabbaths

and Festal Days. Translated from Hebrew and Aramaic by William G. Braude and Israel Kapstein. Philadelphia: Jewish Publication Society, 1975.

Sifra on Leviticus. Edited by I. H. Weiss. Vienna, 1862.

Sifre on Deuteronomy. Edited by Louis Finkelstein. 1939. Reprint, New York: Jewish Theological Seminary of America, 1969.

Sifre on Numbers and Sifre Zuta. Edited by H. S. Horovitz. Leipzig, 1917. Reprint, Jerusalem: Wahrmann, 1966.

Tanakh: A New Translation of the Holy Scriptures according to the Traditional Hebrew Text. Philadelphia: The Jewish Publication Society of America, 1985.

Tanna Debe Eliyyahu. Translated by William G. Braude and Israel Kapstein. Philadelphia: Jewish Publication Society, 1981.

Tosefta. Edited by Saul Lieberman. New York: Jewish Theological Seminary, 1955–1988.

SECONDARY SOURCES

Abramov, S. Zalman. *Perpetual Dilemma: Jewish Religion in the Jewish State.* Rutherford, N.J.: Fairleigh Dickinson University Press, 1976.

Adler, Rachel. *Engendering Judaism: An Inclusive Theology and Ethics.* Philadelphia: Jewish Publication Society, 1998.

———. "Feminist Folktales of Justice: Robert Cover as a Resource for the Renewal of Halakhah." *Conservative Judaism* 45: 3 (1988): 40–56.

———. "The Virgin in the Brothel and other Anomalies: Character and Context in the Legend of Beuriah Traditions." *Tikkun* 3:6 (1988): 28–32, 102–105.

Anderson, Gary. "The Garden of Eden and Sexuality in Early Judaism." In *People of the Body: Jews and Judaism from an Embodied Perspective,* edited by Howard Eilberg-Schwartz, 47–68. Albany: State University of New York Press, 1992.

Baker, Cynthia. "Bodies, Boundaries, and Domestic Politics in a Late Ancient Marketplace." *Journal of Medieval and Early Modern Studies* 26:3 (fall 1996): 391–418.

Bamberger, Bernard. *Proselytism in the Talmudic Period.* New York: KTAV Publishing House, 1968.

Bar Ilan, Meir. *Some Jewish Women in Antiquity.* Atlanta: Scholars Press, 1998.

———. "Witches in the Bible and in the Talmud." In *Historical, Literary, and Religious Studies,* edited by Herbert W. Basser and Simcha Fishbane, 7–32. Approaches to Ancient Judaism, edited by Jacob Neusner, n.s., 5. Atlanta: Scholars Press, 1993.

Baskin, Judith R. *Pharaoh's Counsellors: Job, Jethro, and Balaam in Rabbinic and Patristic Tradition.* Chico, Calif.: Scholars Press, 1983.

———. "Rabbinic Judaism and the Creation of Woman." *Shofar* 13: 4 (fall, 1995): 68–73. Reprinted in *Judaism Since Gender,* edited by Miriam Peskowitz and Laura Levitt, 125–130. New York: Routledge, 1997.

———. "The Rabbinic Transformations of Rahab the Harlot." *Notre Dame English Journal: A Journal of Religion in Literature* 11 (1979): 141–157.

———. "The Separation of Women in Rabbinic Judaism." In *Women, Religion, and Social Change,* edited by Yvonne Yazbek Haddad and Ellison Banks Findly, 3–18. Albany: State University of New York Press, 1985.

———. "Silent Partners: Women as Wives in Rabbinic Literature." In *Active*

Voices: Women in Jewish Culture, edited by Maurie Sacks, 19–40. Urbana and Chicago: University of Illinois Press, 1995.

———. "Women and Ritual Immersion in Medieval Ashkenaz: The Sexual Politics of Piety." In *Judaism in Practice: From the Middle Ages through the Early Modern Period*, edited by Lawrence Fine, 131–142. Princeton: Princeton University Press, 2001.

———. "Woman as Other in Rabbinic Literature." In *Judaism in Late Antiquity*. Part 3, volume 2: *Where We Stand: Issues and Debates in Ancient Judaism*, edited by Jacob Neusner and Alan J. Avery-Peck, 177–196. Leiden: E. J. Brill, 1999.

———. "Women at Odds: Biblical Paradigms." In *Feminist Nightmares: Women at Odds: Feminism and the Problem of Sisterhood*, edited by Susan Ostrov Weisser and Jennifer Fleischner, 209–224. New York: New York University Press, 1994.

Berman, Saul. "The Status of Women in Halakhic Judaism." In *The Jewish Woman*, edited by Elizabeth Koltun, 114–128. New York: Schocken, 1984.

Biale, David. *Eros and the Jews: From Biblical Israel to Contemporary America*. New York: Basic Books, 1992.

Biale, Rachel. *Women and Jewish Law: An Exploration of Women's Issues in Halakhic Sources*. New York: Schocken, 1984.

Bird, Phyllis. "Male and Female He Created Them: Gen 1:27b in the Context of the Priestly Account of Creation." *Harvard Theological Review* 74:2 (1981): 129–159.

Blayney, Jan. "Theories of Conception in the Ancient Roman World." In *The Family in Ancient Rome: New Perspectives*, edited by Beryl Rawson, 230–236. London: Routledge, 1986.

Boyarin, Daniel. *Carnal Israel: Reading Sex in Talmudic Culture*. Berkeley: University of California Press, 1993.

———. "Reading Androcentrism against the Grain: Women, Sex, and Torah Study." *Poetics Today* 12: 1 (spring, 1991): 29–53.

———. *Unheroic Conduct: The Rise of Heterosexuality and the Invention of the Jewish Man*. Berkeley: University of California Press, 1997.

Braude, William. *Jewish Proselyting in the First Five Centuries of the Common Era*. Providence: Brown University, 1940.

Bronznick, Norman, trans. "Annotated *Alphabet of Ben Sira*." In *Rabbinic Fantasies: Imaginative Narratives from Classical Hebrew Literature*, edited by Mark Jay Mirsky and David Stern, 167–202. Philadelphia: Jewish Publication Society, 1990.

Bronner, Leila Leah. "From Veil to Wig: Jewish Women's Hair Covering." *Judaism* 42:4 (fall, 1993): 465–477.

Brooten, Bernadette. "Early Christian Women and their Cultural Context: Issues of Method in Historical Reconstruction." In *Feminist Perspectives on Biblical Scholarship*, edited by Adela Yarbo Collins, 65–91. Chico, Calif.: Scholars Press, 1985.

———. "Könnten Frauen in Alten Judentum die Scheidung betrieben? Überlegung zu Mk 10, 11–12 und I Kor 7, 10–11. *Evangelische Theologie* 42 (1982): 65–80.

———. *Women Leaders in the Ancient Synagogue*. Chico, Calif.: Scholars Press, 1982.

Cadden, Joan. *The Meaning of Sex Differences in the Middle Ages: Medicine,*

Natural Philosophy, and Culture. Cambridge: Cambridge University Press, 1993.

Callaway, Mary. *Sing, O Barren One: A Study in Comparative Midrash.* Society for Biblical Literature Dissertation, s., 91. Atlanta: Scholars Press, 1986.

Camp, Claudia V. "Understanding a Patriarchy: Women in Second Century Judaism Through the Eyes of Ben Sira." In *"Women Like This": New Perspectives on Jewish Women in the Greco-Roman World,* edited by Amy-Jill Levine, 1–39. Atlanta: Scholars Press, 1991.

Cohen, Jeremy. *"Be Fertile and Increase, Fill the Earth and Master It": The Ancient and Medieval Career of a Biblical Text.* Ithaca: Cornell University Press, 1989.

Cohen, Shaye J. D. "Conversion to Judaism in Historical Perspective: From Biblical Isael to Post-Biblical Judaism." *Conservative Judaism* 36:4 (summer, 1983): 31–45.

———. "Judaism to the Mishnah, 135–220 C.E." In *Christianity and Rabbinic Judaism: A Parallel History of Their Origins and Early Development,* edited by Hershel Shanks, 195–224. Washington, D.C.: Biblical Archaeology Society, 1992.

———. "Menstruants and the Sacred in Judaism and Christianity." In *Women's History and Ancient History,* edited by Sarah B. Pomeroy, 273–299. Chapel Hill: University of North Carolina Press, 1991.

———. "Purity and Piety: The Separation of Menstruants from the Sancta." In *Daughters of the King: Women and the Synagogue,* edited by Susan Grossman and Rivka Haut, 103–116. Philadelphia: Jewish Publication Society, 1992.

———. "Purity, Piety, and Polemic: Medieval Rabbinic Denunciations of 'Incorrect' Purification Practices." In *Women and Water: Menstruation in Jewish Life and Law,* edited by Rahel R. Wasserfall, 82–100. Hanover, N.H.: Brandeis University Press, 1999.

———. *The Beginnings of Jewishness: Boundaries, Varieties, Uncertainties.* Berkeley: University of California Press, 1999.

———. "Why Aren't Jewish Women Circumcised?" In *Gender and the Body in the Ancient Mediterranean,* edited by Maria Wykes, 136–154. Oxford: Blackwell, 1998.

Dan, Joseph. "Samael, Lilith, and the Concept of Evil." *Association for Jewish Studies Review* 5 (1980): 17–40.

Daniélou, Jean. "Rahab as a Type of the Church." In idem, *"Sacramentum Futuri": From Shadows to Reality,* 244–260. London: Burns and Oates, 1960.

Daube, David. *The Duty of Procreation.* Edinburgh: The University of Edinburgh Press, 1977.

Davies, Steven. "Women in the Third Gospel and the New Testament Apocrypha." In *"Women Like This": New Perspectives on Jewish Women in the Greco-Roman World,* edited by Amy-Jill Levine, 185–197. Atlanta: Scholars Press, 1991.

De Beauvoir, Simone. *The Second Sex.* Translated and edited by Howard Madison Parshley. New York: Vintage Books, 1989.

Dean-Jones, Lesley Ann. *Women's Bodies in Classical Greek Science.* Oxford: Clarendon Press, 1994.

Diamond, Eliezer. "Hunger Artists, and Householders: The Tension between

Ascetism and Family Responsibility among Jewish Pietists in Late Antiquity." *Union Seminary Quarterly Review* 48 (1996): 28–47.

———. "The World of the Talmud." In *The Schocken Guide to Jewish Books*, edited by Barry W. Holtz, 47–69. New York: Schocken Books, 1992.

Dinari, Yedidyah. "The Customs of Menstrual Impurity: Their Origin and Development." *Tarbiz* 49 (1979–80): 302–304 [Hebrew].

Douglas, Mary. *Purity and Danger: An Analysis of the Concepts of Pollution and Taboo*. New York: Praeger, 1966.

Dresner, Samuel H. *Rachel*. Minneapolis: Fortress Press, 1994.

Eilberg-Schwartz, Howard. *God's Phallus and Other Problems for Men and Monotheism*. Boston: Beacon Press, 1994.

———. *The Savage in Judaism: An Anthropology of Israelite Religion and Ancient Judaism*. Bloomington: Indiana University Press, 1990.

Epstein, Louis. *Marriage Laws in the Bible and Talmud*. Cambridge, Mass.: Harvard University Press, 1942.

———. *Sex Laws and Customs in Judaism*. New York: KTAV Publishing House, 1948, 1967.

Falk, Ze'ev W. *Jewish Matrimonial Law in the Middle Ages*. Oxford: Oxford University Press, 1966.

Feldman, David M. *Marital Relations, Birth Control and Abortion in Jewish Law*. New York: Schocken, 1968, 1975.

Fiorenza, Elizabeth Schussler. *In Memory of Her*. New York: Crossroad, 1984.

Fishbane, Simcha. "Most Women Engage in Sorcery: An Analysis of Female Sorceresses in the Babylonian Talmud." In *Historical, Literary, and Religious Studies*, edited by Herbert W. Basser and Simcha Fishbane, 143–166. *Approaches to Ancient Judaism*, edited by Jacob Neusner, n.s., 5. Atlanta: Scholars Press, 1993.

Fonrobert, Charlotte Elisheva. *Menstrual Purity: Rabbinic and Christian Reconstructions of Biblical Gender*. Stanford: Stanford University Press, 2000.

———. "Yalta's Ruse: Resistance against Rabbinic Menstrual Authority in Talmudic Literature." In *Women and Water: Menstruation in Jewish Life and Law*, edited by Rahel S. Wasserfall, 60–81. Hanover, N.H.: Brandeis University Press, 1999.

Fraade, Steven D. "Ascetical Aspects of Ancient Judaism." In *Jewish Spirituality: From the Bible Through the Middle Ages*, edited by Arthur Green, 253–288. New York: Crossroads Press, 1986.

Friedman, Mordechai A. *Jewish Polygyny in the Middle Ages: New Documents from the Cairo Genizah* [Hebrew]. Jerusalem: The Bialik Institute, Tel Aviv University, 1986.

———. "Marriage as an Institution: Jewry under Islam." In *The Jewish Family: Metaphor and Memory*, edited by David Kraemer, 31–45. Oxford: Oxford University Press, 1989.

———. "Tamar, a Symbol of Life: The 'Killer Wife' Superstition in the Bible and Jewish Tradition." *Association for Jewish Studies Review* 15:1 (spring, 1990): 23–61.

———. *Jewish Marriage in Palestine: A Cairo Genizah Study*. 2 vols. Tel Aviv: Tel Aviv University; New York: The Jewish Theological Seminary of America, 1980.

Friedman, Richard Elliot. *Who Wrote the Bible?* New York: Summit Books, 1987.

Frymer-Kensky, Tikva. *In the Wake of the Goddesses: Women, Culture and the Biblical Transformation of Pagan Myth.* New York: The Free Press, 1992.

———. "Pollution, Purification, and Purgation in Biblical Israel." In *The Word of the Lord Shall Go Forth: Essays in Honor of David Noel Freedman,* edited by Carol Meyers, 399–414. Winona Lake, Ind.: Eisenbraun's, 1983.

Gafni, Isaiah M. "The Institution of Marriage in Rabbinic Times." In *The Jewish Family: Metaphor and Memory,* edited by David M. Kraemer, 21–25. New York: Oxford University Press, 1989.

———. "The World of the Talmud: From the Mishnah to the Arab Conquest." In *Christianity and Rabbinic Judaism: A Parallel History of Their Origins and Early Development,* edited by Hershel Shanks, 225–266. Washington D.C.: Biblical Archaeology Society, 1992.

Gaster, Theodor. *The Holy and the Profane.* New York: William Sloane Associates, 1955.

Ginzberg, Louis. *The Legends of the Jews.* 7 vols. Philadelphia: Jewish Publication Society, 1909–1937.

Goitein, Shlomo Dov. *A Mediterranean Society.* Vol. 3, *The Family.* Berkeley: University of California Press, 1978.

Goldenberg, Robert. "Talmud." In *Back to the Sources: Reading the Classic Jewish Texts,* edited by Barry W. Holtz, 128–175. New York: Summit Books, 1984.

Goodblatt, David. "The Beruriah Traditions." *Journal of Jewish Studies* 26 (1975): 68–85.

Green, Arthur. "Bride, Spouse, Daughter: Images of the Feminine in Classical Jewish Sources." In *On Being a Jewish Feminist: A Reader,* edited by Susannah Heschel, 248–260. New York: Schocken, 1983.

Gruber, Mayer. "The Status of Women in Ancient Judaism." In *Where We Stand: Issues and Debates in Ancient Judaism,* 151–176. Vol. 2., pt. 3 of *Judaism in Late Antiquity,* edited by Jacob Neusner and Alan J. Avery-Peck. Leiden: E. J. Brill, 1999.

Hackett, Jo Ann. "Rehabilitating Hagar: Fragments of an Epic Pattern." In *Gender and Difference in Ancient Israel,* edited by Peggy L. Day, 12–27. Minneapolis: Fortress Press, 1989.

Hartman, Geoffrey H. and Sanford Budick, eds. *Midrash and Literature.* New Haven: Yale University Press, 1986.

Hasan-Rokem, Galit. *Web of Life: Folklore and Midrash in Rabbinic Literature.* Translated by Batya Stein. Stanford: Stanford University Press, 2000.

Hauptman, Judith. "Feminist Perspectives on Jewish Studies: Rabbinics." In *Feminist Perspectives on Jewish Studies,* edited by Shelly Tenenbaum and Lynn Davidman, 40–51. New Haven: Yale University Press, 1994.

———. "Images of Women in the Talmud." In *Religion and Sexism: Images of Women in Jewish and Christian Tradition,* edited by Rosemary Radford Ruether, 184–212. New York: Simon and Schuster, 1974.

———. *Rereading the Rabbis: A Woman's Voice.* Boulder, Colo.: Westview Press, 1998.

———. "Some Thoughts on the Nature of Halakhic Adjudication: Women and Minyan." *Judaism* 42:4 (fall, 1993): 396–413.

———. "Women and Prayer: An Attempt to Dispel Some Fallacies." *Judaism* 42:1 (winter 1993): 94–103.

Hengel, Martin. "Maria Magdelena und die Frauen als Zeugen." *Abraham Un-*

ser Vater: Festschrift für O. Michel. Arbeiten Zur Geschichte des Spätjuden-
tums und Urchristentums 5 (1963): 243–256.

Hoffman, Lawrence A. *Covenant of Blood: Circumcision and Gender in Rab-*
binic Judaism. Chicago: The University of Chicago Press, 1996.

Holtz, Barry W. "Midrash." In *Back to the Sources: Reading the Classic Jewish*
Texts, edited by Barry W. Holtz, 177–211. New York: Summit Books, 1984.

Idel, Moshe. "Sexual Metaphors and Praxis in the Kabbalah." In *The Jewish*
Family: Metaphor and Memory, edited by David Kraemer, 197–224. Oxford:
Oxford University Press, 1989.

Ilan, Tal. "The Historical Beruriah, Rachel, and Imma Shalom." *Association for*
Jewish Studies Review 22:1 (1997): 1–17.

———. *Integrating Women into Second Temple History.* Texts and Studies in
Ancient Judaism 76. Tübingen: J.C.B. Mohr, 1999.

———. *Jewish Women in Greco-Roman Palestine: An Inquiry into Image and*
Status. Texts and Studies in Ancient Judaism 44. Tübingen: J.C.B. Mohr,
1995.

———. "Matrona and Rabbi Jose: An Alternative Interpretation." *Journal for*
the Study of Judaism 25 (1994): 18–51.

———. *Mine and Yours are Hers: Retrieving Women's History from Rabbinic*
Literature. Brill: Leiden, 1997.

———. "Notes and Observations on a Newly Published Divorce Bill from the
Judean Desert." *Harvard Theological Review* 89:2 (1996): 195–212.

———. "The Quest for the Historical Beruriah, Rachel, and Imma Shalom."
Association for Jewish Studies Review 22:1 (1997): 1–17.

Joseph, Norma Baumel. "Mehitzah: Halakhic Decisions and Political Conse-
quences." In *Daughters of the King: Women and the Synagogue,* edited by
Susan Grossman and Rivka Haut, 103–116. Philadelphia: Jewish Publication
Society, 1992.

Kimelman, Reuven. "The Seduction of Eve and the Exegetical Politics of Gender." *Biblical Interpretation* 4:1 (1996): 1–39.

King, Helen. "Reading the Female Body." In *Gender and Body in the Ancient*
Mediterranean, edited by Maria Wykes, 136–154. Oxford: Blackwell, 1998.

Koren, Sharon. "Mystical Rationales for the Laws of Niddah." In *Women and*
Water: Menstruation in Jewish Life and Law, edited by Rahel S. Wasserfall,
101–121. Hanover, N.H.: Brandeis University Press, 1999.

Kraemer, Ross Shepard. *Her Share of the Blessings: Women's Religions among*
Pagans, Jews, and Christians in the Greco-Roman World. New York: Oxford
University Press, 1992.

———. *Maenads, Martyrs, Matrons, Monastics: A Sourcebook on Women's Re-*
ligions in the Greco-Roman World. Philadelphia: Fortress, 1988.

———. "Jewish Women and Christian Origins: Some Caveats." In *Women and*
Christian Origins, edited by Ross Shepard Kraemer and Mary Rose
D'Angelo, 35–49. New York: Oxford University Press, 1999.

———. "Jewish Women in the Diaspora World of Late Antiquity." In *Jewish*
Women in Historical Perspective. 2nd ed., edited by Judith R. Baskin, 46–
72. Detroit: Wayne State University, 1998.

———. "Jewish Women and Women's Judaism(s) at the Beginning of Christianity." *Women and Christian Origins,* edited by Ross Shepard Kraemer
and Mary Rose D'Angelo, 50–79. New York: Oxford University Press,
1999.

Kugel, James L. *In Potiphar's House: The Interpretive Life of Biblical Texts.* New York: HarperCollins, 1990.

Langer, Ruth. *To Worship God Properly: Tensions between Liturgical Custom and Halakhah in Judaism.* Cincinnati: Hebrew Union College Press, 1998.

Lesses, Rebecca. "Exe(o)rcising Power: Women as Sorceresses, Exorcists, and Demonesses in Babylonian Jewish Society of Late Antiquity." *Journal of the American Academy of Religion* 69:2 (2001):343–375.

Levine, Molly Myerowitz. "The Gendered Grammar of Ancient Mediterranean Hair." In *Off with Her Head! The Denial of Women's Identity in Myth, Religion, and Culture*, edited by Howard Eilberg-Schwartz and Wendy Doniger, 76–130. Berkeley: University of California Press, 1995.

Levinas, Emmanuel. *In the Time of the Nations.* Translated by Michael B. Smith. Bloomington: University of Indiana Press, 1994.

———. *Nine Talmudic Readings.* Translated and with an introduction by Annette Aronowicz. Bloomington: University of Indiana Press, 1990.

Lewis, Naphtali, ed. *The Documents from the Bar Kokhba Period in the Cave of Letters: Greek Papyri.* Judean Desert, 2nd ser. Jerusalem: Israel Exploration Society; Hebrew University of Jerusalem; Shrine of the Book, 1989.

McCarter, P. Kyle, Jr. "The Patriarchal Age: Abraham, Isaac and Jacob." In *Ancient Israel: A Short History from Abraham to the Roman Destruction of the Temple*, edited by Hershel Shanks, 1–30. Washington D.C.: Biblical Archaeology Society; Englewood Cliffs, N.J.: Prentice-Hall, 1988.

Meacham, Tirzah. "An Abbreviated History of the Development of the Jewish Menstrual Laws." In *Women and Water: Menstruation in Jewish Life and Law*, edited by Rahel S. Wasserfall, 23–39. Hanover, N.H.: Brandeis University Press, 1999.

———. "Woman More Intelligent than Man: Creation Gone Awry." In *Historical, Literary, and Religious Studies*, edited by Herbert W. Basser and Simcha Fishbane, 143–166. *Approaches to Ancient Judaism*, edited by Jacob Neusner, n.s., 5. Atlanta: Scholars Press, 1993.

Meeks, Wayne. "The Image of the Androgyne: Some Uses of a Symbol in Early Christianity." *History of Religions* 13 (1974): 165–208.

Meyers, Carol. *Discovering Eve: Ancient Israelite Women in Context.* New York: Oxford University Press, 1988.

Neusner, Jacob. *Androgynous Judaism: Masculine and Feminine in the Dual Torah.* Macon, Ga.: Mercer University Press, 1993.

———. *How the Rabbis Liberated Women.* Atlanta: Scholars Press, 1998.

———. *In Search of Talmudic Biography: The Problem of the Attributed Saying.* Chico, Calif.: Scholars Press, 1984.

———. *Midrash in Context: Exegesis in Formative Judaism.* Philadelphia: Fortress Press, 1983.

———. *The Midrash: An Introduction.* Northvale, N.J.: Jason Aronson, 1990.

———. *Method and Meaning in Ancient Judaism.* Brown Judaic Studies 10. Missoula, Mont.: Scholars Press, 1979.

Niditch, Susan. "Portrayals of Women in the Hebrew Bible." In *Jewish Women in Historical Perspective.* 2nd ed., edited by Judith R. Baskin, 25–45. Detroit: Wayne State University Press, 1998.

Ortner, Sherry. "Is the Female to Male as Nature is to Culture?" In *Women,*

Culture and Society, edited by Michelle Zimbalist Rosaldo and Louise Lamphere, 67–87. Stanford: Stanford University Press, 1971.

Pardes, Ilana. *Countertraditions in the Bible: A Feminist Approach*. Cambridge: Harvard University Press, 1992.

Patai, Raphael. "Jewish Folk-cures for Barrenness." Pts. 1 and 2. *Folklore* 54 (1943): 117–124; 56 (1945): 208–218.

Peskowitz, Miriam. *Spinning Fantasies: Rabbis, Gender, and History*. Berkeley: University of California Press, 1997.

Plaskow, Judith. *Standing Again at Sinai: Judaism from a Feminist Perspective*. New York: Harper & Row, 1990.

Porton, Gary G. *The Stranger Within Your Gates: Converts and Conversion in Rabbinic Literature*. Chicago: University of Chicago Press, 1994.

———. *Understanding Rabbinic Midrash: Texts and Commentary*. Hoboken: KTAV Publishing House, 1985.

Reinhartz, Adele. "From Narrative to History: The Resurrection of Mary and Martha." In *"Women Like This": New Perspectives on Jewish Women in the Greco-Roman World*, edited by Amy-Jill Levine, 161–184. Atlanta: Scholars Press, 1991.

Rosaldo, Michelle Zimbalist. "Women, Culture, and Society: A Theoretical Overview." In *Women, Culture, and Society*, edited by Michelle Zimbalist Rosaldo and Louise Lamphere, 17–42. Stanford: Stanford University Press, 1971.

Rubenstein, Jeffrey L. *Talmudic Stories: Narrative Art, Composition, and Culture*. Baltimore: The Johns Hopkins University Press, 1999.

Rubin, Gayle. "The Traffic in Women: Notes on the 'Political Economy' of Sex." In *Toward an Anthropology of Women*, edited by Rayna R. Reiter, 157–210. New York: Monthly Review Press, 1975.

Safrai, Hannah. "Women and the Ancient Synagogue." In *Daughters of the King Women and the Synagogue*, edited by Susan Grossman and Rivka Haut, 39–50. Philadelphia: Jewish Publication Society, 1992.

Satlow, Michael. *Jewish Marriage in Antiquity*. Princeton: Princeton University Press, 2001.

———. *"Tasting the Dish": Rabbinic Rhetorics of Sexuality*. Atlanta: Scholars Press, 1995.

Scholem, Gershom. *Origins of the Kabbalah*. Edited by R. J. Zvi Werblowsky. English edition. Princeton: Princeton University Press, 1987.

Soler, Jean. "The Dietary Prohibitions of the Hebrews." In *Food: A Culinary History*, edited by Jean-Louis Flandrin and Massimo Montanari, 46–54. New York: Columbia University Press, 1999. First published in *The New York Review of Books* 26 (14 June, 1976): 29–33.

Strack, Hermann Leberecht and Paul Billerbeck. *Kommentar zum Neuen Testament aus Talmud und Midrasch*. 6 vols. Munich: Beck, 1922–1926.

Trachtenberg, Joshua. *Jewish Magic and Superstition: A Study in Folk Religion*. 1939. Reprint, New York: Atheneum, 1970.

Trenchard, Warren C. *Ben Sira's View of Women*. Chico, Calif.: Scholars Press, 1982.

Umansky, Ellen M. "Jewish Feminist Theology." In *Choices in Modern Jewish Thought: A Partisan Guide*. 2nd ed., edited by Eugene B. Borowitz, 313–340. West Orange, N.J.: Behrman House, 1995.

Umansky, Ellen M. and Dianne Ashton, eds. *Four Centuries of Jewish Women's Spirituality: A Sourcebook*. Boston: Beacon Press, 1992.

Urbach, Ephraim E. *The Sages: The World and Wisdom of the Rabbis of the Talmud*. Cambridge: Harvard University Press, 1987.

Valler, Shulamit. "Business Women in the Mishnaic and Talmudic Period," *Women in Judaism: A Multidisciplinary Journal* 2:2 (2001).

Wegner, Judith Romney. *Chattel or Person? The Status of Women in the Mishnah*. New York: Oxford University Press, 1988.

———. "Dependency, Autonomy and Sexuality: Woman as Chattel and Person in the System of the Mishnah." In *New Perspectives on Ancient Judaism* 1, edited by Jacob Neusner, Peter Borgen, Ernest S. Frerichs, and Richard Horsley, 89–102. Lanham, Md.; New York; London: University Press of America, 1987.

———. "The Image and Status of Women in Classical Rabbinic Judaism." In *Jewish Women in Historical Perspective*. 2nd ed., edited by Judith R. Baskin, 73–100. Detroit: Wayne State University Press, 1998.

———. "Philo's Portrayal of Women—Hebraic or Hellenic." In *"Women Like This": New Perspectives on Jewish Women in the Greco-Roman World*, edited by Amy-Jill Levine, 41–66. Atlanta: Scholars Press, 1991.

Weisberg, Dvora. "Men Imagining Women Imagining God: Gender Issues in Classic Midrash." In *Agendas for the Study of Midrash in the Twenty-First Century*, edited by Marc Lee Raphael, 63–83. Williamsburg, Va.: Department of Religion, William and Mary College, 1999.

Weissler, Chava. "The Religion of Traditional Ashkenazic Women: Some Methodological Issues." *Association for Jewish Studies Review* 12 (1987): 73–94.

———. "The Traditional Piety of Ashkenazic Women." In *Jewish Spirituality: From the Sixteenth Century to the Present*, edited by Arthur Green, 245–275. New York: Crossroad, 1987.

———. *Voices of the Matriarchs: Listening to the Prayers of Early Modern Women*. Boston: Beacon Press, 1998.

SUBJECT INDEX

Abaye's foster mother, 198n8
R. Abba, 152
R. Abba bar Kahana, 157
R. Abbahu, 63, 117
Abba Saul, 69–70
Abel, 57–58, 181n32
Abigail, 31, 151
R. Abihu, 57
R. Abin, 132
Abishag, 117
Abraham, 78, 122, 126. *See also*
    Sarah
Adam: creation, 46–49, 184n22;
    death, 78–79, 183–84nn14–15; Lil-
    ith, 58–59; potential for wicked-
    ness, 52–53
Adler, Rachel, 8, 83, 86
Adultery, 98–99, 182–83n4; associ-
    ated with study, 81; conception,
    124–25, 195n12; divorce, 92,
    189n13; at funerals, 70; as
    punishment, 112; witchcraft, 33
Aggadic midrash, 1, 4–7; contradic-
    tions, 41–43, 54, 180n31; multivo-
    cality, 5, 11, 161, 179n19; named
    women, 84, 179n19; real life inter-
    pretations, 7, 182n47
R. Aha, 31, 106, 115
R. Aha b. R. Kattina, 123
Alcestis (Euripides), 104, 191–92n39
Alcohol use, 108
R. Alexandri, 117, 157

Alphabet of Ben Sira, 58–60
Alterity of women, 12, 161–63. *See
    also* Otherness of women
R. Ammi, 14, 21–22, 127, 128, 130–
    31
Amnon, 34–35
Amulets, 58–59. *See also* Witchcraft
Anderson, Gary, 64, 178n7
Androgynous first human, 46–47, 50,
    60–64, 95, 177n5
Animals, 77–78, 187n50
Apocrypha, 173–74n49
R. Aqiva, 27, 101
R. Aqiva's wife, 101–2, 104, 191n34
Aristotle, 20–21
R. Ashi, 98
Autonomous women. *See* Indepen-
    dent women
R. Azariah, 132

Babata, 41, 176n74, 193n63
Babylonian Talmud, 3–4, 69, 89–90,
    189n13. *See also* Study
Baker, Cynthia, 113, 186n47, 187–
    88n2
Bar Ilan, Meir, 69, 145, 183n11,
    185n30
Barrenness. *See* Infertility
Bathsheba, 173n44
Ben-Azzai, 81–82, 96, 104
Ben Sira, 32–33, 36–37, 58–60, 173–
    74n49, 183n6

Benedictions. *See* Prayer
R. Benjamin bar Yapat, 10
R. Berekhiah, 38–39, 52, 152
Berenice, 41
Berkowits, Eliezer, 143, 198n6
Berman, Saul, 80
Beruriah, 82–83, 186n36
Betrothal, 89
Biale, David, 26, 93, 102, 190n21
Biale, Rachel, 124, 135
Bilhah, 146
Birth, 66–67
Blayney, Jan, 20
Blessings. *See* Prayer
Boaz, 30
Bodily functions, 8, 18–19, 33–35, 161–62, 199n17. *See also* Childbirth; Menstruation
Boyarin, Daniel: celibacy, 96–97; creation narratives, 63–64, 177n5; female study, 29, 82–83; male study *vs.* procreation, 96–97, 102–4, 191–92n39; rabbinic attitudes towards women, 36–37, 39–40, 56; sexuality, 107–8; three commandments of women, 73; Yalta, 84
Bronner, Leila Leah, 68, 182–83n4
Brooten, Bernadette, 41–42

Cain, 57, 181n32
Celibacy, 96–97, 102, 104, 190n29
Childbirth, 14–15, 66–67, 70–75, 184n16, 184n22
Childlessness. *See* Infertility
Children. *See* Procreation
Christian writings about Rahab, 200–201n29
Circumcision, 15, 18–19, 22, 24, 44, 219
Cohen, Jeremy, 62
Cohen, Shaye J. D., 2, 19, 24–25, 28
Collusion by women in their subordination, 40, 176n70
Conception/embryology, 13–14, 20–21, 112
Concubinage, 67–68, 76. *See also* Polygyny

Conversion, 11, 154–60, 163, 173n44, 200nn21–24, 200n26, 200–201n29
Corporeality. *See* Bodily functions
Co-wives, 145–50. *See also* Polygyny
Cozbi the Midianite, 154, 160, 199n18
Creation narratives, 9, 177n3; androgynous first human, 46–50, 60–64, 95, 177n5; first woman, 44–56; inferiority of women, 49–56; justification for women's disempowerment, 65–67, 162; of man in God's image, 49–56, 125, 181n39; need for two narratives, 49–56, 180n26; serial creation of man and woman, 49–56, 65–67; simultaneous creation of man and woman, 46–50, 57, 177n5; of woman in God's image, 61–62
Cultural contexts of midrashic interpretations, 163, 166n7; conversion to Judaism, 155–56; creation in the divine image, 63; ethnic diversity of outside world, 114; female rituals, 72; funerals, 68–69; infertility, 199n16; menstruation, 27, 172–73n39; misogyny, 36–40, 175n56; patriarchal structure, 162; political impotence of Jewish men, 38–40; polygyny, 116; procreation, 20–21; sexuality, 32–33, 190n21, 192n45; veils, 68, 182–83n4, 185n29; witchcraft and magic, 198n8
Curses of women, 73–79, 184n22

Dan, Joseph, 60
Dance, 70, 183n12
Daughters, 32–33, 51–52; inheritance of property, 138; of Lot, 124; of Mar Samuel, 179n19; of R. Nahman, 33, 142–43; of Saul, 30; study of the Torah, 81–83, 176n68, 190–91n31; of Zelophehad, 11, 143–45, 160, 162
David, King of Israel, 30, 117, 154–55, 173n44

Death: childbirth, 72–73, 184n16; women as cause, 24–25, 35, 38, 66, 68–73, 179n17, 183n6

De Beauvoir, Simone, 1

Deborah, 31–32, 54, 179n18

Demonization of women, 33–35, 38, 142–43, 160, 183n6, 185n29. *See also* Lilith

Descendants, 156–60, 200–201n29, 200n25

Dietary laws, 24, 71–72, 110, 183n13

R. Dimi, 25–26, 74–78

Dinah, 11, 51–53, 109, 121, 147–49, 160, 178n14

Discipleship, 138–39, 197n34

Disempowerment of women, justifications for, 65–87; creation narratives, 65–67, 162; light mindedness, 51–52, 56

Divorce, 2, 18, 30, 33, 68, 188–89n12, 193n62; bad wives, 113–18, 193n55; financial aspects, 90; infertility, 10, 94, 104, 119–23, 126–30, 196n21; initiation by wives, 127–28; legal issues, 91–93, 127–28, 188–89nn12–13; preference not to divorce, 128–30, 196n21; sexuality, 108

Domestic duties. *See* Household responsibilities of women

R. Dostai, 15

Dowry, 90. See *Ketubbah*

Dress: immodesty, 112–14, 167–68n2, 173n41, 189n16, 190n18, 193n57; veils, 66, 68, 113–14, 182–83n4, 185n29

Economics. *See* Financial aspects of women's lives

Eden, 64

Eilberg-Schwartz, Howard, 19, 24, 139

R. Eleazar, 72, 116, 121, 124–25

R. Eleazar b. 'Azariah, 111

R. Eleazar b. R. Simeon, 125

R. Eliezer, 81–83, 91, 117, 192n49

Elijah, 25, 97

Emancipated slave story, 123–24

Enabling role of women. *See* Nurturing role of women

Epstein, Louis, 195–96n20

Esther, 151

Euripides, 104, 191–92n39

Eve, 1–2, 9, 44–60; disobedience, 50; nature of women, 57–58, 122, 175n56; polygamy, 116; procreation, 178n7; ten curses, 75–79, 184n22; three precepts, 183–84n14, 184n15. *See also* Death

Falk, Ze'ev W., 195–96n20

Feldman, David M., 124, 125

Female beauty, 132–33

Female prophets, 158–59

Feminization of Israel, 39, 99–100, 130, 136–38, 175n64, 197n37

Financial aspects of women's lives: divorce, 90; household responsibilities, 90–91, 188n10; independent women, 42; marriage, 89–92, 94. *See also* Legal aspects of women's lives

First women. *See* Eve; Lilith

Fishbane, Simcha, 143

Fonrobert, Charlotte Elisheva, 28, 166n7, 199n17

Food. *See* Dietary laws

Foreign women. *See* Gentile women

Fraade, Steven D., 102

Friedman, Mordechai A., 37–38, 40, 177n3, 183n6, 195–96n20

Friendships. *See* Groups of women

Frymer-Kensky, Tikva, 36

Funerals, 66, 68–70, 183n11

Gafni, Isaiah M., 116

Galen, 20–22

Gemara, 3

Gentile women, 11, 163; Cozbi the Midianite, 154, 160, 199n18; Hagar the Egyptian, 150–54, 160; immorality, 157–58, 199n17; Rahab, 11, 31, 54, 151, 154–60, 163,

Gentile women (*continued*)
200nn22–26, 200–201nn29–30;
Ruth the Moabite, 154–55, 157;
Zipporah, wife of Moses, 154
R. Gershom b. Judah, 188–89n12,
195–96n20
Governance, women's roles in, 76–79
Great Demon, 60
Greco-Roman culture, 155–56; men-
struation, 172–73n39; misogyny,
36–40, 175n56; procreation, 20–21
Groups of women, 10–11, 141–43,
160, 173–74n49–50, 197–98n1
Gruber, Mayer, 29, 38–41, 92,
168n2, 189nn13–14
Gynophobia. *See* Misogyny

Hadlaqah, 66, 71–72, 80, 184n15
Hagar, 11, 126, 131, 150–54, 160
Hair, 34–35, 68, 113–14, 179–
80n22, 182–83n4, 185n29
Hallah, 66, 71–72, 80, 184n15
R. Hanan, 115, 147
R. Hananiah b. Hakinai, 103, 111,
191–92n39, 193n54
R. Hanina, 52–53, 132
R. Hanina b. Pappa, 115
Hannah, 131, 135, 136
Hannah's prayer, 80, 106, 124–25,
136, 149, 185n30, 197n30
Hasan-Rokem, Galit, 69
Hauptman, Judith: marriage, 89,
188n9; multivocality of rabbinic
literature, 11, 179n19; procreation,
194n4, 195n16; religious practice
of women, 80–81, 83–84, 185n32;
rights of women, 17, 188n9; rules
of separation, 26–27, 31
Hebrew, knowledge of, 185n30
R. Helbo, 98, 132
Hezekiah, King of Judah, 159
R. Hilkiah, 53
R. Hillel, 143
Hippocrates, 20–21
R. Hisda, 1, 21, 54, 114
R. Hiyya, 100, 110–11

R. Hiyya b. Abba, 132
R. Hiyya b. Gomdi, 96
R. Hiyya bar Yosef, 94
Homa, 40
Household responsibilities of women,
76–79, 96–97; childrearing, 111; fi-
nancial responsibilities, 90–91,
188n10; marketing, 112–14,
183n13, 186n47. *See also* Nurtur-
ing role of women; Religious prac-
tices by women
Huldah, 31–32, 54, 158–59, 179n18
Humanity achieved through mar-
riage, 62–64, 88, 95–96
R. Huna, 132
R. Huna the Elder, 53

R. Idi, 132
Idolatry, 198n5
Ilan, Tal, 82–83, 102, 180n31,
191n34
R. Ile'a, 120–21, 125
Imma Shalom, 106, 192n49
Immodesty: behavior, 109, 149, 167–
68n2; dress, 112–14, 167–68n2,
173n41, 189n16, 190n18, 193n57;
hair, 34–35, 68, 113–14, 182–
83n4, 185n29
Immorality, 157–58, 163, 198n4,
199n17
Impurity of women, 22–29, 39–40,
71–72, 168n3, 171nn32–33. *See
also* Light mindedness of women;
Menstruation
Independent women, 40–43, 84–87;
Beruriah, 82–83, 186n36; daughters of Zelophehad, 143–45; infertility, 133. *See also* Leaders,
women as
Inferiority of women, 3, 5, 9, 12, 64,
161–63, 178n8; creation narratives, 49–56, 179n17; female collusion, 40, 176n70; Greco-Roman
culture, 36–37; justification for, 65–
87
Infertility, 10, 94, 104, 119–40, 163;

divorce, 120–23, 126–30, 196n21; matriarchs, 132–38, 148, 197n37; miracles, 137–38; polygyny, 126–27, 195–96n20; prayer, 129–30, 132–36, 139–40, 148, 196–97n29; as punishment, 130–36, 195n17; remedies for, 196n26; slaves and servants, 150–54, 199n16
Infidelity. *See* Adultery
Inheritance. *See* Property
Isaac, 78, 134, 150
R. Isaac, 14, 21–22, 34, 69–70, 117, 123, 152
R. Isaac b. Abdimi, 74
R. Isaac b. Joseph, 25–26
R. Isaac ben Jacob ha-Kohen, 60
Isaiah, 34
Ishmael, 150–51, 153
R. Ishmael, 122
Israel, feminization of, 39, 99–100, 130, 136–38, 175n64, 197n37
Issachar, 108–9, 199n12

Jacob, 78, 109, 135, 145–49, 191n34
R. Jeremiah, 132
R. Jeremiah b. Leazar, 46–48
Jethro the Midianite, 154–58
Jewelry, 167–68n2
Jewish identity through circumcision, 19, 22, 44
R. Johanan: creation narratives, 46, 78; inferiority of women, 21; infertility, 126, 128, 132–33; marriage, 96, 106, 112, 115–17; Rachel, 146; religious practices by women, 85; sexuality, 30; teachers, 138–39
R. Johanan b. Beroqah, 51, 120–22
R. Johanan b. Dahabai, 106–7
R. Jonathan, 108
R. Jose, 57, 97, 112
R. Jose b. Abin, 32
R. Jose b. Hanina, 80, 117
R. Jose b. Zimra, 51, 121
Joseph, 30, 173n44
R. Joseph, 32–33, 106, 168n3

R. Joseph son of Rava, 104
R. Jose the Galilean, 56, 111
Joshua, 154–60
R. Joshua, 66, 98, 178n8
R. Joshua b. Levi, 39, 96, 138–39
R. Joshua b. R. Nehemiah, 61, 111
R. Joshua of Siknin, 53, 96
R. Josiah, 106
Rav Judah, 112, 117
R. Judah, 69, 115–16, 152, 158, 159
R. Judah b. Batra, 116
R. Judah b. R. Simon, 63, 147
R. Judah b. Rabbi, 57
R. Judan, 152

Kashrut, 71–72
Ketubbah, 89–93, 113–14, 127, 188n5, 188nn7–9, 189n13, 190n19
Kiddush, 85–86, 187n50
Kimelman, Reuven, 50
Kraemer, Ross Shepard, 41, 72, 183n13, 198n8

Laban, 145–46
Langer, Ruth, 185n30
Language knowledge, 185n30
Leaders, women as, 9, 41–43, 54, 76–79, 84–87, 143–45, 162
Leah, 78, 145–49, 160, 199n10, 199n14; fertility, 130–31, 134; friendships, 11; immodesty, 109, 149
R. Leazar, 51, 61, 121
Legal aspects of women's lives: divorce, 91–93, 127–28, 188–89nn12–13; marriage, 89–95, 188n5, 188nn7–9, 188–89nn12–13, 190n19, 194n2; polygyny, 74, 116, 195–96n20; procreation, 194n3, 195n16; sexual intercourse, 190n19
Lesses, Rebecca, 185n29, 198n3, 198n8
R. Levi, 48–49, 96, 108, 132

R. Levi b. Zechariah, 131
Levinas, Emmanuel, 163–64, 178n6
Levine, Molly Myerowitz, 182–83n4
Levirate marriage, 18
Light mindedness of women: Beruriah, 82; justification for female disempowerment, 51–52, 56; justification for separation, 91, 173n45; sexual unreliability, 30, 35, 98–99, 160, 170n12, 190n22
Lilith, 9, 58–60, 181n33, 185n29
Lot's daughters, 124

Magical power. *See* Witchcraft
Maidservants, 150–54, 199n16. *See also* Slavery
Maimonides, 196n21
Male assumptions, 7, 11, 36–40, 56; justifications for women's disempowerment, 16–18, 51–52, 56, 65–87; sexuality, 29–36, 67–68, 173n44, 173n45, 190n18, 190n22, 190n23; unreliability of women, 30, 35, 98–99, 160, 170n12, 190n22
Male dominance, 178n8; marriage, 30, 59, 80–81, 89, 93; prayer and study, 17; procreation, 18–22, 120–22; relationship with God, 44; sexual intercourse, 50–51, 59, 125, 194n2
Male sexual desire, 29–36, 173nn44–45, 190n22
Man's creation in God's image, 49–50, 62
Marketplace, 112–14, 162, 183n13, 186n47, 187–88n2
Marriage, 2, 8–10, 88–118; achievement of human status, 62–64, 88, 95–96; adultery, 33, 70, 81, 92, 98–99, 112, 124–25, 182–83n4, 189n13, 195n12; companionate/intellectual relationship, 59, 100–101, 106, 110; creation narratives, 46, 54–55, 60–64; discord, 110–12; financial aspects, 89–92, 94; with

gentiles, 150–51; legal aspects, 89–95, 127, 188n5, 188nn7–9, 188–89nn12–13, 190n19, 194n2; levirate, 18; love, 97–98; male dominance, 30, 59, 80–81, 89, 93; male obligation to study, 95–97, 101–5, 162, 191n38; metaphoric interpretations, 99–100; monogamy, 67–68, 76, 116, 145; polygamy, 74, 116; polygyny, 67–68, 76, 90, 116–17, 126–27, 145–50, 189n13, 193n63; preordainment, 112; sacred significance, 88; social order, 95–99, 113–14. *See also* Divorce; Nurturing role of women; Procreation; Sexuality; Wives
Mar 'Ukba b. Hiyya, 114
Mary Magdalene, 200–201n29
Matchmaking, 96
Maternal role. *See* Nurturing role of women
Matriarchs, infertile, 132–38, 148, 197n37
Matrona, 57, 180n31
McCarter, P. Kyle, Jr., 199n16
Meacham, Tirzah, 27, 54–56
Meeks, Wayne, 177n5
R. Meir, 15, 22–23, 82, 101, 113, 132
Menstruation, 22–29, 74–75; punishment for Adam's blood, 15, 183–84n14; ritual impurity, 71–72, 105–6, 168n3, 171nn32–33. *See also Niddah*
Merab, 30
Metaphoric aspect of marriage, 99–100
Meyers, Carol, 70
Michal, 30, 31, 132
Middle Eastern culture. *See* Cultural contexts of midrashic interpretations
Mikveh, 172n38
Miracles, 137–38
Miriam, 54
Misogyny, 56, 175n56, 175n61; bod-

ily functions, 33–35; cultural contexts, 36–40
Monogamy, 67–68, 76, 116, 145
Moses, 144, 154
Motherhood. *See* Nurturing role of women
Multivocality of rabbinic literature, 5, 11, 161, 179n19

Naaman, 158
R. Nahman: daughters, 33, 142–43; divorce, 114, 117, 128; female sexuality, 31–32; infertility, 134; Yalta, 85
R. Nahman b. Isaac, 50, 120, 123
R. Nahman b. R. Hisda, 47–48
R. Nahman bar Abba, 131
Named women in midrashic texts, 84, 179n19
Naomi, 154–55
Nature of women, 23–24, 43, 53; alterity, 12, 161–63; impurity, 22–29, 39–40, 71–72, 168n3, 171n32, 171n33; inferiority, 3, 5, 9, 12, 49–56, 64, 161–63, 178n8, 179n17; intellectual strengths, 54–55, 82–83; otherness, 8–9, 12–43, 23, 69–70, 73, 75–79, 167–68n2, 175n61; spirituality, 36; weakness, 67, 142, 179n17; wisdom, 54; witchcraft, 10–11, 32–34, 141–43, 160, 162, 173–74n49, 198nn3–4, 198n8. *See also* Light mindedness of women
Nebuchadnezzar, 58–59
Nehemiah, 115
Neusner, Jacob, 4, 17, 30, 38–40, 99–100
Niddah, 22–29, 71–72, 80, 93, 163; sexuality, 105–6; white days, 25–29, 172n38. *See also* Ritual impurity
Nocturnal emissions, 57, 59, 181n33
Nurturing role of women, 8, 54, 161; motherhood, 17–18, 74–75, 184n22; study, 95–97, 101–5, 162,

168n7, 169–70n11, 176n68, 191n38

Objectification of women, 31–32
'Onah, 93–94
Otherness of women, 8–9, 12–43, 161–63, 167–68n2, 175n61. *See also* Misogyny
Outhouse, 33, 142, 198n5

Palestinian Talmud, 4. *See also* Study
Palti/Paltiel, 30
Pandora, 175n56
R. Pappa, 98, 100, 110
Pappus b. Judah, 113
Paternal roles. *See* Daughters
Patriarchal culture, 2, 162, 166n7
Peace, 122–25
Penina, 131
Perfume, 66–67, 167–68n2, 174n51
Personification of Israel, 39, 99–100, 130, 136–38, 175n64, 197n37
Philo of Alexandria, 63
Phinehas, 154
R. Phinehas, 53
R. Phinehas bar Hama ha-Kohen, 112
Plaskow, Judith, 8
Polygamy, 74, 116
Polygyny, 193n63; ban, 195–96n20; infertility, 126–27, 145–50; male sexual freedom, 67–68, 76; obligations to wives, 90; *vs.* divorce, 116–17
Potiphar, 173n44
Prayer, 2, 79–83, 185n30, 185n32, 197n37; Hannah's, 80, 106, 124–25, 136, 149, 185n30, 197n30; infertility, 129–30, 132–36, 139–40, 148, 196–97n29; morning prayer, 16–17, 76–77, 169n8, 180n23; voice, 35; wedding blessings, 48–49
Preuss, Julius, 124
Privy. *See* Outhouse
Procreation, 9–10; commandments, 194n3, 195n16; Eve, 178n7; with

Procreation (*continued*)
  gentiles, 150–60, 163; infertility,
  94, 104; male obligations, 51, 96–
  97, 102–5, 119–26, 147; male potency, 18–21; maternal death in
  childbirth, 59; secondary role of
  women, 67–68, 179–80n22; status
  of women, 130–31, 145, 156–60;
  women's obligations, 119–26,
  194n4, 195n16. *See also* Infertility
Property, 90–92, 138–39
Prophets, female, 158–59
Proselytism. *See* Conversion
Prostitution, 94, 113–14, 156–57,
  160, 173n44, 200n21–23, 201n29
Puberty, 70
Pubic hair, 34–35
Public domain. *See* Marketplace
Public roles of women, 75–79. *See
  also* Leaders, women as
Punishment: by death in childbirth,
  72–73; for failure to observe rituals, 72–73, 184n16; for immodesty, 167–68n2; by infertility, 130–
  36, 195n17; of Leah and Rachel,
  148–49; within marriage contract,
  93, 95; of Moses, 154; for neglect
  of wives, 103–4, 191–92n39; rules
  of separation, 173n41; three precepts, 183–84nn14–15; of wives,
  111–12, 193n55

Rabbah b. Abbuha, 114, 133
Rabbah b. Bar Hannah, 96, 112
Rabban Gamliel, 192n49
Rabban Simeon b. Gamliel, 91
Rabbinic social order. *See* Social
  order
Rabbi Samuel's daughters, 179n18
Rabina, 108
Rachel, 53, 78, 160, 191n34; infertil-
  ity, 109, 124, 131–36; and Leah,
  11, 145–49, 199n10
Rachel, wife of R. Aqiva, 101–2,
  104, 191n34

Rahab, 31, 54, 151; conversion, 11,
  154–60, 163, 200nn22–24, 200n26;
  descendants, 200n25, 200–
  201nn29–30
Rape, 34–35, 51–52, 108, 192n52
Rashi (Shlomo ben Isaac), 6, 82–83
Rav, 97–98, 110–12
Rava, 40, 103–5, 114, 127
Rebecca, 78, 135, 136
Religious practices by women, 3, 29,
  70–72, 76–83, 185n32, 187n50;
  exemptions, 142; funerals, 68–70;
  menstruation, 28–29, 35–36, 172–
  73n39; prayer, 80, 106, 124–25,
  129–40, 185n30, 196–97nn29–30,
  197n37; repentance, 156–58;
  Sabbath precepts, 66, 71–72, 80,
  183–84n14, 184n15; worship, 2,
  9, 76–79, 168n3, 168n7
Reproduction. *See* Procreation
Resh Laqish, 98, 109, 112
Reuben, 109
Ritual impurity, 163; birth, 13–15,
  20, 23, 168nn3–4; ethnic differences, 199n17; *niddah*, 25–29, 71–
  72, 80, 93, 105–6, 163, 172n38;
  spiritual death of men, 24–25, 35.
  See also Menstruation
Rosh Hodesh, 70
Rules of separation, 9, 26–29, 31,
  173n45; ritual purity, 171n27,
  171n33; worship, 35–36, 172–
  73n39, 174n53. *See also* Ritual impurity
Ruth the Moabite, 154–55, 157

Sabbath bread (*hallah*), 66, 71–72,
  80, 184n15
Sabbath lights (*hadlaqah*), 66, 71–72,
  80, 184n15
Sabbath precepts, 66, 71–72, 80, 183–
  84nn14–15
Samael, spouse of Lilith, 60
Samson's mother, 136
Samuel, 106, 132, 135

R. Samuel, 153
Samuel b. Unya, 99
R. Samuel b. R. Isaac, 112
R. Samuel b. Nahmani, 30, 38–39, 46–47, 95, 108
Sarah, 11, 53, 78, 160, 187n50; and Hagar, 150–54; infertility, 126, 131–38; punishment, 195n17; sexuality, 122
Satlow, Michael: ethnicity, 199n17; light mindedness of women, 30, 98–99, 190n22; sexuality, 94, 104–6, 190n21
Separateness of women, 12, 26, 69–79, 162–63. *See also* Rules of separation
Septuagint, 61, 181n39
Sexual intercourse, 15–16, 171n26; coercion, 73–74; contraception, 107, 123–24; legal issues, 190n19; male dominance, 50–51, 59, 125, 194n2; marital obligations, 93–95; orgasm, 21–22; overt, by women, 98–99, 108–9, 124–25; passive, by women, 55–56, 66–67, 73–75, 106–9, 161–62, 184n22, 193n53; pleasure, 94, 178n7; polygyny, 67–68, 76, 193n63; purposes, 107, 192n50; rape, 34–35, 51–52, 192n52; Sabbath, 103; vs. spiritual life, 102; witchcraft, 198n4. *See also* Light mindedness of women
Sexuality, 2, 5–6, 8, 105–9, 175n56; cultural contexts of midrashic interpretations, 32–33, 190n21, 192n45; food metaphors, 106, 113; immodesty, 112–14, 167–68n2, 173n41, 189n16, 190n18, 193n57; immorality, 157–58, 163, 199n17; male aspects, 29–36, 67–68, 173nn44–45, 190n18, 190nn22–23; *niddah*, 105–6; objectification of women, 31–32
Shekhinah, 62–63
R. Shila, 132

R. Shiman b. Abba, 116–17
Shittim, 115, 154, 193n61
Shlomo ben Isaac (Rashi), 6, 82–83
Shoken-Zeb, eight elegies of, 69
R. Simeon, 53, 96, 120–21, 153
R. Simeon b. Laqish, 106
R. Simeon b. Yohai, 14–15, 138
R. Simeon ben Shetah, 198n5
R. Simeon ben Yohai, 129, 159
R. Simlai, 63
Sin, 179n17
Single women, 40, 123–24
Sisters, 32–33, 144–50, 162
Slavery, 16–17, 76–77, 81, 169n8, 183n13; infertility, 199n16; maidservants, 150–54, 199n16; story of the emancipated slave, 123–24
Social inequality of women. *See* Inferiority of women
Social order, 2, 7–9, 47, 83, 173n45, 175n56, 179n17; idealized male construct, 13, 28, 35, 41–44, 51; potential turmoil caused by women, 56, 88, 143, 149, 161–62; procreation, 122–25; single women, 40, 123–24
Soler, Jean, 23–24
Sotah. See Adultery
Spirituality of women, 36
Spousal roles. *See* Marriage
Status of women, 130–31, 145, 156–60
Study, 164; alternative to procreation, 138–39, 197n34; R. Aqiva's wife, 101–2; celibacy, 96–97, 102, 104; daughters, 81–83, 176n68, 190–91n31; exclusion of women, 2, 9, 28–29, 39–40, 79–84, 190–91n31; impact on marriage, 95–97, 101–5, 162, 168n7, 169–70n11, 176n68, 191n38; by women, 81–83, 142, 144–45, 176n68, 186n35, 186n37, 190–91n31
Synagogues, 35–36, 174n53

Takkanot, 188–89n12
Talmud of the Land of Israel, 4. *See also* Study
Tamar, 34–35, 54, 124
R. Tarfon, 101
Teachers, 102, 138–39, 191n36, 197n34
Ten curses of women, 73–79
R. Tifdai, 61–62
Torah. *See* Study
Traveling salesmen, 33
Tzitzit, 200n21

'Ulla, 21, 23, 34, 167–68n2; Yalta, 85–86, 126, 187n50
Umansky, Ellen M., 8
Unreliability of women. *See* Light mindedness of women
Urbach, Ephraim E., 179n17
Urination, 74, 77–78

Veils, 66, 68, 113–14, 182–83n4, 185n29
Virginity, 74–75
Voice, 35, 66–67, 113, 182n2, 193n57; keening, 68–70, 183n11

Weakness of women, 67, 142, 179n17
Wedding prayers, 48–49
Wegner, Judith Romney: divorce, 92–93, 95; intelligence of women, 55; marriage, 89, 190n23, 194n2; po-

lygyny, 195–96n20; religious practice by women, 81; women's gatherings, 142
Weisberg, Dvora, 185n30
Weissler, Chava, 196–97n29, 197n37
Wickedness, 52–53, 187n52
Widows, 40
Wisdom, 54
Wisdom of Ben Sira, 32–33, 36–37, 173–74n49, 183n6
Witchcraft, 10–11, 32–34, 141–43, 160, 162, 173–74n49, 198nn3–5, 198n8
Wives, 32–33, 91; bad, 107, 109–15, 193n55; co-wives, 145–50; good, 100–105; initiation of divorce, 127–28; legal status, 91–93, 116–17; polygyny, 116–17. *See also* Marriage; Nurturing role of women; Procreation; Sexuality
Women's gatherings, 10–11, 141–43, 160, 173–74n49–50, 197–98n1
Worship. *See* Religious practices by women

Yael, 31, 35, 54
Yalta, 83–87, 126, 187n51, 187n54

Zavot, 27
Zebulun, 199n12
Zipporah, wife of Moses, 154
Zohar, The, 59

INDEX OF PRIMARY SOURCES

Hebrew Bible

Genesis
1 66
1:26 46, 47, 62, 177n1, 178n16,
  181n39
1:26–27 44
1:27 47, 48, 49, 60, 61, 63, 164
1:28 45, 50, 51, 61, 63, 119, 120,
  121, 124, 125, 129, 194n5
1:31 53
2:1 45
2:7 45, 47, 48, 63
2:11 180n28
2:18 1, 45, 56, 95, 97, 111
2:19 177n6
2:19–20 47
2:20 47
2:21 46, 47, 56, 65
2:21–22 1, 45
2:22 1, 21, 47, 48, 53, 54, 55, 63,
  178n7
2:23 45, 57
2:24 45, 63, 115
3:16 74, 75, 99, 133, 184n22,
  193n53
3:20 45
4:7 99
4:8 57
4:17 57
5:1 58
5:1–2 46

5:2 46, 49, 61, 95, 96, 120
9:1 120, 194n3
9:6 96, 183n14
9:7 96, 120, 194n3
11:30 134, 136
12:16 98
12:17 151
15:2 152
16:1 152
16:2 133
16:3 126
16:5 151
16:6 152
16:8 152
17 19
18 187n50
18:10 53
18:12 122
18:13 122
19:31–36 124
21:7 136, 137
21:8 137
21:9 153
21:21 152
25:19 138
29:2 146
29:16–17 199n10
29:31 130, 131, 147
30:1 53, 124
30:6 150

30:7   150
30:8   146
30:14   134
30:15   148
30:16   109, 149
30:16–18   109
30:21   148
30:22   133, 146
30:22–23   131
30:24   148
30:25   147
30:28   14
31:19   53
34   149
34:1   51, 53, 109, 121, 149,
   178n14
35:11   120, 121
38   124
39   173n44
39:7–13   30
46:30   192n39
47:31   147
49:14   108

Exodus
   15:1   38
   18:11   158
   21:10   93, 188n7
   22:17   142
   26:20   46
   28:31–35   180n30
   28:34   57

Leviticus
   11:44   20
   11–15   172n35
   12   171n32
   12:1–3   20
   12:2   21, 171n26
   12:6–8   70
   12:6–12   168n4
   11–15   24
   12–18   168n3
   15   171n32
   15:33   25

16:11   96
18   172n35
18:6   26
18:19   24, 25, 26, 27, 105
18:29   24
20:18   24, 27

Numbers
   5:28   124, 125, 195n12
   15:39   108
   25   11, 154
   25:1–2   193n61
   25:7–8   154
   25:15   154
   27   11
   27:1   144
   27:8   138
   36:1–12   145

Deuteronomy
   1:13   108
   1:15   108
   7:3   21
   7:13   85
   14:25   95
   20:16   159
   24:1–4   92

Joshua
   2:4   158, 200n24
   2:6   201n30
   2:10   156, 200n22
   2:10–11   155
   2:11   156, 158
   2:12   157
   213   157
   2:18   158
   5:1   200n22
   6:23   159, 200n27
   6:25   155, 156

Judges
   2:9   159
   11:39–40   70
   21:20–21   70

1 Samuel
  1   80
  1:6   131
  1:11   80, 124
  1:27   106
  2   136
  2:5   134, 136
  2:5-6   149
  2:6   134
  25:6   96
  25:44   30

2 Samuel
  3:15   30
  6:16   132
  12   173n44
  13:15   34

2 Kings
  5:15   158
  6:23   14
  20:2   159
  22:14   158
  22:15   159

Isaiah
  3:16   34, 53
  3:17   34
  3:23   34
  16:1   14
  26:1   39
  30:22   27
  34:14   58
  49:21   136
  54:1   136
  54:5   99
  54:6   117
  57:7   193n55
  58:9   97

Jeremiah
  5:2   157
  9:4   111
  11:11   114
  18:6   199n13

Ezekiel
  16:31   157
  16:44   109
  18:6   171n32
  20:38   108
  22:7   157
  22:10   171n32
  44:30   96

Zephaniah
  1:15   138

Zechariah
  3:2   70
  12:12-14   183n11
  13:2   26, 105

Malachi
  2:13   115
  2:13-14   116
  2:16   115, 193n62

Psalms
  1:6   52
  9:9   157
  39:13   153
  45:13   112
  55:18   80
  55:20   138, 197n33
  68:6   163
  68:7   96, 112
  69:34   130
  96:1   39
  99:6   106
  113:9   136
  125:3   112
  128:3   112
  136:24   144, 161
  139:5   46, 48, 177n4
  145.9   144, 161
  145:14   131
  146:4   26, 105

Proverbs
  1:25   53

5:18 117
6–7 173n44
9:8 121
11:21 50, 178n11
15:15 110
17:2 157
18:22 97, 110
22:10 114
27:15 114
31 33
31:15 101
31:29 30
31:30 30

Job
  5:24 97
  12:18 137
  18:6 117
  18:7 117
  21:32–33 66
  31:1 116
  31:32 200n25
  35:11 74, 77, 184n23

Song of Songs
  1:4 130
  2:14 15, 29, 132, 182n2
  7:11 99

Ruth
  3:8–15 30

Lamentations
  1:8 171n32
  1:14 114
  3:39 69

Ecclesiastes
  7:26 110, 117
  9:9 96
  11:9 78

1 Chronicles
  4:21 201n30
  12:33 108

Apocrypha

Wisdom of Ben Sira
  9:8–9 33
  11:32 33
  25:24 33, 183n6
  25:28 179n17
  26:1 32

  26:3 32
  26:7 32
  42:9–10 32
  42:12–14 33
  42:13 187n51

New Testament

Mark
  10:11–12 189n13

Matthew
  1:4–5 201n29

Hebrews
  11:31 201n29

James
  2:24–26 201n29

Ancient Authors

Plato
Symposium
  189d, 190d   182n41

Euripedes
Alcestis   104, 191n39

Josephus
Antiquities
  15.7   189n13
  18.4   189n13

Philo
De Opificio mundi
  134   63, 182n42

Mishnah

Berakhot
  3:3   79, 185n27
  9:3   147

Shabbat
  2:6   71, 72
  6:3   167n2
  9:1   27

Pesahim
  8:7   142

Sukkah
  2:7   185n27

Ta'anit
  4:8   183n12

Hagigah
  1:1   76

Yevamot
  6:6   97, 120, 126, 195n16
  6:7   51
  14:1   92

Ketubbot
  4:4   69
  4:5   89
  5:5   71, 91
  5:6   93, 103, 190n19

  5:7   94
  5:8   90
  5:9   71, 90
  7:1–5   91
  7:6   113, 189n16
  7:6–7   93
  7:10   91

Sotah
  3:4   81, 83, 98, 176n68, 190n30
  3:8   68
  6:1   142

Gittin
  5:6   96
  5:9   201n1
  9:10   91

Qiddushin
  1:1   89
  4:12   30, 69

Bava Metzi'a
  2:11   102

Sanhedrin
  2:2   31

Shevuot
  4:1   76

Avot
2:7   143, 145, 150

Niddah
3:5–7   168n3
3:7   13, 14

Kelim
11:4   186n36

Tosefta

Berakhot
2:12   28

Yevamot
8:4   194n4
8:4–6   195n16
8:5   126
8:5–6   195n18
8:6   126

Ketubbot
4:7   188n10
7:6–7   193n57

'Eduyyot
3:4   191n36

Kelim Bava Metzi'a
1:6   186n36
4:17   18n36

Talmud of the Land of Israel

Berakhot
4:4, 35a   159

Shabbat
2:6, 8b   70

Ta 'anit
1:6, 64c   71

Hagigah
2:2, 77d   198n5

Yevamot
6:6, 7c   195n18

Ketubbot
2:6, 13a   179n19
5:2, 29b   188n10
11:3, 34b   193n55

Babylonian Talmud

Berakhot
10a   186n36
17a   17, 101
20a–b   135
20b   79
22a   29
24a   35, 68, 182n2

31a   136, 197n30
31a–b   124, 185n29
31b   80, 125
51a   70, 75
51b   21, 126
60a   147
61a   47, 48, 49, 50, 179n22

Shabbat
  11a 110
  13a 25
  25a 101
  31b–34a 72
  32a 72, 73
  51b 84, 85
  62a 12, 13, 167n2
  62b 34, 86, 174n51
  64b 173n47
  66b 198n8
  110a 28
  151b 181n33
  152a 34

'Eruvin
  18a 48, 49
  18b 50, 58
  53b 179n20
  53b–54a 186n36
  64b 142
  100b 65, 68, 73, 75, 76, 77, 78,
    177n79, 181n33, 185n29,
    192n52, 193n53

Pesahim
  62b 186n36
  110a 142
  111a 27, 142
  113b 130

Yoma
  47a 17, 68

Ta'anit
  2a–b 133
  24a 32

Megillah
  13b 146
  14a 151
  14b 31, 159, 179n19
  15a 31, 35, 151

Mo'ed Qatan
  28b 69

Hagigah
  16b 187n50

Yevamot
  61b 192n50
  61b–64a 97
  62b 95, 96, 97, 100, 190n29
  62b–63a 111
  63a 97, 100, 110
  63b 107, 114, 133, 194n3
  64a 196n24
  64a–b 133
  64b 132
  65a 127
  65b 120, 121, 125, 126, 128,
    178n10, 194n4
  65b–66a 120, 122, 123
  66a 123
  77a 151
  113a 98
  118b 98
  122a 201n30

Ketubbot
  5a 194n3
  8a 48, 64
  23a 179n19
  57a 89
  59b 100
  61a–b 91
  62b 103, 192n39
  62b–63a 103, 104
  63a 191n34
  64b 94
  65a 40, 68
  72b 113, 193n57
  75a 98

Nedarim
  20a 31
  20a–b 106, 173n47
  20b 100, 107, 108, 109, 199n14
  50a 101
  64b 130, 194n8

Nazir
  59a 35, 174n52

Sotah
  2a 96, 112, 190n27
  21a 101, 169n11
  22a 40
  26a 195n12
  32a–33a 185n30

Gittin
  6b 35
  45a 33, 142
  70a 192n50
  90a–b 68, 113, 115, 193n62
  90b 113

Qiddushin
  2a 90
  70a–b 84, 187n54
  80b 69, 70, 98

Bava Metzi'a
  59a 97, 110
  87a 137, 151, 187n50

Bava Batra
  16b 33
  73b 181n33
  116a 138
  119b 144
  123a 146
  145b 110

Sanhedrin
  19b 139
  19b 197n34
  19b–20a 29, 31
  21a 34, 132

  22a 96
  22a–b 116
  22b 99
  36b 130
  39a 179n20
  67a 142
  76b 190n29
  82a 154
  99b 197n34
  100b 32

'Avodah Zarah
  18b 82

Shevuot
  18b 20, 170n22

Zevahim
  116a–b 156

Menahot
  43b 16
  44a 173n44, 200n21

Me'ilah
  17b 153

Niddah
  20b 85
  24b 181n33
  30b 14
  31a 21, 22
  31b 14, 15, 16, 17, 18, 21, 23,
     29, 35, 50, 125, 168n4, 168n6,
     182n1, 182n2

Midrashic Works

Mekhilta de-Rabbi Ishmael
  Pisha 14 181n39
  'Amalek 3 158, 200n22

Sifra
  Lev 1:5 187n50

Sifre Numbers
  78 159, 200n25, 201n30
  115 200n21
  133 144, 161

Sifre Zuta on Numbers
  10:28   156, 200n28, 201n30

Avot de-Rabbi Nathan A
  ch. 1   184n22
  ch. 2   25, 26, 93

Avot de-Rabbi Nathan B
  ch. 2   116
  ch. 9   65, 67, 68, 71, 168n6,
    178n8, 182n1, 184n15
  ch. 42   78, 79, 184n22

Genesis Rabbah
  1:28   178n10
  8:1   46, 60, 61, 63, 95
  8:3   53
  8:4   52
  8:9   62
  8:11   61
  8:12   51, 63, 121, 125, 178n10
  17:2   95
  17:3   56, 111
  17:4   47, 53
  17:6   56
  17:7   57, 128
  17:8   65, 66, 67, 68, 69, 70, 71,
    75, 76, 168n6, 178n8, 179n17
  18:1   54, 76
  18:2   53, 54, 55, 67, 170n12
  18:3   1, 21, 54
  18:4   56
  18:5   115
  18:12   51
  20:11   58
  22:2   62, 181n32
  22:7   57
  24:6   58, 61
  40:7   152
  45:1   133
  45:3   151, 195n18
  45:4   131, 132, 133
  45:5   151, 179n17
  45:6   152
  45:10   151, 153
  53:8   137

  53:9   137
  53:10   137
  53:11   153
  53:14   153
  53:15   152
  70:19   147
  71   145
  71:1   130, 199n12
  71:2   131, 147, 199n12
  71:5   130
  71:6   196n23
  71:8   146
  71:16   146
  72:1   134, 149
  72:3   148
  72:5   199n14
  72:6   148, 199n13
  73.4   146
  73:5   131
  80:1   109, 149
  95   192n39
  80:1–12   178n14

Exodus Rabbah
  19:4   200n25

Leviticus Rabbah
  8:1   190n26
  34:14   193n55

Numbers Rabbah
  8:9   158
  16:25   181n33
  20:24   154
  21:3   199n18
  21:10   144
  21:11   144

Deuteronomy Rabbah
  2:26–27   158

Lamentations Rabbah
  Proem 24   146

Song of Songs Rabbah
  1:4 §2   130

1:5 §3   38
2:14 §8   133
7:11§1   99

Ruth Rabbah
  2:1   158, 201n30

Ecclesiastes Rabbah
  3:3   73
  5:6   159
  8:10   200n26

Midrash on Psalms
  146:4   26, 105

Tanhuma
  Noah 1   183n14
  Vayishlah 36   112

Tanhuma (ed. Buber)
  Noah 1   184n14

Pesiqta de-Rav Kahana
  13:4   157
  20:1   136
  22:2   129

Pesiqta Rabbati
  40:3   157

Eliyyahu Rabbah
  18   134, 196n27

Midrash HaGadol to Genesis
  1:74   180n24

Medieval Codes

Mishneh Torah
  Women 15:7   196n21

Shulhan Arukh
  Eben ha-Ezer 154:10   196n21

Lightning Source UK Ltd.
Milton Keynes UK
UKHW011156070222
398311UK00001B/16